John Millington
SYNGE

a reference guide

A
Reference
Publication
in
Literature

Ronald Gottesman
Editor

John Millington
SYNGE

a reference guide

EDWARD A. KOPPER, JR.

G.K.HALL &CO.

70 LINCOLN STREET, BOSTON, MASS.

Library of Congress Cataloging in Publication Data
Kopper, Edward A
   John Millington Synge: a reference guide.

   (Reference publications in literature)
   Bibliography: p.
   Includes index.
   1. Synge, John Millington, 1871-1909 — Bibliography.
Z8857.8.K66   [PR5533]   016.822'9'12   78-21968
ISBN 0-8161-8199-5

This publication is printed on permanent/durable acid-free paper
MANUFACTURED IN THE UNITED STATES OF AMERICA

Contents

Introduction

The impact of Synge on established twentieth century authors is much greater than has previously been suggested, and one purpose of this reference guide is to provide workpoints for future critics who might wish to trace the threads of this influence. Pirandello judged Synge to be his "favorite" among "modern dramatists" (1923.2). William Faulkner could quote Synge from memory and felt that Synge's power came at least in part from his depiction of a definite "locality." Faulkner purchased Synge's complete works to read during the winter of 1938 (1974.1). Thomas Wolfe's schooling was saturated with Synge, and an entry in Wolfe's Pocket Notebook 2 (October 1926 to September 1927) judges The Playboy of the Western World "The best play for poetry...." And in 1928, under "Term Paper, Drama," appears this assignment: "Compare the use of suspense, irony, and fate in Riders to the Sea with the use of them in The Agamemnon...Oedipus the King...or The Trojan Women..." (1970.17). Steinbeck admired Synge, and at his funeral service in 1968, Henry Fonda, "who had played Tom Joad in the film version of The Grapes of Wrath, read...selections from J. M. Synge..." (1975.8). And, of course, the influence of Synge on Eugene O'Neill has been cited often, though never fully developed.

The difficulty with the informed opinions of even "classic" writers is that they often obfuscate Synge's true worth and meaning. Theodore Dreiser and H. L. Mencken, for example, tend to impress upon Synge their own visions of what a modern artist should be. Dreiser saw Synge as a Naturalist: Synge had the "same approach" as a man "who would plant himself in front of any insect trapped by anything-- a wasp dragging a grub across a field, a moth beating itself free from a spider's web--and half chortling and half sighing over the cold and seemingly enforced mechanism of it all, proceed to talk" (1959.3). Mencken, probably over-emphasizing the social relevance of Synge, finds him to be "the one undoubted genius of the Neo-Celtic movement--not a fantastic, pale green mystic like W. B. Yeats..." (1911.61). Ezra Pound viewed Synge as a victim of Dublin's "stupidity" (1967.16), and Joyce scored Synge's tepidity, calling him "John Milicent Synge" (1912.26).

Thus many early appreciations of Synge's work are suspect: several verdicts were delivered in haste to answer and to taunt crowds protesting The Playboy of the Western World; many were inspired by the romance of Synge's visits to the Aran Islands and by his early death. In 1905, George Moore, speaking of Synge's dialogue in The Well of the Saints, stated, "Mr. Synge has discovered great literature in barbarous idiom as gold is discovered in quartz..." (1905.8). And in 1911, in answer to the Boston crowds who protested the appearance of Synge's works on the stage during the Abbey's 1911-12 trip to America, Moore stated that The Playboy of the Western World is "the most original piece of stage literature that has been written since Elizabethan times..." (1911.64). Ford Madox Ford histrionically contrasted Shaw with Synge: "Not one of his [Shaw's] plays will leave as much mark upon the emotions as, let us say, 'The Playboy of the Western World'..." (1911.43). And with typical overstatement, Shaw wrote in 1911 that Synge's satire has a "joyousness and a wild wealth of poetic imagery that Swift never achieved" (1911.75).

In contrast, two sound, early judgments of Synge's worth came from unexpected sources. P. D. Kenny, who surfaced as "Pat" in 1907 Dublin newspaper columns, reveals a remarkably acute critical sense when he proposes the idea that The Playboy of the Western World contains "two plays, one within another...." He also predicts--correctly--that the work is "a play on which many articles could be written" (1907.32). T. W. Rolleston found the play "profoundly tragic.... There is cynicism on the surface, but a depth of ardent sympathy and imaginative feeling below..." (1907.33).

Synge's plays are cultural events as well as literary ones, and any study of his literary reputation must deal at least in part with the climates of opinion--American and Irish--in which Synge's works had their life. This guide documents the reception of Synge's work in order to demonstrate that in many instances the riots over Synge's plays, acted out in theaters and after spelled out in newspapers, besides helping to explain the drastically differing opinions of Synge's work, present dramas almost as compelling and self-revealing as parts of his plays. This book, then, attempts to present facts that might allow the reader to trace the reasons that Synge, as Peter Kavanagh justly maintains, was the "most hated" (1950.3) of the Abbey dramatists. It tries, too, to peel away the layers of prejudice--both derogatory and laudatory--that have blurred Synge's contribution for decades.

Some reasons for the mob's hatred of Synge have been known for some time: Synge's Protestant Ascendancy background, which made him and the two other directors of the Abbey, Lady Gregory and Yeats (both also Protestant), outsiders in Catholic Dublin; his "blasphemies"; his "vile" picture of Irish womanhood; his paganism (supposedly imported, packaged from France); his revival of the Stage Irishman at a time when Ireland was fighting for Home Rule (when has the country not been?); his purported lack of knowledge of the true Irish soul; his use of the word "shift" in <u>The Playboy of the Western World</u>; and his Peeping Tomery, a charge that came from Synge's statement in the Preface of <u>The Playboy of the Western World</u> that, when he was writing <u>In the Shadow of the Glen</u>, he listened through a "chink in the floor of the old Wicklow house...that let [him] hear what was being said by the servant girls in the kitchen."

This reference guide details all of the above charges (at times quoting and paraphrasing newspaper accounts long ago out of circulation), and it also records other reasons, some subtle, to account for the frenzied reactions to Synge by people who did not read the works, who did not hear them during commotions in theaters, and who could not state correctly either Synge's name or the title of his most loathed work, <u>The Playboy of the Western World</u>.

Synge was attacked for many reasons, several of them very trivial. Arthur Griffith, editor of <u>The United Irishman</u> and the most vocal of Synge's Dublin opponents, complained that Synge needlessly introduced a drowned "body" onto the stage in <u>Riders to the Sea</u> (1904.4). Others blamed the riots over <u>The Playboy of the Western World</u> on the realism that brought Old Mahon onto the stage with his head wrapped in a large bandage (because of the wound inflicted by Christy's loy), on the fact that Pegeen and Christy are left unchaperoned while her father goes off for the night, on the village girls' performing in <u>The Playboy of the Western World</u> in America without shoes and stockings, on the possible encouragement of emigration that Synge's plays might have (a charge also levelled against Joyce's <u>A Portrait of the Artist as a Young Man</u> [1916]), and on the appearance on the stage of actors portraying drunks.

Others attacked Synge on broader philosophical and psychological bases. <u>The Freeman's Journal</u> maintained that Synge was as "preoccupied with the sex problem as any of the London school of problem playwrights" (1905.1). O. W. Firkins saw the theme of <u>Deirdre of the Sorrows</u> as the "modern fear of living...it is hard to forgive Deirdre and Naisi for crossing the threshold of the lazarhouse" (1920.3). George Russell grouped Synge with those who "turn from the hearth and...roam in uncharted regions of the psyche." About <u>The Playboy of the Western World</u> Russell wonders, "how many playboys may yet come out of that lawless imagination!" (1937.1). Maud Gonne attacked Synge because he (supposedly) did not understand the Irish soul--as did Yeats (1971.18). And Father George O'Neill cites the commendations that the Abbey principals heaped on the works of one another (1912.31), an embarrassing practice that Synge was sensitive to when he asked that Yeats not write prefaces to some of his (Synge's) works.

The problem with the Dublin audience was aggravated by Synge's unwillingness to "explain" his work. In fact, in a hasty interview with a reporter from <u>The Dublin Evening Mail</u>, Synge said that his purpose in <u>The Playboy of the Western World</u> was "nothing" and that the work was meant merely to "amuse." When asked about the use of

police by the Abbey Directors to quell the protestors--a gesture
that infuriated Irish Nationalists--Synge is reported to have said,
"it does not matter a rap," words that made headlines in Dublin
(1907.21). We still do not know, in fact, what Synge really thought
of the disturbances over his play. He did feel that the famous
Debate over The Playboy of the Western World, initiated by Yeats and
held at the Abbey Theatre on February 4, 1907, was a mistake, and he
does mention in a letter to his fiancée, Maire O'Neill (Molly Allgood) that the crowds consisted of "low ruffians"; but in 1907 the
ill Synge was so consumed with his passion for Miss Allgood that he
never did specifically state his views about the audiences' reactions
to his work (1971.41).

It is no wonder, then, that Synge's work was open to many misin-
terpretations. Dublin's The Daily Express argued that Martin Doul's
second blinding in The Well of the Saints is caused by his desiring
to elope with Molly Byrne (1905.2). Theodore Roosevelt, who attend-
ed a showing of The Playboy of the Western World with Lady Gregory in
New York, apparently missed the point when he laughed until his face
was red as Christy attacked his father for the second time (1911.26).
Some American protesters, entirely ignorant of the plot, illogically
hissed even louder when a noose was prepared for Christy. Others
waited (with a noose) outside the Maxine Elliott Theatre in New York
for the appearance of the playwright, not realizing that Synge had
been dead for over two years. Euphemia Van Rensselaer Wyatt, in
1946, saw the Mayo girls in the play as the "equivalent of bobby-
soxers..." (1946.7). And two Englishmen were expelled from a per-
formance for protesting the line "loosèd kharki cut-throats," a
reference to the British army (1911.10). Yeats summarizes much of
his disappointment over the reception of The Playboy of the Western
World by stating: "The failure of the audience to understand this
powerful and strange work has been the one serious failure of our
movement..." (1907.41).

This difficulty of understanding Synge continues, with his works
suffering badly in translation and with his views still being distorted to fit an ideology. Procrustean East Berliners stress Christy's role as killer and interpret Pegeen's ending lament that she
has lost the only playboy of the western world to mean that the last
murderer of the West has now gone and that an era of peace will begin
(1972.32). And "behind the Iron Curtain, Christy Mahon has been
frequently portrayed as a Marxist revolutionary who has raised a
loy...against petit-bourgeois capitalism" (1974.22).

Attacks on Synge led, in Dublin, to a good deal of humor, both
intentional and unintentional. Arthur Griffith shrieked out "the
fact which all of us know--that Irishwomen are the most virtuous
women in the world" (1903.6). Griffith also became embroiled in an
argument over Synge's "language of the gutter." As Griffith states,
"The father of the hero [Christy Mahon] refers to his son in one
place as a 'dirty__lout.' The word omitted is so obscene that no

man of ordinary decency would use it..." (1907.22). It turned out
that Griffith misheard the word "stuttering" and thought it was
"fucking." Again, "A Western Girl," in a Letter to the Editor of
The Freeman's Journal, complained about Molly Allgood's use of the
word "shift": it indicated "an essential item of female attire,
which the lady would probably never utter in ordinary circumstances,
even to herself" (1907.38). And Hilary Pyle, in his biography of
Jack Yeats, relates how Synge told of the janitress of the Abbey
calling Synge a "bloody old snot" for having included the word
"shift" in The Playboy of the Western World (1970.11).

On the other hand, reactions of many Dubliners do indeed show a
willingness to try to understand Synge's work, or failing this, an
attempt to diffuse the protests against it with humor. One point
that clearly emerges in this study is the contrast between Dublin
audiences and American ones. There were boors a-plenty in Dublin and
in New York, but the wrongheaded anger of the Irish Irelanders seems
preferable to the patronizing attitudes of Irish-Americans, typified
by Mayor Fitzgerald of Boston, who sent his secretary, William A.
Leahy, to act as censor of The Playboy of the Western World. Leahy
did not find the work obscene--only coarse and vulgar. The quality
of Leahy's literary appreciation is seen in his report to his supe-
rior: Pegeen "sheltered two men in her heart and wavered when she
might have chosen" (1911.7). Leahy's obtuseness is shared by New
Yorkers who complained about "G. N. Synge's 'Plowboy of the Western
World'" (1911.56) and who argued that Irish do not lionize a "para-
site." It is seen, too, in the thug who, in Chicago, threatened Lady
Gregory through an anonymous letter with murder for staging The Playboy of the Western World; and in the "wholesale liquor dealer," from
Philadelphia, Joseph McGarrity, who secured an injunction against the
Irish Players on the charge of immorality, then upon cross examina-
tion in a magistrate's court revealed that he had not read or seen
the work (1912.3).

More sensitive attitudes of Dubliners who became rabid only occasionally are seen in the parody written by "Conn" and called "In a
Real Wicklow Glen," which appeared in the October 24, 1903 issue of
The United Irishman (1903.3). This skit pictures Nora, the protagonist of In the Shadow of the Glen, years after the play with several
children, entertaining "John," a "figure all in rags," whom she tries
to wean from the bottle. Another clever parody of Synge, probably
written by George Russell (AE), appeared in the February 9, 1907 issue of Sinn Féin, edited by Arthur Griffith (again!) after The United
Irishman folded. Called "Britannia Rule-the-Wave" [sic], the skit
satirizes Synge and Yeats, using the incantatory language of Cathleen
ni Houlihan to refer to Lady Gregory: "I never saw anybody like her
before. Wanting to be a charwoman, maybe" (1907.34). Here the allu-
sion is to Shaw's complimentary description of Lady Gregory as the
"charwoman of the Abbey Theatre." Again, The Evening Telegraph on
February 2, 1907 published the broadside "The Man That Killed His
Da," a humorous ballad commemorating the disturbances over The Playboy

of the Western World: the piece is written in "Synge-y song"
(1907.8). These three pieces are typical of much of the criticism
directed at Synge in Ireland by intelligent men and women who could
laugh occasionally at passing foibles. Even Arthur Griffith showed
that, while he could condemn with his Nationalistic side, he could
also respond to a significant literary event.

Although the best sources for understanding the cultural impact
that Synge's work had remain the Irish newspapers from 1903 through
1907 and American newspapers of 1911-12, there have been a number of
important studies made of the culture shock that Synge's works occa-
sioned. Lady Gregory describes at length the problems of The Playboy
of the Western World in America (1913.9). Gerard Fay, in The Abbey
Theatre: Cradle of Genius (1958.2), provides important background
information to define Synge's place amidst the squabbles. Daniel J.
Murphy (1960.9) examines protests over The Playboy of the Western
World in the context of other plays considered at one time detriment-
al to Irish causes. Ida G. Everson (1966.7) assesses the role of
Lennox Robinson in taking the play to America for the first Abbey
Tour (1911-12). Her essay includes a Program of the Abbey Players
made from a "typescript copy in [the] Secretary's Office, Abbey
Theatre Dublin." Richard M. Kain, in two articles (1966.13 and
1972.28), has shared the contents of his "scrapbook" of newspaper
clippings dealing with the 1907 Dublin performances of The Playboy of
the Western World. Hilary Berrow (1972.2) synthesizes several accounts of the riots. Malcolm Kelsall (1975.14) shows how the acting
of the play in 1907 contributed to the audiences' angry reactions:
"the riots were natural, even, dare one suggest, healthy."

The most useful source of information about the problems caused
by The Playboy of the Western World is James F. Kilroy's The 'Playboy'
Riots, Number 4 in the Irish Theatre Series (1971.22). Kilroy not
only reprints many important 1907 Dublin newspaper accounts but also
offers a useful commentary on them. Unfortunately, his book is
limited to 1907 and does not include any of the early reviews of
Synge's work. This lacuna is partially obviated in the Frayne and
Johnson edition of the Uncollected Prose of W. B. Yeats, Vol. 2
(1976.30) and by E. H. Mikhail's collections of Interviews and Recol-
lections--of Synge and of Yeats (1977.7, 10). What is needed in
Synge scholarship is a slender but useful volume reprinting all of
the reaction to Synge's works in Dublin appearing in newspapers in
1903-05.

While reactions to Synge's works assist in limning traits of a
civilization, they also help to explain the most important single
force which has led for decades to a distorted view of Synge's writing: the picture presented of him by Yeats. Yeats's portrait of
Synge as a combination of Keats shattered by hostile critics and an
Adonais assumed into a vague Greek heaven (1911.83 and 1928.6) is so
moving that we are tempted to believe it and to discount the evidence
in Synge's published letters and other sources that demonstrate that

Synge was less than a saint and that occasionally Yeats and Synge
were less than unquestioning soul brothers. Perhaps an analogue for
Yeats's depiction of Synge is found in the Duke of Venice's answer to
Brabantio after Othello has recited the "magic" stories with which he
won Desdemona's hand: "I think this tale would win my daughter too."

But the Yeats image remains, and so strong is it still that Robin
Skelton, writing in 1977 about the politics of Synge, feels required
to dispel the notion that Synge was (as Yeats maintained) "unfitted
to think a political thought" (1977.13). Yeats's image of Synge as a
wounded and wandering Byron has become so entrenched that some critics actually see in the black lock of Synge's hair that graces his
forehead in many of his photos the guise of a Gothic hero. In reality, Synge wore a hairpiece to compensate for the loss of hair caused
by his treatment for Hodgkin's Disease.

Of Synge's intimate friends Lady Gregory has offered one of the
most balanced, though too pejorative, verdicts on Synge's work. In
an amazingly candid interview with Mary O'Connor Newell of the Chicago Sunday Record-Herald (1912.29), she said of The Playboy of the
Western World, "it is a masterpiece of literature...full of poetry
and imagery.... The question is not whether you like it or not. I
do not ask people to like it. As a matter of fact, there are other
plays in our repertory I much prefer, but it has been made necessary
for us now to give 'The Playboy' in order to show that it is not what
it has been called, indecent, unfit for presentation." Lady Gregory
was exhausted from defending a play which ruffled her Victorian principles, and she never does spell out just which plays she "much" prefers, but she seems to have meant what she told Ms. Newell. In fact,
Wilfrid Scawen Blunt in his Diaries (1921.3) reports that Lady Gregory told him it was "a mistake to produce the play...."

The widely differing opinions of Synge's work, inspired in part
by his suggestion that The Playboy of the Western World has "several
sides" (1907.37), have given rise to a multiplicity of interpretations of Synge's masterpiece. Some find archetypal myths in the
work; some view it through Christocentric symbolism. Others look
upon The Playboy of the Western World as the autobiographical record
of the fated love affair between Synge and Molly Allgood, finding co
confirmation in her playing of the role of Pegeen Mike. Other critics see the work as the growth of a poet; some find the modern search
for identity to be the play's central theme. A few critics point out
analogues in The Playboy of the Western World with other works as
varied as Huckleberry Finn and Bonnie and Clyde. A few Synge scholars attack the structure of the work, feeling that it might well have
been a shorter, two-act play. Others focus on the love poetry in the
work, believing that Christy's dialogue in wooing Pegeen rivals that
with which Romeo courts Juliet.

Myth critics of Synge often emphasize the ritual murder of Old
Mahon by his son. Norman Podhoretz (1953.10) finds that The Playboy

<u>of the Western World</u> develops the paradox that "individual achieve-
ment and communal progress depend on [symbolic] murder." Patricia
Meyer Spacks delineates fairy tale elements in the play, especially
those surrounding the ritual murder, which help to form Christy as a
"constructed man" (1961.11). Henry Popkin (1967.15) maintains that
Christy "'kills' his father to escape another of those loveless Irish
marriages; at the same time, he is participating in one of the most
archetypal patterns of all--the conflict between father and son."
Mary Rose Sullivan (1969.18) scrutinizes many parallels between
<u>Oedipus Rex</u> and <u>The Playboy of the Western World</u>. Augustine Martin
asserts that Christy's leaving Pegeen at the conclusion of the work
evidences a victory of the Dionysian view of life over the Apollonian,
his "escape to freedom between the Scylla and Charybdis of loneliness
on the one hand and domination on the other" (1972.42). And Donald
Gutierrez (1974.9) sees <u>The Playboy of the Western World</u> as a "pu-
berty rite of passage," in which Christy passes from "boyhood to manhood."

Other myth critics, defining archetypes in a more limited manner,
find analogues for Christy's problems in ancient Irish saga materials.
M. J. Sidnell (1965.24) sees in <u>The Playboy of the Western World</u> the
mythological "Championship of Ulster"--from the cycle of legends surrounding Cuchulain, the Irish Achilles. Diane E. Bessai (1968.3)
takes up where Sidnell leaves off and finds that Christy is Cuchulain,
in his many exploits and in his relationship with father figures.

Hugh H. MacLean (1954.4) is one of the first critics to develop
the idea that Christian references form the scaffolding of <u>The Playboy of the Western World</u>. Citing several specific parallels between
Christ's mission and Christy's, he feels that Synge's Mayo villagers
discover by the play's end that their salvation cannot come from an
outside source (Christy) but must originate in themselves. Howard D.
Pearce (1965.19) sees irony in Synge's use of Christocentric materials and casts Christy in the role of mock-hero. Stanley Sultan
(1968.30; 1969.19) traces the theme of the Deliverer or Messiah in
the work and discusses several specific parallels between Christy and
Christ, e.g. Palm Sunday happenings and the Good Samaritan Parable.
And Robin Skelton (1971.46) summarizes many references to Christ in
the play.

The desire to find out exactly what <u>The Playboy of the Western
World</u> is all about has led not only to myth criticism and to exegeses
of the work's religious elements but also to the unearthing of more
mundane analogues, some inspired by the hectic 1960s. Ronald G. Rollins compares Christy to Huckleberry Finn (1966.19): "Perhaps the
most manifest parallelism is that both fictions focus on two young
men...who desire to break away from conformity and confinement...."
Rollins also finds several similarities between Christy and O'Casey's
Donal in <u>The Shadow of a Gunman</u>. Both works express the Irish "tendency to mistake sham heroes and false patriots for men of real conviction and courage" (1966.20). Harry W. Smith (1969.17) cites

parallels between the villagers' thirst for violence in The Playboy of the Western World and the uprisings of the 1960s: "The archetypal attitudes of Synge's mythical villagers resemble our own." Donna Gerstenberger (1971.11), examining similarities between Bonnie and Clyde and the work, believes that both center upon the unlikely folk-hero who is venerated by rural groups: dispossessed mid-Americans of the Great Depression and impoverished villagers of Western Ireland.

The overall form and design of The Playboy of the Western World still trouble Synge critics. Francis Bickley early on held that the work moves too slowly, especially the last act (1912.10). T. R. Henn also has reservations about the play's structure, seeing it as a "deliberately distorted tragedy, all the joints wrenched out of place by a comic vision that Synge imposed upon it..." (1966.11). Some solid comments about the play's plan have been offered by Jon Rogers Farris (1974.4), who analyzes the process of composition of the work by examining the over one thousand typewritten pages which make up Synge's thirteen drafts for the play; and by Paul M. Levitt (1975.17), who points out that Synge was forced by the requirements of the theater to write the play in three acts: it should be a two-act work, Levitt maintains, with the first entrance of Old Mahon the point of division.

Some of these organizational difficulties are obviated, however, when we see that the central purpose of the play is to limn the growth of a poet. In other words, language is the true protagonist of The Playboy of the Western World, just as the language and the ideas in Eilert Lövborg's manuscript about the future are the real principals in Ibsen's Hedda Gabler. As early as 1935, Francis J. Colligan pointed out that Christy is a "fainthearted lad with a poetic strain in his undeveloped soul..." (1935.3). James F. Kilroy's excellent article, "The Playboy as Poet" (1968.17), develops the motif of Christy as incipient poet: the play "dramatizes the gradual development of the poet's craft...." On the other hand, R. Reed Sanderlin (1968.28) argues that Christy is not at all enlightened by the end of the play and that Synge's intention was to stress the delusion of the Irish villagers. And Bruce M. Bigley (1977.2) sees the work as a "Bildungsdrama," which permits us to comprehend Synge's attitude towards Christy.

The critical reception of Riders to the Sea has also been mixed, though reactions to it are less frenetic. Max Beerbohm praises the play's simplicity and points out its poetic elements (1904.2). Francis Bickley (1912.10) feels that Riders to the Sea is "one of those achievements before which the voice of criticism is dumb...." On the other hand, P. P. Howe (1912.24) says that the play violates unity of time, so many deaths taking place in so short a work. Denis Johnston (1965.15) scores the characters' "disregard for the weather reports...." And Malcolm Pittock (1969.12) believes that Maurya's vision is implausible because its effect depends upon the audience's assenting to the superstitions of the Aran islanders. Some commentators have wondered, too, whether the play is indeed a tragedy. Denis

Donoghue (1955.2), for example, maintains that it is not one in the classical sense but that it does capture the pathos of the characters' losing struggle against the sea. In spite of its flaws, however, Riders to the Sea is, apart from The Playboy of the Western World, the most widely anthologized play by Synge.

Much sound criticism of Riders to the Sea has dealt with the play's overall format. Paul M. Levitt (1969.10) finds that the work is unified by its Biblical allusions, especially those to Revelations and Exodus: Synge "compresses past and present action into the closing moments of a tragedy long unfolding. It is this organization, combined with the biblical imagery...which gives Riders its extraordinary compactness and intensity...." Elsewhere, he maintains that the play gives the "impression of an unbroken cycle of death inevitably working itself out..." (1971.26). David R. Clark, also, has discussed references to Revelations in the play (1972.10), and T. R. Henn (1972.23) mingles Biblical allusions with symbolic physical "props" when analyzing the plan of Riders to the Sea.

A good deal of criticism has centered upon Maurya. William H. Combs (1965.5) sees Synge's portrayal of Maurya as an example of his pessimism. Ryder Hector Curry and Martin Bryan (1968.5) find that she has affinities with Morrigu, the ancient Irish crow of battle, and with Eddic Mara or "hag." Errol Durbach (1972.14) points out that Maurya embodies the figure of the Pietà. David R. Clark's Casebook on Riders to the Sea (1970.1) reprints several critical analyses of the play.

With both The Playboy of the Western World and Riders to the Sea, informed critical opinion has managed to pass through the scrim of irrelevant materials and to ask important questions about the literary worth of the plays. In the Shadow of the Glen, however, has been less fortunate and still seems to attract more than its share of sociologists. In the beginning, the work was seen by its detractors as a variation of the ancient story of wifely infidelity, the Widow of Ephesus, and as a part of the Decameron imported into Ireland by Yeats and his decadent friends. Synge's supporters viewed his play as an attack on the Irish institution of the loveless marriage--another tangential issue. Later, Daniel Corkery (1931.1) issued the oft quoted statement that Nora wears "her lusts upon her sleeve...." Denis Johnston (1965.15), approaching In the Shadow of the Glen with the same meteorological expertise that marked his discussion of Riders to the Sea, calls Synge's language in In the Shadow of the Glen a "depressing weather report...."

Some critics approach In the Shadow of the Glen through its symbolism. Robin Skelton (1969.15 and 1971.46) sees the work as a forerunner of black or dark comedy; Nicholas Grene (1974.8) examines its anti-pastoral elements and its use of the symbolic shadow; Paul N. Robinson (1974.24) points out elements of the medieval play Everyman in In the Shadow of the Glen; and Jean Alexander (1972.1) says that the work "is basically concerned with the acceptance of risk for the sake of vital existence." David H. Greene (1947.8) offers a judicious analysis of the work, pointing out that its ending swings the play "from its logical and somber conclusion into the realm of romantic symbolism. To do that it was necessary that the entire emphasis be withdrawn from the guilty lovers and refocused on the tramp and the lonely girl who finds release from her bondage in his company."

The Well of the Saints, too, has mystified critics, and differing opinions of its worth are often strident. Francis Bickley (1912.10) finds that it "is not so interesting as any of the others...." Denis Johnston (1965.15) thinks that it is too long for its scanty plot. On the other hand, Daniel Corkery (1931.1) feels that the play is a true picture of Ireland and that Martin Doul is a much more plausible character than Christy Mahon. Alan Price (1961.9) believes that The Well of the Saints is "perhaps Synge's most profound and sombre work...."

Synge critics are only beginning to realize the full complexity of The Well of the Saints. Vincent Nash (1972.48) warns that the theme of the work is much more complex than the bland antithesis between saving illusion and unpleasant reality. M. J. Sidnell (1972.67) examines the blindness motif in the work, tracing analogues in Tiresias, Oedipus, and Gloucester. And Grace Eckley (1973.1) maintains that "...Synge combines in this one play the symbols of holy water on the eyes and reflective water in a pool to develop his preference for confronting one's fate in one's own fashion and in a short, full life...."

The Tinker's Wedding has not fared well with Synge critics. P. P. Howe (1912.24) finds it the "smallest" of Synge's plays. Daniel Corkery (1931.1) says that the play is "scarcely worth considering...." David H. Greene (1947.9) summarizes his views on the work: "A fair estimate of The Tinker's Wedding is that it contains a crude farcical element which is typical of Synge, little or no deftness of characterization, perhaps one good scene at the end where the tinkers rush off in confusion with the priest's curses ringing in their ears, and a few passages of lyric vigor such as one associates with Synge's best writing."

Recent critics, though, have tried to rehabilitate the play. Robin Skelton (1971.46) sees The Tinker's Wedding as expressive of the "movements of May" in conflict with a sterile Establishment. And Vivian Mercier (1972.44) presents an excellent analysis of the character of the priest in the play.

Criticism of Deirdre of the Sorrows is still influenced by Yeats's comments on the play (1910.5): had Synge lived, his "masterwork" would have been Deirdre of the Sorrows, "so much beauty is there in its course, and such wild nobleness in its end, and so poignant is an emotion and wisdom that were his own preparation for death." Many other critics, as well, treat the work as the autobiographical log of Synge's last years. P. P. Howe (1912.24) excuses the play's faults on the basis that Synge died before he had a chance to correct the occasional lapses into hackneyed diction. Daniel Corkery (1931.1) holds that Deirdre of the Sorrows reveals a "ripened artistry": "But then he [Synge] died." Edward M. Stephens (1954.8) sees in the play Synge's union in nature with Molly Allgood at Glen Cree, with this idyllic episode inspiring "the dramatization of Naisi in the woods with Deirdre."

Those who find Deirdre of the Sorrows to be successful frequently emphasize its theme of joy in the midst of death. Cornelius Weygandt (1913.18) feels that Synge combines "mordancy" with joy in this play (and others) and compares him to Hardy and Donne. Jon R. Farris (1971.8) holds that "...Deirdre has a most intense joy in life, and that...is to be the very cause of her death...self-fulfillment is ultimately self-destruction." Brenda Murphy (1974.19) sees the "major theme" in the play as death's "transcendence of time and decay...." And Herbert V. Fackler (1969.3) finds "existential pantheism" in the characters' union with nature.

Favorable commentary on Deirdre of the Sorrows emphasizes that the play is dramatic in spite of its lyricism, which, according to negative criticism, often impedes the action. Francis Bickley (1912.10) stresses the dramatic nature of Synge's work, opposing it to the merely poetic renderings of the Deirdre legend by Yeats and George Russell. David H. Greene (1948.3) finds that the play is much underrated and says that Synge's "sense of theater [is] nowhere so sound" as in Deirdre of the Sorrows. Harold Orel (1961.8) expresses a similar view: "For all its faults," the play "succeeds in being compassionate, in charging the text with life, and in moving outward from the emotion of Lavarcham's final speech...to a final meeting, uniting stoicism, asceticism, and ecstasy." Pejorative views of Deirdre of the Sorrows are exemplified by Denis Johnston (1965.15), who wonders whether Deirdre is "a woman at all and not a transvestite."

Synge's prose, basically The Aran Islands, has not received the attention that it deserves and has often been analyzed merely as source material for the plays or as a statement about the folklore of the islands' inhabitants. P. A. Ó Síocháin (1962.15) finds that Synge's attitude towards the islands was that of a "literary dilettante and aspirant" and stresses Synge's apartness from the people and their indifference to him and his writings. Richard Bauman (1963.3) analyzes traditional folkloric patterns in The Aran Islands, including riddles and superstition. Yet Donna Gerstenberger(1964.8) devotes a chapter in her Twayne book on Synge to his prose; Robin Skelton spends a chapter in The Writings of J. M. Synge (1971.46) on The Aran Islands; and Alan Price, in Emerald Apex (1966.17), reprints a good deal of the prose, with Price maintaining that the writings possess "an intrinsic worth that would remain even if he had written nothing else...."

Two recent analyses indicate a direction that future critics of Synge's prose might profitably follow. Ann Saddlemyer (1972.64) details the "systematic arrangement" of Synge's prose, finding that he was influenced by the "aesthetic doctrines of...great nineteenth century synthesizers...." And Jeanne Flood (1976.6) applies the techniques of psychoanalysis to the prose and opens up many areas of approach.

Not a great deal of criticism has been expended on Synge's poetry, but one wonders whether the corpus merits even the analysis that it has received. Many of the poems are embarrassingly poor, even "Danny," Synge's best known piece, which concerns a youthful womanizer who is stomped to death by irate (and jealous?) village lads. Often critics have turned the very awkwardness of the poetry into a virtue, citing its "brutality" (as did Synge) and its reaction against traditional poetic forms. But one wonders, again, whether Synge was being deliberate or whether he simply lacked talent for writing poems. Others have pointed out the influence of Synge's vigorous meters on Yeats, but no one has convincingly documented such an hypothesis.

A good number of critics, however, have taken the poems seriously, some, such as Denis Donoghue (1957.2), emphasizing their fluctuations between the "romantic" and the "earthy." William Lyon Phelps (1918.3) relates Synge's poetical abilities to his training in musical composition. Robert Farren (1947.5) speaks of his poetry of "bitch and ditch" and compares Synge favorably with Hopkins. For Donald A. Davie (1952.2), Synge remains "one of the very few poets, writing in English since the end of the eighteenth century, who have talked sense about the question of diction in poetry." And Robin Skelton (1962.17) summarizes what he feels is Synge's contribution to poetry: Synge "left behind him a couple of dozen poems that will last out centuries, and that will always keep his name in mind as one of the great renewers of tradition."

Debate over the nature and quality of Synge's dialogue (and language generally) divides along predictable lines. Denis Johnston (1965.15) snidely says that "It is probably true that he [Synge] had heard all the words he uses, though probably not in the same order." Alan J. Bliss, however, believes that "Synge, like many other writers before him and after him, was creating a special language to suit his special artistic purpose..." (1972.4).

Of more interest to the student of Synge are the "hard" data presented in several scientific analyses of his style. As early as 1912, for example, A. G. van Hamel (1912.34) thought Synge's dialect sufficiently distinctive to merit detailed comments on his "very realistic and vigorous Western Anglo-Irish...." Later, P. L. Henry (1965.14) explored at length the "rhythmical structure of Synge's prose...." Pat Barnett (1967.2), in discussing In the Shadow of the Glen, shows how Synge's lyrical dialogue is quite functional, e.g. it mirrors the poetic nature of Nora and the Tramp. Alan J. Bliss'

Glossary (1972.5) to the plays and poems contains 282 head-words.
Lorna Reynolds (1972.62) offers a detailed scansion of Synge's language patterns in relation to the Elizabethans and to the Authorized
Version of the Bible. Jiro Taniguchi's sprawling grammatical analysis of Gaelic-English (1972.74) devotes page after page to charts of
all types dealing with Synge's work. And Joachim Kornelius (1976.15)
lists proper names in Synge's plays and includes a pronunciation
guide and other helpful tools.

The student who is trying to elucidate the meaning of Synge's
works does have a number of excellent biographical sources. Those
who knew Synge personally have left accounts of their dealings with
him: Yeats (1900.1; 1905.12; 1911.84; 1924.10; 1928.6); John Masefield, the poet (1911.60; 1912.28; 1915.4); Lady Gregory (1913.9);
George Moore (1914.4); Cherrie Matheson Houghton, to whom Synge pro-
posed marriage (1924.3 [though her account disappoints those looking
for insight into Synge's makeup]); William G. Fay, the actor, and
Catherine Carswell (1935.6); Joseph Holloway, the indefatigable
chronicler of the Abbey (1963.9; 1967.10); Mary Walker (Maire Nic
Shiubhlaigh), the actress (1955.7); Lennox Robinson, who became one
of the Directors of the Abbey Theatre in 1923 (1951.4); and Max Meyerfeld, who translated The Well of the Saints into German (1924.6).

The standard biography of Synge is that by David H. Greene and
Edward M. Stephens, Synge's nephew (1959.5), but a number of important sources of information about Synge have been published since,
and the need for a definitive biography of Synge is obvious. Andrew
Carpenter (1974.29) has edited Stephens' massive life of his uncle,
John; Ann Saddlemyer has published Synge's letters to Molly Allgood
and some of his letters to Yeats and Lady Gregory (1971.41, 42);
W. R. Rodgers' Irish Literary Portraits (1973.15) contains comments
on Synge by Oliver Gogarty (Buck Mulligan in Joyce's Ulysses), the
publisher George Roberts, and others. Elizabeth Coxhead (1965.6) in
her Daughters of Erin, provides background on the Synge-Allgood engagement; and Ronald Ayling, in an article (1963.2), discusses the
Synge-Matheson relationship.

Also, there is no dearth of bibliographical studies, both primary
and secondary, devoted to Synge. Maurice Bourgeois (1913.3) early on
set a standard of sorts for Synge scholars with his sometimes inaccu-
rate but always exhaustive tome. M. J. McManus (1930.4) lists and
describes twelve of Synge's works, from 1904 to 1910. O. F. Babler
(1946.1) provides data on Czech translations of Synge's plays. David
H. Greene (1946.4) points out gaps in the four editions of Synge's
works published up to 1946 and calls for an adequate text. P. S.
O'Hegarty (1947.11) provides an important note on the first edition
of The Well of the Saints. A. E. Weldon (1949.3) gives data on first
productions of Synge's plays through 1910. Ian MacPhail (1959.8)
comments on translations of Synge's works and on their various English editions. Lawrence Wilson's slim collection of Synge's letters
and other documents (1959.14) has been published by Redpath Press and

McGill University Library. And Frances-Jane French (1970.5) provides
important data on The Well of the Saints and The Playboy of the Western World in her description of the Abbey Theatre Series of Plays.

Trinity College, Dublin, is the single most important storehouse
of Synge materials, and several scholars have described its holdings.
Trinity College has issued a brief check-list (compiled by Hester M.
Black) of first editions of Synge's works and those of George Russell
(1956.1). Ian MacPhail and M. Pollard (1959.9) have compiled A Cata-
logue of an Exhibition Held at Trinity College Library Dublin on the
Occasion of the Fiftieth Anniversary of His [Synge's] Death. Nicholas Grene has prepared the most significant single source of information about Trinity's Synge holdings in The Synge Manuscripts in the
Library of Trinity College Dublin (1971.50). And Grene and Ann Saddlemyer (1974.7; 1971.39) have worked with the Trinity papers to
elucidate Synge's writings.

Two recent, excellent books of secondary criticism on Synge are
J. M. Synge: A Bibliography of Published Criticism (1974.17) by
Paul M. Levitt, and J. M. Synge: A Bibliography of Criticism
(1975.18) by E. H. Mikhail. The second is a model of completeness;
the first, an example of unblemished accuracy. A third indispensable source of information about Synge criticism is Weldon Thornton's
chapter on Synge in Anglo-Irish Literature: A Review of Research
(1976.27), a judicious commentary on published work on Synge. Also,
Thornton has reviewed the Levitt and Mikhail books (1974.31; 1976.28).

Other useful secondary bibliographies are found in the following
books and articles: Adelaide Duncan Estill's doctoral dissertation,
The Sources of Synge (1939.3); Donna Gerstenberger's Twayne book on
Synge (1964.8); Mikhail's article, "Sixty Years of Synge Criticism,
1907-1967" (1970.10); and S. B. Bushrui's A Centenary Tribute to John
Millington Synge, 1871-1909: Sunshine and the Moon's Delight
(1972.8).

Finally, any student of Synge should be familiar with two ongoing
projects dealing with Anglo-Irish literature: the Work in Progress
handlists published by the Royal Irish Academy Dublin, Committee for
the Study of Anglo-Irish Language and Literature (1969.14), and the
Bibliography Bulletins issued by the International Association for
the Study of Anglo-Irish Language and Literature, compiled by M. Pollard (1972.57).

This present volume of Synge criticism is complete through 1976,
with several items from 1977. All of the works listed have been read.
But while the work is complete, it is not exhaustive. However, it
does annotate anything of importance said or written on Synge. The
Index is exhaustive in one respect: it lists all authors, editors,
and translators connected with criticism on Synge. Important works
dealing with Synge are listed under "Bibliography," "Biography,"
"Poetry," "Language," "The Aran Islands," and each of the six major

plays. Since the effort, however, was to be helpful without becoming puerile, a few of the items of small significance have been omitted from the rest of the Index. The book, then, should be read from cover to cover.

Acknowledgments

The following persons offered assistance in the preparation of this book, and I am most grateful to them: the library staff at Slippery Rock State College, and especially Ms. Janice E. Druschel, interlibrary loan librarian, whose efforts made it possible for me to obtain the materials cited in the book; many other libraries that expeditiously sent materials, but especially the National Library of Ireland, the Boston Public Library, the Pennsylvania State University Library, the University of Pennsylvania Library, the Temple University Library, and the Library of Youngstown State University; Slippery Rock State College, for helping to defray the costs of Xeroxing the manuscript; Eben Bass and Kenneth E. Harris, for the task of proofreading the book; and Joseph E. Geist and Jeanne Flood, for suggestions of inclusion of entries. Thanks, too, to Ms. Anita Miller, editor of the <u>Arnold Bennett Newsletter</u>, for permission to reprint the note on Arnold Bennett (1933.1).

List of Abbreviations

AI	American Imago
AntigR	Antigonish Review
Archiv	Archiv für das Studium der Neueren Sprachen und Literaturen
ArQ	Arizona Quarterly
BB	Bulletin of Bibliography
BNYPL	Bulletin of the New York Public Library
CahiersI	Cahiers Irlandais (Lille)
CathW	Catholic World [Now New Catholic World]
CEA	CEA Critic
CEMW	Columbia Essays on Modern Writers
CentR	The Centennial Review (Michigan State University)
CLQ	Colby Library Quarterly
ContempR	Contemporary Review (London)
CritQ	Critical Quarterly
DAI	Dissertation Abstracts International
DM	The Dublin Magazine [Formerly The Dubliner]
DR	Dalhousie Review
E&S	Essays and Studies by Members of the English Association
EDH	Essays by Diverse Hands
EI	Etudes Irlandaises (Lille)
EIC	Essays in Criticism (Oxford)
Éire	Éire-Ireland: A Journal of Irish Studies (St. Paul)
EJ	English Journal
ELN	English Language Notes
ELT	English Literature in Transition (1880-1920)
EngRev	English Review
ES	English Studies
ESA	English Studies in Africa (Johannesburg)
ETJ	Educational Theatre Journal
FJS	Fu Jen Studies (Republic of China)
FT	Finsk Tidskrift
GRM	Germanisch-romanische Monatsschrift, Neue Folge

HSL	Hartford Studies in Literature
IUR	Irish University Review
JEGP	Journal of English and Germanic Phi- lology
JIL	Journal of Irish Literature
JML	Journal of Modern Literature
LHY	Literary Half-Yearly
LWU	Literatur in Wissenschaft und Unterricht (Kiel)
MD	Modern Drama
MHRev	Malahat Review
MLN	Modern Language Notes
MR	Massachusetts Review (University of Massachusetts)
MTJ	Mark Twain Journal
N&Q	Notes and Queries
NEQ	New England Quarterly
NM	Neuphilologische Mitteilungen
NY	New Yorker
NYFQ	New York Folklore Quarterly
Pensée	La Pensée: Revue du Rationalisme Moderne
PhoenixC	Phoenix: The Classical Association of Canada
PLL	Papers on Language and Literature
PMLA	Publications of the Modern Language Association of America
PP	Philologica Pragensia
QJS	Quarterly Journal of Speech
QQ	Queen's Quarterly
RDM	Revue des Deux Mondes [Now Nouvelle Revue des Deux Mondes]
REH	Revista de Estudios Hispánicos (Univer- sity of Alabama)
RES	Review of English Studies
RHM	Revista Hispánica Moderna
RLC	Revue de Littérature Comparée
SAQ	South Atlantic Quarterly
SatR	Saturday Review
SFQ	Southern Folklore Quarterly
SHR	Southern Humanities Review
SoQ	The Southern Quarterly (University of Southern Mississippi)
SoR	Southern Review (Louisiana State Univer- sity)
SR	Sewanee Review
TCI	Twentieth Century Interpretations
TCL	Twentieth Century Literature
TEAS	Twayne's English Authors Series
ThR	Theatre Research/Recherches Théâtrales
TLS	Times Literary Supplement
TN	Theatre Notebook
TQ	Texas Quarterly (University of Texas)

Abbreviations

TUSAS	Twayne's United States Authors Series
TWAS	Twayne's World Authors Series
UWR	University of Windsor Review (Windsor, Ontario)
WascanaR	Wascana Review (Regina, Sask.)
WHR	Western Humanities Review
WN	A Wake Newslitter (Newcastle U. Coll., N.S.W.)
YR	Yale Review

Major Works by Synge

In the Shadow of the Glen, produced 1903; published 1904.

Riders to the Sea, published 1903; produced 1904.

The Well of the Saints, produced and published 1905.

The Aran Islands, published 1907.

The Playboy of the Western World, produced and published 1907.

The Tinker's Wedding, published 1908; produced, in London, 1909.

Poems and Translations, published 1909.

Deirdre of the Sorrows, produced and published 1910.

The Works of John M. Synge, 4 Vols., published 1910.

John M. Synge: Collected Works, 4 Vols., published 1962-68.

"Letters of John Millington Synge," published 1924.

Letters to Molly: John Millington Synge to Maire O'Neill,
    1906-1909, published 1971.

Some Letters of John M. Synge to Lady Gregory and W. B. Yeats,
    published 1971.

The Synge Manuscripts in the Library of Trinity College Dublin,
    published 1971.

Writings about Synge, 1900-1977

1900

1 YEATS, W. B. "Irish Witch Doctors." The Fortnightly Review, 74 (September), 440-456.
    Yeats mentions having spoken to a Mr. Synge, who provided him with information about the Aran Islands. Reprinted: 1976.30.

1903

1 ANON. "Irish National Theatre Society." Dublin The Daily Express (9 October), p. 5.
    Calls In the Shadow of the Glen a "gem" and defines the Irishness of the play: "the actions and characters are quite possible in real life, consequently in Irish life." Hints at the "polemical significance" of In the Shadow of the Glen, which the audience sensed, but avers that it is nevertheless "agreeable fooling."

2 ANON. "Irish National Theatre Society." Dublin The Freeman's Journal (9 October), pp. 5-6.
    Synge "must be congratulated on the success of his first effort." Calls In the Shadow of the Glen "a quaint Irish comedy" which is "true to nature." Describes the end of the play as "continuing the festivities of the 'wake.'" "...Mr. Synge was called before the curtain and received a most flattering ovation."

3 CONN. "In a Real Wicklow Glen." Dublin The United Irishman (24 October), p. 3.
    Pictures Nora, the protagonist of In the Shadow of the Glen, years later with several children, being visited by John, a "figure all in rags," whom she tries to coax from drink.

1903

4   [GRIFFITH, ARTHUR.] "All Ireland." Dublin The United Irish-
     man (10 October), p. 1.
        "During five years we have fought the prostitution of
     the stage in Ireland, and the defenders of the filth and
     abomination with which it abounded have been the...Inde-
     pendent and the...Freeman's Journal." Play in question is
     Sappho, starring Olga Nethersole. About In the Shadow of
     the Glen: "we have not ourselves yet seen or read." The
     diatribe foreshadows attacks upon Synge's work.

5   _____. "All Ireland." Dublin The United Irishman (17 Octo-
     ber), p. 1.
        A lengthy attack upon Synge and Yeats, implying that
     they are West-Britons, i.e. English sympathizers living in
     Ireland and accepting the plaudits of the British press.
     In the Shadow of the Glen is simply a page out of The De-
     cameron, an un-Irish product of European decadence and
     cynicism. In short, the play, influenced by the ancient
     story of the Widow of Ephesus, is an inferior substitute
     for Cathleen ni Houlihan, Yeats' earlier, patriotic work.

6   _____. Reply to W. B. Yeats's "The Irish National Theatre
     and Three Sorts of Ignorance." Dublin The United Irishman
     (24 October), p. 2.
        Contains the famous (or notorious) declaration of "the
     fact which all of us know--that Irishwomen are the most
     virtuous women in the world." Argues that Synge's Nora of
     In the Shadow of the Glen is not at all typical of Irish
     women. See 1903.12.

7   _____. Reply to J. B. Yeats's Letter, "The Irish National
     Theatre Society." Dublin The United Irishman (31 October),
     p. 7.
        Attacks Synge's portrait of the faithless Irish wife:
     "in no country are women so faithful to the marriage bond
     as in Ireland." Refuses to accept the plaudits of even a
     sympathetic English theatre critic: "being a Briton, he
     is our enemy, and the people who allows itself to be influ-
     enced by the praise or censure of its enemies maims its own
     soul." Contrasts Padraic Colum, the good Irishman, with
     Synge, who "spends most of his time away from Ireland...
     under the operation of foreign influences...." See 1903.9.

8   M., R. "The National Theatre Society: Last Night's Plays."
     The Dublin Evening Mail (9 October), p. 2.
        "If loveless marriage and marital infidelity have ever
     formed the chief ingredients of a problem play--and, Shades
     of Pinero and Jones, how often have they not done so!--the

'Shadow of the Glen' is of this school." Mentions that the play was received with some hissing.

9   YEATS, J. B.   "Correspondence: The Irish National Theatre Society." Dublin The United Irishman (31 October), p. 7.
        Attacks on In the Shadow of the Glen are really caused by the play's castigation of the loveless marriage and the fact that "anything like impulse or passion is discredited..." by "our thrifty elders." Yeats complains that Synge did not go far enough: he should have made it unmistakably clear that "the wife will not return to the house into which she should never have entered...." See 1903.7.

10   _____. "Ireland Out of the Dock." Dublin The United Irishman (10 October), p. 2.
        Contrasts Synge's peasant with the fictitious peasant described superficially by previous Irish writers. Sees In the Shadow of the Glen as an attack on the "foulness" of the "loveless marriage." Applauds Nora's departure with the tramp: "morality will often gain its end by loosening the ligatures."

11   YEATS, W. B.   "An Irish National Theatre." Dublin The United Irishman (10 October), p. 2.
        Writing to prepare Dublin for In the Shadow of the Glen, Yeats pleads for freedom of artistic expression. Also, the theme of the faithless wife is a "subject that inspired Homer and about half the great literature of the world." And about Synge's satiric picture of Ireland: "Aristophanes held up the people of Athens to ridicule, and...they invited the foreign ambassadors to the spectacle." Yeats calls himself a Nationalist, a person "who is ready to give up a great deal" for his country. Subsequent columns in The United Irishman attacked Yeats for not offering to give up "all" for his nation, as was counseled by his heroine Cathleen ni Houlihan.

12   _____. "The Irish National Theatre and Three Sorts of Ignorance." Dublin The United Irishman (24 October), p. 2.
        Analyzes the "obscurantism" of different types of Irishmen, including the once intellectually liberated nationalists who now attack Synge. Argues that women in a loveless marriage do indeed occasionally take on lovers; Yeats cites as evidence the lyrics of "The Red-haired Man's Wife." In fact, Synge "softened" the tales he had heard in the west of Ireland. Yeats uses the metaphor of the "shadow" to describe Ireland's dim opinion of Synge. See 1903.6. Reprinted: 1976.30.

1904

1   ANON. "Irish National Theatre Society," Dublin The Freeman's
     Journal (26 February), p. 6
         Small audience came to see George Russell's Deirdre and
     and Synge's Riders to the Sea, "a story mournful almost to
     weirdness."

2   BEERBOHM, MAX. "Some Irish Plays and Players." London The
     Saturday Review (9 April), pp. 455-457.
         About Yeats's The King's Threshold and Synge's Riders
     to the Sea and In the Shadow of the Glen: "quite simple
     and quite strange." "There was in none of the plays any
     structural complexity...." Praises the simplicity of the
     plays. In Riders to the Sea, "Mr. Synge, being an Irish-
     man, is content to show us the pathos of his theme: he
     does not...try to rouse any indignation." Beerbohm finds
     "plenty of poetry" in Riders to the Sea and compares its
     theme to that of Heijermans' play "The Good Hope." In the
     Shadow of the Glen is a "farce" but illustrates the ina-
     bility of the Irish to be "vulgar." Reprinted: 1953.1.

3   CONNOLLY, JAMES. "Some Plays and a Critic." Dublin The
     United Irishman (7 May), p. 6.
         Praises the effect of Riders to the Sea on the audience
     and adds that Synge's success in the play "lies chiefly...
     in the complete withdrawal, or rather concealment, of his
     own personality...."

4   [GRIFFITH, ARTHUR.] "All Ireland." Dublin The United Irish-
     man (5 March), p. 1.
         Praises the "tragic beauty" of Riders to the Sea but
     complains that Synge should have been able to produce this
     effect "without the introduction of the body of a drowned
     man on the stage...." He calls this ploy a "cheap trick."

5   JOY, MAURICE. "The Drama." Dublin The United Irishman
     (21 May), p. 3.
         Praises In the Shadow of the Glen and points out that
     viewing the play from the outside only caused a main point
     to be missed, that Nora "was formerly in love with the ro-
     mantic Michael Dara, and that she saw in the tramp who came
     now a resemblance to him...."

6   JOYCE, JAMES. "The Holy Office," in The Critical Writings of
     James Joyce. Edited by Ellsworth Mason and Richard Ellmann.
     New York: The Viking Press, pp. 149-150.
         Joyce calls Synge "him who sober all the day/Mixes a
     naggin in his play." See 1964.9.

7   O'D., D. "The Irish National Theatre Company." Dublin The
    United Irishman (9 April), p. 6.
        In contrast to In the Shadow of the Glen, which "rings
    true" artistically although it is not at all a picture of
    Irish life, Riders to the Sea is "false."

8   _____. "Some Plays and a Critic." Dublin The United Irishman
    (21 May), p. 3.
        Spells out evidence for the universality of The Well of
    the Saints and reiterates the complaint about Riders to the
    Sea: "can anyone catch the soul of the hour who has not
    lived the life of the years [of deprivation on the Aran
    Islands]?"

9   WEYGANDT, CORNELIUS. "The Irish Literary Revival." SR, 12,
    no. 4 (October), 420-431.
        Calls Synge's "'In a Wicklow Glen' [sic] a bitter sketch
    of the loveless marriages of the Irish peasants, and
    'Riders to the Sea' a tragic day in the gray life of the
    Aran fisher folk....'"

                              1905

1   ANON. "Ireland's National Theatre: Mr. Synge's New Play."
    Dublin The Freeman's Journal (6 February), p. 5.
        Questions whether Synge is an Irish dramatist at all and
    maintains that Synge knows nothing of the Irish peasant's
    religious nature, which lacuna is evidenced in all of his
    plays. Also, Synge "is as preoccupied with the sex problem
    as any of the London school of problem playwrights."
    Again, Synge's plays are "gruesome, not tragic." In short,
    Synge cannot pretend that he is portraying true Irish na-
    tional character in his work. The Well of the Saints re-
    flects Synge's nearness to the "unhealthy" elements in a
    country's life, and the play is not effective artistically
    since it has almost no action and only one character--
    Martin Doul.

2   ANON. "Irish National Theatre Society: 'The Well of the
    Saints.'" Dublin The Daily Express (6 February), p. 6.
        Says that The Well of the Saints is Irish in "garb,
    flavour and atmosphere." Explains that "Doul" is Gaelic
    for "blind." Maintains that Martin's second blinding is
    caused by his "sin" of wishing to elope with Molly Byrne.
    And feels that the Douls are driven away by the villagers
    because of Martin's irreverent act of kicking over the holy
    water can proffered by the Saint.

1905

3 [GRIFFITH, ARTHUR.] "All Ireland." Dublin <u>The United Irish-</u>
   <u>man</u> (28 January), p. 1.
       Contains Yeats's letter arguing to the universality of
   <u>The Well of the Saints</u> and Griffith's retort.

4 _____. "All Ireland." Dublin <u>The United Irishman</u> (11 February), p. 1.
       Comments on <u>The Well of the Saints</u>' wearisome and uneven
   dialogue, its atypical portrait of Irish people, its sensu-
   al atmosphere, the grossness of confounding loss of sight
   with regained imagination, and the blunder of having Martin
   Doul, long blind, recognize people by the color of their
   hair. Notes that Synge needs "compassion." Concludes with
   a thinly veiled reference to Synge's European studies and
   his Protestant background: the Irish National Theatre "can
   now only alternate a decadent wail with a Calvinistic
   groan."

5 _____. Reply to Yeats's Letter. Dublin <u>The United Irishman</u>
   (4 February), p. 1.
       Response to Yeats's demand that Synge's letter giving the
   Aran Islands source of <u>In the Shadow of the Glen</u> be printed.
   See 1905.6, 10, and 11.

6 _____. Reply to the Letters of Yeats and Synge. Dublin <u>The</u>
   <u>United Irishman</u> (11 February), p. 1.
       Says that he did not know that Synge wanted his letter
   made public and then states that he is refusing to publish
   Synge's description of his source because "of insufficient
   merit to entitle it to a place in our columns." For
   Yeats's involvement, <u>see</u> 1905.5; for Synge's, <u>see</u> 1905.5,
   10, and 11.

7 M., R. "At the Abbey Theatre: Production of 'The Well of the
   Saints.'" <u>The Dublin Evening Mail</u> (6 February), p. 2.
       Finds <u>The Well of the Saints</u> difficult to fit into any
   genre: "although it is cast in dramatic manner it is not
   a play in the accepted sense of the term. It lacks action
   and incident...[and is] a moral told from behind the foot-
   lights." Synge's intention is not worth searching out because "out of such intangible and fantastic material it
   will never be possible to build up a national Irish drama."

8 MOORE, GEORGE. "The Irish Literary Theatre." Dublin <u>The</u>
   <u>Irish Times</u> (13 February), p. 6.
       Moore sees Synge's work as a "new growth." Praises
   Synge's dialogue in <u>The Well of the Saints</u>: "Mr. Synge
   has discovered great literature in barbarous idiom as gold
   is discovered in quartz...."

9   SCUDDER, VIDA D. "The Irish Literary Drama: An Address De-
     livered at the Opening of the Twentieth Century Club Series
     of Plays." Poet Lore, 16, no. 1 (Spring), 40-53.
          Riders to the Sea purifies "by pity and terror," with
     the play being unified by the caoin of the dead and by the
     horrifying significance given to common objects. Riders
     to the Sea ends in the calm of a tragic catharsis.

10   SYNGE, J. M. Letter about the Source of In the Shadow of the
     Glen. Dublin The United Irishman (11 February), p. 1.
          Synge maintains that the source of In the Shadow of the
     Glen is a story he heard on the Aran Islands in 1898. See
     1905.5, 6, and 11.

11   YEATS, W. B. Letter to the Editor Concerning In the Shadow of
     the Glen. Dublin The United Irishman (4 February), p. 1.
          Yeats reiterates his claim that Synge's source for In
     the Shadow of the Glen was the Aran Islands. Arthur Grif-
     fith repeats his view that the play is a "prurient" revival
     of Petronius. See 1905.5, 6, and 10.

12   _____. "Introduction: Mr. Synge and His Plays," in The Well
     of the Saints by J. M. Synge. Being Volume Four of Plays
     for an Irish Theatre. London: A. H. Bullen, pp. iv-xvii.
          Yeats explains how he urged Synge to leave Paris and go
     to the Aran Islands, then discusses Synge's dialogue at
     length. Also, sees Synge's characters as driven by inde-
     finable dreams. Nora, of In the Shadow of the Glen, "feels
     an emotion that she does not understand." Reprinted:
     1912.36; 1924.9; 1961.14.

1907

1   ANON. "Abbey St. 'Parricide.'" Dublin The Evening Telegraph
     (1 February), p. 2.
          Describes the singing of the "Celtic War Cry," "O'Don-
     nell Abu," during the showing of The Playboy of the Western
     World, the mixture of cheering and jeering in the audience
     accompanied by the strains of "A Nation Once Again," and
     the arrests of two protestors. Prints William Boyle's let-
     ter withdrawing his plays from the Abbey because of Synge's
     "vilification of any section of the Irish people...," a
     disclaimer by Ambrose Power, the actor, on the matter of
     his using bad language during the performance, and a letter
     maintaining that only degraded people will frequent the
     Abbey in the future.

1907

2   ANON. "The Abbey Theatre: 'The Playboy of the Western
        World.'" Dublin The Freeman's Journal (28 January), p. 10.
           Contains most of the charges that were to be brought
        against the play. Calls the work "squalid," points out
        that the audience rebelled at the violence in Act III,
        complains about the "barbarous jargon," and demands a "cen-
        sor" at the Abbey. Reprinted: 1971.22.

3   ANON. "The Abbey Theatre: Uproarious Scenes." Dublin The
        Freeman's Journal (29 January), p. 7.
           Complains that Christy Mahon is left alone in Flaherty's
        publichouse with Pegeen. Reports Willie Fay's failing at-
        tempts to mollify the crowd. Reprinted: 1971.22.

4   ANON. "Another 'Playboy' Matinee." Dublin The Evening Tele-
        graph (2 February), p. 5.
           Interesting account of a hearing for Edward Dillon, ac-
        cused of causing a disturbance, having been arrested by
        Constable Dillon [sic]. Touches on the questions of
        whether the opposition to The Playboy of the Western World
        was organized and of Pegeen's being left unchaperoned with
        Christy.

5   ANON. "The Aran Islands." TLS (28 June), p. 202.
           Synge's book is "near" to beautiful, but "the ultimate
        sense of intimacy with these islanders is not communicated."
        "We feel also that the style of the book might be simpler,
        more transparent." Calls The Aran Islands too "objective"
        an account.

6   ANON. "'Freedom of the Theatre.'" Dublin The Evening Tele-
        graph (31 January), p. 4.
           Announcement of Yeats's discussion, "The Freedom of the
        Theatre and Mr. Synge's Play," to be held "on Monday
        next...." Announcement appeared on Thursday.

7   ANON. "Last Night's Disturbances." Dublin The Evening Tele-
        graph (2 February), p. 5.
           Notes that those sympathetic to The Playboy of the West-
        ern World had been given free admission tickets.

8   ANON. "'The Man That Killed His Da.'" Dublin The Evening
        Telegraph (2 February), p. 5.
           A humorous ballad commemorating the events that trig-
        gered the uproar over Synge's play--done in "Synge-y song."

9   ANON. "Parricide and Public: Discussion at the Abbey Thea-
      tre." Dublin The Freeman's Journal (5 February), pp. 6-7.
          Shows how the debate over The Playboy of the Western
      World was participated in by many important figures, from
      "Pat" to Conor Cruise O'Brien. This account reports Yeats's
      famous plea to the noisy crowd: "The author of 'Kathleen
      Ni Houlihan' [sic] appeals to you...." Yeats supports with
      an anecdote his insistence that Synge's play has a source
      in the Aran Islands. Reprinted: 1971.22 .

10   ANON. "Passing of the 'Parricide.'" Dublin The Evening Tele-
      graph (4 February), p. 2.
          Contains several important letters to the editor about
      controversy over The Playboy of the Western World.

11   ANON. "'Pegeen Mike'--A Parricide--Personalities--and Pre-
      tences." Belfast The Irish News and Belfast Morning News
      (31 January), p. 4.
          Provides background on P. D. Kenny, who, sympathetic to
      The Playboy of the Western World, surfaced as "Pat" in the
      newspaper columns. After a snide attack on Yeats and Lady
      Gregory, says flatly, "But the public are the jury, and
      their verdict must be accepted." Reprinted: 1971.22.

12   ANON. "The Playhouses: The Dublin Abbey Theatre Company at
      Great Queen Street." The Illustrated London News (22 June),
      p. 956.
          Describes first London performance of The Playboy of the
      Western World "last Monday evening at the Great Queen
      Street Theatre, where the famous Abbey Theatre company is
      established this week for its customary annual visit."
      Calls Synge's play "an exceedingly diverting, if rather
      cynical, exploitation of--what is undoubted fact--the hero-
      worship which some men and many women are ready to lavish
      on the criminal." The play has "robust humour and realis-
      tic observation" and its condemners lack "all appreciation
      of humour."

13   ANON. "Uproarious...Abbey Theatre Again Confusion Last Night."
      Dublin The Irish Independent (31 January), p. 5.
          A lengthy article about the disturbances over the fourth
      production of The Playboy of the Western World and the fol-
      lowing litigation. Surprisingly, audience was aware of
      precisely where the cuts in the play had been made. Also,
      mentions the arrest of Padraic Colum's father and prints
      the son's letter of protest.

1907

14   AVIS. "The Playboys in the Abbey." Dublin The Leader (2 Feb-
     ruary), pp. 387-388.
          Calls the Abbey and Synge "neurotic" and refers to the
     building which the Abbey Theatre took over in 1904 and
     turned into a theater: "the Movement in the Morgue...."
     Reprinted: 1971.22.

15   BIRMINGHAM, GEORGE A. "The Literary Movement in Ireland."
     The Fortnightly Review, NS 82, no. 492 (December), 947-957.
          Praises the "virile" Synge and calls him "By far the
     boldest and most original of our Irish dramatists...."
     Feels that Synge should be consoled over the attacks on his
     works: he must be a great figure to merit such ire.

16   BOYLE, WILLIAM. "Mr. William Boyle's Protest." Dublin The
     Freeman's Journal (1 February), p. 6.
          Boyle withdraws his plays because of the Abbey Theatre's
     "vilification" of a "section of the Irish People...."
     Also, uses the reception by the audience as the best test
     of a playwright's worth: "the Irish public has accepted my
     criticisms...." Reprinted: 1971.22.

17   COLUM, PADRAIC. "Letter from Mr. Padraic Colum, Author of
     'The Land.'" Dublin The Freeman's Journal (31 January),
     p. 8.
          A balanced letter which, while it deplores the use of
     police at the Abbey, pleads for a hearing of Synge's play
     so that it might be judged accurately. Reprinted: 1971.22.

18   D., H. S. "A Dramatic Freak: First Night at the Abbey Thea-
     tre." The Dublin Evening Mail (28 January), p. 2.
          Suggests an allegorical meaning for The Playboy of the
     Western World, in which the parricide represents "some kind
     of nation-killer" and Synge "may have been pulling our leg
     with his theme...." Mr. Synge himself is "apparently, 'The
     Playboy of the Western World'...." Reprinted: 1971.22.

19   DUNCAN, ELLEN. "The 'Playboy.'" Dublin The Irish Times
     (31 January), p. 5.
          The dialogue, though masterful at times, tends to ob-
     scure the incompletely developed theme of the play: "the
     stimulating effect of hero worship, following upon a life-
     time of suppression...." Reprinted: 1971.22.

20   ELTON, OLIVER. "Mr. J. M. Synge's Plays," in Modern Studies.
     London: Edward Arnold, pp. 308-312.
          Praises Synge's art, which is "as yet short of its full
     maturity," and traces in The Aran Islands sources for
     Synge's plays.

21   F., A. "'I Don't Care a Rap': Mr. Synge's Defence." The
     Dublin Evening Mail (29 January), p. 2.
          The beleaguered Synge, in a hasty interview with a des-
     perate reporter, made several comments about his work that
     were to be held against him. His object in The Playboy of
     the Western World was "'nothing.'" About the use of police
     to quell the disturbances: "'it does not matter a rap.'"
     Synge cites his Aran Islands source for his play and then
     says that it is an "'extravaganza, made to amuse....'" Re-
     printed: 1971.22; 1977.7.

22   [GRIFFITH, ARTHUR.] "The Abbey Theatre." Dublin Sinn Féin
     (2 February), p. 2.
          Calls The Playboy of the Western World the work of a
     "moral degenerate" told in the "language of the gutter."
     (Part of the attack was based upon a mishearing of the word
     "stuttering," with Griffith thinking he had heard "fuck-
     ing.") As Griffith states, "The father of the hero, refers
     to his son in one place as 'a dirty lout.' The word
     omitted is so obscene that no man of ordinary decency would
     use it...." Reprinted: 1971.22.

23   GWYNN, STEPHEN. "Mr. Boyle and Mr. Synge: Letter from Mr.
     Stephen Gwynn, M.P." Dublin The Freeman's Journal (2 Feb-
     ruary), p. 2.
          Argues that The Playboy of the Western World is based
     on reality, that Boyle's plays have done more than Synge's
     to harm Ireland's image, and that Boyle should have read
     Synge's play before denouncing it. Reprinted: 1971.22.

24   HORNIMAN, A. E. F. "The Abbey Theatre: Letter from Miss
     Horniman." The Dublin Evening Mail (12 February), p. 3.
          Believes that "The accusation of the too light and fre-
     quent use of sacred names is out of place from people who
     hoot and hiss 'God Save Ireland' or 'God Save the King.'"
     Maintains that "No jury would bring in a verdict of wilful
     murder against Christy Mahon...."

25   AN IRISHWOMAN. "A Lady Defender of the Play." Dublin The
     Evening Telegraph (31 January), p. 4.
          Distinguishes between Synge's play and those containing
     Stage Irishmen.

26   JUSTITIA. "The Prestige of the Abbey." Dublin The Evening
     Telegraph (4 February), p. 2.
          Compares the Abbey Directors to shop keepers and says,
     without irony, that they should serve merchandise that
     pleases the customers.

1907

27   MARKHAM, THOMAS. "'Singed His Wings.'" Dublin The Evening
      Telegraph (31 January), p. 4.
         Calls Synge "a mystic whose creations are formed in the
      ebb of shadowy waters."

28   MILLIGAN, ALICE. "Letter from Miss Milligan." Dublin The
      Freeman's Journal (4 February), p. 4.
         Shrewdly says that Yeats is using the controversy over
      The Playboy of the Western World for "advertising." Says
      that Synge's play is similar to a "squalid" story, "The
      Hero of Hamilton street" [sic]. Feels that "English maga-
      zine literature is now greatly concerned with the criminal
      and his surroundings." Reprinted: 1971.22.

29   O'DONOGHUE, D. J. "Letter from Mr. O'Donoghue." Dublin The
      Freeman's Journal (4 February), p. 4.
         Argues that there is no comparison between The Playboy
      of the Western World and Boyle's "masterpieces," adding,
      "I am afraid Mr. Synge's play is due to ignorance of public
      life." Reprinted: 1971.22.

30   OMAOLÁIN, MICEÁL. "Mr. Synge's Knowledge of the West." Dub-
      lin The Evening Telegraph (31 January), p. 4.
         Letter to the editor asking Synge to defend his claim
      that Aran Islanders give refuge to murderers.

31   ORYZA. "'A Tramcar Conversation.'" Dublin The Evening Tele-
      graph (4 February), p. 2.
         Reports two remarks by Synge that were overheard by
      people seated near him in the theater. One was, "'The
      Irish seem to have lost all sense of humour; we shall soon
      have to establish a Society for the Preservation of Irish
      Humour!'"

32   PAT [P. D. KENNY]. "That Dreadful Play." Dublin The Irish
      Times (30 January), p. 9.
         Posits the theory that The Playboy of the Western World
      contains "two plays, one within another...." Synge has
      "shot his dreadful searchlight into our cherished accumula-
      tion of social skeletons.... The merciless accuracy of his
      revelation is more than we can bear." Pegeen turns to
      Christy out of desperation; her other choice is the "trem-
      bling," cowardly Shawn. Adds, prophetically, that The
      Playboy of the Western World "is a play on which many arti-
      cles could be written." Reprinted: 1971.22.

33   ROLLESTON, T. W. "The 'Playboy' as a Book." Dublin The Irish
      Independent (6 March), p. 7.

A crucial judgment on The Playboy of the Western World, which is "profoundly tragic.... There is cynicism on the surface, but a depth of ardent sympathy and imaginative feeling below, and vistas of thought are opened up that lead from the West of Ireland shebeen to the stars."

34   [RUSSELL, GEORGE (AE)]. "Britannia Rule-the-Wave: A Comedy (in One Act and in Prose)." Dublin Sinn Féin (9 February), p. 3.
     A parody of Synge and Yeats using the incantatory language of Cathleen ni Houlihan in which Lady Gregory becomes the Old Lady of Ireland: "I never saw anybody like her before. Wanting to be a charwoman, maybe." Unsigned. Possible author is George Russell (AE). Reprinted: 1971.22.

35   S.-S., F. [FRANCIS SHEEHY-SKEFFINGTON]. "An Impression of 'The Playboy.'" Dublin The Irish Times (29 January), p. 8.
     While pleading for a week's hearing for The Playboy of the Western World, points out its poor construction, its thinness over three acts, and Synge's "obsession by the sexual idea...." Reprinted: 1971.22.

36   SHANGANAGH [ARTHUR GRIFFITH]. "The Fable of the Fiddler." Dublin Sinn Féin (9 February), p. 3.
     Parodies Yeats's and Synge's view of the uneducated masses. Reprinted: 1971.22.

37   SYNGE, J. M. "Letter from Mr. Synge." Dublin The Evening Telegraph (31 January), p. 4.
     Synge says that although parts of The Playboy of the Western World are "extravagant comedy...a great deal more that is behind it, is perfectly serious, when looked at in a certain light." Adds the often quoted line: "There are, it may be hinted, several sides to 'The Playboy.'" Reprinted: 1971.22.

38   A WESTERN GIRL. Letter to the Editor. Dublin The Freeman's Journal (28 January), p. 10.
     Miss Allgood (Pegeen Mike in The Playboy of the Western World) has been forced to use a word [shift] "indicating an essential item of female attire, which the lady would probably never utter in ordinary circumstances, even to herself." Reprinted: 1971.22.

39   YEATS, W. B. "The Controversy over the Playboy." The Arrow, 1, no. 3 (23 February), 1-2, 6-9.
     "I have reprinted in the present Arrow my speech at the Debate in the Abbey Theatre on the 4th of February upon the

1907

Playboy, and the measures taken to preserve order, and certain extracts from the 'Samhain' of 1905, and from patri-
otic papers of various dates." Places The Playboy of the
Western World securely in the long history of attacks by
those who have tried to censor the artist.

40   _____. "Interview with Mr. W. B. Yeats: Synge's Version of
the Objectionable Passage." Dublin The Freeman's Journal
(30 January), p. 8.
    Maintains, citing Lady Macbeth as an example, that all
"great literature...dealt with exaggerated types...."
Synge says that the objectionable word, shift, was used by
Douglas Hyde, in Irish, in Love Songs of Connacht. Reprinted: 1971.22; 1977.10.

41   _____. "Notes." The Arrow, 1, no. 4 (1 June), 1-2.
    About The Playboy of the Western World: "The failure of
the audience to understand this powerful and strange work
has been the one serious failure of our movement...," and
this failure was caused not by the regular patrons of the
Abbey, but by groups organized by the politicians. Reprinted: 1976.30.

1908

1   UNTERMEYER, LOUIS. "J. M. Synge and The Playboy of the Western World." Poet Lore, 19 (September), 364-367.
    Praises Synge's unrestrained, bold, and virile poetry;
compares Christy Mahon to Peer Gynt; and maintains that
Synge embodies Shaw's Life Force in his characters--but
without Shaw's pretensiveness. The Playboy of the Western
World is a comedy but effectively commingles most other
genres as well.

1909

1   ANON. "The Playhouses: Irish Theatre Society at the Court."
The Illustrated London News (12 June), p. 870.
    Praises the acting of the Irish Theatre Company "last
Monday night" in The Playboy of the Western World, which
is Synge's "good-natured indictment" and not a work of
vilification. Praises the farcical humor and the poetry,
as well.

2   CONNELL, F. NORREYS. "John Millington Synge." EngRev, 2
    (June), 609-613.
        Praises The Playboy of the Western World as "the joy of
    a child's dream of chivalry" and "one of the finest love-
    comedies in the English language," but finds Riders to the
    Sea thin and not intellectually stimulating. The Tinker's
    Wedding is a failure with the "sinister ugliness of sheer
    farce" characterizing the last act.

3   YEATS, W. B. "John M. Synge," in Poems and Translations by
    John M. Synge. Churchtown: Cuala Press, pp. vi-[xiv].
        In addition to Yeats's moving reverie on Synge's death,
    the section includes a letter from Synge about his own
    poetry and crucial comments by Yeats on Synge's plays.
    Synge was a "solitary, undemonstrative man, never asking
    pity, nor complaining, nor seeking sympathy...all folded u[
    in brooding intellect, knowing nothing of new books and
    newspapers...." See 1910.4. Reprinted: 1912.36; 1924.9;
    1961.14.

1910

1   ANON. "The Playhouses: 'Deirdre of the Sorrows,' at the
    Court." The Illustrated London News (4 June), p. 854.
        "...rarely, if ever, did Mr. Synge achieve such exqui-
    site phrasing and prose-rhythm." Complaint is that "the
    action is inclined to drag and limp along." Synge over-
    emphasized the literary side of his play at the expense of
    the dramatic.

2   ARCHER, WILLIAM. "The Drama: The Art of the Artless." The
    Nation (4 June), pp. 346-347.
        Calls Deirdre of the Sorrows "a thing of extraordinary
    beauty, a permanent enrichment of our dramatic literature."

3   BICKLEY, FRANCIS. "Synge and the Drama." The New Quarterly,
    3 (February), 73-84.
        Synge's writings describe a life that is "Close to the
    earth and within hearing of the song of the stars...."

4   HODGSON, GERALDINE E. "Some Irish Poetry." ContempR, 98
    (September), 323-340.
        Comments briefly on Synge's Poems and Translations: "I
    is no 'pathetic fallacy' into which Mr. Synge has fallen,
    but rather that coincidence of human sorrow with painful
    surroundings...which...furnishes a thread in the texture
    of much Irish thought." See 1909.3.

1919

5   YEATS, W. B. "Preface," in <u>Deirdre of the Sorrows: A Play by</u>
    <u>John M. Synge</u>. Churchtown: Cuala Press, n.p.
        An important comment on the role of Owen in <u>Deirdre of</u>
    <u>the Sorrows</u>. Had Synge lived, the play would have been his
    "masterwork, so much beauty is there in its course, and
    such wild nobleness in its end, and so poignant is an emo-
    tion and wisdom that were his own preparation for death."

6   _____. "The Tragic Theatre." <u>The Mask</u>, 3 (October), 77-81.
        Points out matters in <u>Deirdre of the Sorrows</u> that the
    audience missed. Yeats says, for example, that the third
    act pleased Synge most but that no reviewer detected its
    excellence. Before the third act Yeats found that <u>Deirdre</u>
    <u>of the Sorrows</u> was "a master's unfinished work, monotonous
    and melancholy, ill arranged, little more than a sketch of
    what it would have grown to...." The third act, however,
    rises to a "tragic ecstasy." Reprinted: 1912.36; 1976.30.

                            1911

1   ANON. "The Abbey Theatre." <u>Boston Evening Transcript</u> (3 Oc-
    tober), p. 13.
        Article contains Yeats's explanation of how Synge re-
    wrote <u>The Playboy of the Western World</u> to match the scenery
    necessitated by Yeats's theory of stage design and setting.

2   ANON. "Acting of the Irish Players." <u>The New York Times</u>
    (26 November), Part 7, p. 2.
        The Irish actors are strictly amateurs--although they
    have been exalted by those with a cause--and such provin-
    cial types should not expect to be considered professionals
    by metropolitan playgoers. <u>The Playboy of the Western</u>
    <u>World</u> is delightful entertainment and must not be viewed
    as part of a cause.

3   ANON. "Approves the Irish Play." <u>Boston Evening Transcript</u>
    (17 October), p. 3.
        Mayor Fitzgerald, acting upon a report of his secretary,
    who attended <u>The Playboy of the Western World</u>, found noth-
    ing damaging to public morals in the work, even though his
    secretary thought the biting of "Shane's [sic]" leg "mon-
    strous and disgusting." Sees the play as not realistic,
    but, rather, symbolic--and an extravaganza. <u>See</u> 1911.7.

4   ANON. "The Aran Islands." <u>The Independent</u>, 71 (6 July), 44.
        Synge's book is "a travel narrative full of zest, vivid
    portraiture and admirable descriptions of nature."

5   ANON. "Attractions at the Theatres: 'The Playboy of the West-
     ern World' at the Plymouth." The Boston Sunday Globe
     (15 October), p. 58.
          Defines the term "playboy." Says that the work should
     be read as a "satiric fable."

6   ANON. "Comes to Direct Irish Players." The Boston Daily
     Globe (30 September), p. 4.
          Brief comment by Lady Gregory to a reporter that Synge
     had been to the "island of Aran." (Important because this
     datum is the one that stood out in the reporter's mind.)
     Reprinted: 1913.9.

7   ANON. "Doesn't need Expurgation: Boston Opinion of 'The
     Playboy.'" The Boston Daily Globe (17 October), p. 6.
          Mayor Fitzgerald's secretary, William A. Leahy, sent by
     the mayor to act as censor of The Playboy of the Western
     World, did not find it obscene, although coarse and vulgar.
     Piece includes a long quotation from Leahy's report to his
     superior. The quality of Leahy's appreciation is exempli-
     fied in his comment that Pegeen "sheltered two men in her
     heart and wavered when she might have chosen." See 1911.3.

8   ANON. "Drama." The Nation (12 October), pp. 346-347.
          Praises the "refined, simple, vigorous prose" of The
     Aran Islands; maintains that Riders to the Sea is overrated,
     not truly a tragedy, but that it still has "theatrical value
     of a very high order." The Tinker's Wedding is simply a
     "broad farce" and may be "dismissed briefly."

9   ANON. "Drama." The Nation (30 November), pp. 528-529.
          Synge's plays are too limited to present a true picture
     of Ireland; his talents are descriptive and poetic, but not
     dramatic. The Well of the Saints contains "a wandering
     friar," who is a "grotesque creation." Any possible mean-
     ing behind the fantasy of The Playboy of the Western World
     "is not suggested either by the dialogue or the players."

10   ANON. "How Ireland Turned from Politics to Playwriting." The
     New York Times (3 December), Part 5, p. 5.
          Describes an interview with Lady Gregory backstage dur-
     ing a performance of The Playboy of the Western World.
     Lady Gregory states at one point: "Two of those who were
     arrested for rioting" against the play "were Englishmen,
     who didn't like the reference to khaki-clad cutthroats."
     Article develops Lady Gregory's belief that the Irish lit-
     erary movement began with Parnell's death. The slight
     morbidity in Synge's plays is not due to the French

1911

influence, but, Lady Gregory maintains, to the "shadow of
his early death." Lady Gregory believes that the Irish
Players defended Synge's plays during his lifetime and that
they will scarcely fail to do so now that he is dead.

11 ANON. "An Irish Anthology." Boston Evening Transcript
    (19 October), p. 12.
        Complains that "Even the Playboy's lovemaking is not
    love, but love of the words love uses."

12 ANON. "The Irish Players." Boston Evening Transcript
    (23 September), p. 9.
        Brief plot summary of The Well of the Saints, Synge's
    "ironic and bitter comedy."

13 ANON. "Irish Players as Wild Westerners." The New York Times
    (24 November), p. 13.
        Audience simply didn't understand The Well of the Saints
    and found it merely laughable.

14 ANON. "Irish Players at the Plymouth." The Boston Daily
    Globe (3 October), p. 17.
        Includes details about the dark stage scenery in Riders
    to the Sea.

15 ANON. "Irish Players Fear no Riot." The New York Times
    (26 November), Part 1, p. 15.
        Cites The Gaelic American, which warned Lady Gregory on
    November 11 that "rotten eggs may not be so scarce in other
    places as Boston or Providence." Announces that The Play-
    boy of the Western World will open the next day at Maxine
    Elliott's Theatre. William Flynn, general manager of the
    Irish Players, said that the New York Police Department
    would prevent a riot--in contrast to the one in New Haven,
    where Yale Students wrecked the Hyperion Theatre.

16 ANON. "Irish Players in New Bill." Boston The Christian
    Science Monitor (3 October), p. 5.
        Riders to the Sea is a "masterly monotone, a Whistler
    drama."

17 ANON. "Irish Players to Act 'The Playboy.'" Boston The
    Christian Science Monitor (14 October), p. 14.
        Provides background, including an account of the Dublin
    protests, for The Playboy of the Western World, a "satiric
    fable."

18   ANON. "The Irish Players: The Victory for 'The Playboy.'"
      Boston Evening Transcript (18 October), p. 23.
         Says that the performance of the play the previous even-
      ing was "altogether undisturbed" and sees the performance
      as a great example of freedom of expression.

19   ANON. "An Irish Playwright." The Independent (13 April),
      pp. 792-793.
         Praises The Tinker's Wedding (in the Luce, 1910 edition
      of Synge's work) but says that it has less poetry than any
      of "the dramas of this master of stinging and idealistic
      prose." Contrasts the "salt" of Synge's dialogue with the
      vapidity of modern dramatists.

20   ANON. "New Plays and New Music: Signs in the Irish Heavens."
      Boston Evening Transcript (5 October), p. 14.
         Defends Synge's knowledge of the Irish mind and points
      out that Synge was not trying for photographic realism.

21   ANON. "Playboy Dead as a Nail in a Door." New York The Gael-
      ic American (9 December), p. 1.
         Besides this premature headline, the front page story
      contains an attack on Lady Gregory's Ascendancy background
      and a large pictorial caricature of the Irish Theatre's
      principals.

22   ANON. "'The Playboy' in New York." Boston Evening Transcript
      (28 November), p. 14.
         Provides a full account of the riots in New York: "Bos-
      ton only hissed; Manhattan threw eggs." And: "Yet so un-
      reasoning was the opposition that even when the villagers
      were about to hang the parricide, hitherto the object of
      the disturbers' wrath, they only hissed the more." One man
      shouted that the rope should be put around Synge's neck,
      "pronouncing the author's name with a soft 'g.'"

23   ANON. "'The Playboy of the Western World.'" Boston The
      Christian Science Monitor (17 October), p. 4.
         Sees The Playboy of the Western World as "an ironic epic
      of loneliness and the grotesque yet imaginative effort of
      the peasants of a gray countryside to escape from it...."

24   ANON. "The 'Playboy' Row." The New York Times (29 November),
      p. 10.
         Complains of the unfairness of Gaelic-Americans, who
      will not permit others to see and appreciate Synge's play,
      "this queer, partly droll, partly pathetic piece by the
      dead poet."

1911

25   ANON. "The Poetry of Ireland." The Living Age, 271 (7 October), 15-24.
     Comments on Synge's depiction of nature in The Well of the Saints, on tragedy in Riders to the Sea, and on Shakespearean comedy in The Tinker's Wedding: "Mr. Synge stands by himself in a niche in the literary Temple of Fame...."

26   ANON. "Pursuing 'The Playboy.'" Boston Evening Transcript (29 November), p. 22.
     A lengthy article. States that the majority of people had bought their tickets after the previous night's rioting because they wanted to see more police action. Lady Gregory and Colonel Roosevelt sat side-by-side, with Roosevelt laughing till his face was red when Christy went to attack his father for the second time. Article relates how the audience had sat with their backs turned to the stage and how not one actor appeared in the center of the stage. One woman with a "stink bomb" had kept repeating, "'I'm waiting till the author comes out.'" One man had complained that The Playboy of the Western World was "indelicate" because the peasant girls appeared on the stage without shoes and stockings. Another critic, however, had stressed the fact that no real violence appears in the play and that Pegeen probably knew from the start that Christy did not really kill his father.

27   ANON. "Representative Boston Men Criticise 'The Playboy of of the Western World.'" The Boston Daily Globe (17 October), p. 9.
     A committee of men appointed by the Boston Globe to witness the first night's performance of The Playboy of the Western World at the Plymouth Theatre (16 October). See individual entries: 1911.38, 51, 55, 65, 71.

28   ANON. "Riot in Theatre over an Irish Play." The New York Times (28 November), pp. 1, 3.
     Describes the "Donnybrook Fair" at the first production of The Playboy of the Western World at the Maxine Elliott Theatre on the evening of November 27th. The disturbances in other places were "as prayer meetings in comparison with the reception it got here [New York]." Mentions the cries of "shame," the throwing of vegetables and asafoetida balls, the violent ejections of demonstrators, the beginning reluctance of police to interfere, the repetition of the first act (the "first time such a thing has happened in the history of the stage in this country"), the fining of several demonstrators, and the condemning of Pegeen's vile language by Seumas MacManus (see 1911.59), the Irish author.

"One of the witnesses against [a demonstrator who threw eggs] was Miss Emmett, a niece of Robert Emmett" [sic]. Account is followed by a commentary deploring the rioting and pointing out the merits of The Playboy of the Western World: its use of imagination and the humanity of the love scenes.

29   ANON. "Satiric Drama by the Irish Players." The Boston Daily Globe (17 October), p. 15.
       Negative comments on the "construction" of The Playboy of the Western World, especially on Old Mahon's appearance in Act 2, which tends to kill interest. The play is better in the library "than on the stage."

30   ANON. "Simple and Real." The Boston Sunday Globe (24 September), p. 9.
       Praises the realism and construction of In the Shadow of the Glen and its faithful recording of Irish character: "Synge is freely granted recognition as the greatest of Irish dramatists and he must also be given consideration as among the ablest of any nationality."

31   ANON. "Some Hisses, Some Cheers." The Boston Daily Globe (17 October), p. 9.
       Describes the mild disapproval at the Plymouth, especially in the last act of The Playboy of the Western World, with further disturbance quelled, however, by the "quick turns in the 'situations.'"

32   ANON. "The Theatrical World: Irish Players Change Bill." Boston The Christian Science Monitor (27 September), p. 12.
       Stresses the symbolic content of The Well of the Saints.

33   ANON. "This Week at the Theatres." Boston The Sunday Herald (1 October), p. 24.
       Calls Riders to the Sea the "most universally liked" of Synge's plays.

34   ANON. "The Works of J. M. Synge." The Living Age, 269, no. 3484 (15 April), 163-166.
       Though Synge is no Shakespeare, his work will definitely live on. Comments at length on Deirdre of the Sorrows, calls "Danny" a "striking" poem and praises Synge's poetry generally, finding that in three poems Synge comes "nearer to the true spirit of the ballad than any poet of our time."

1911

35   BLAKE, WARREN BARTON. "John Synge and His Plays." The Dial,
     50 (16 January), 37-41.
          Contrasts Synge's contributions with those of the ephem-
     eral new dramatists such as Padraic Colum, then sketches
     several parts of Synge's biography: Synge's Protestant
     background, which lent him individuality; his wanderings;
     his rejection of the Symbolists; Synge's practice of learn-
     ing the ways of the poorer classes, which assisted him in
     characterization; and his meeting with Yeats, which led to
     his going to the Aran Islands. Compares In the Shadow of
     the Glen to Hedda Gabler; mentions that, because of Synge's
     art, the audience is not bothered by the rapid changes
     which the characters undergo; and compares the deprived
     Nora with Christy Mahon. Synge's dramas resemble those of
     the Elizabethans, with their dramatic poetry, and his form
     benefited from his study of the French critics. Synge's
     language could revitalize the English stage.

36   BRANN, HENRY A. "The Modern Literary Conscience." America,
     6, no. 2 (21 October), 30-31.
          The Playboy of the Western World is "vulgar and loath-
     some." Synge's Preface alone "damns him.... Imagine Synge
     lying on the floor, now listening, now peering through a
     hole in it at the poor innocent girls, to get a plot for an
     indecent play! An eavesdropper and a peeping Tom combined!"

37   CAZAMIAN, MADELEINE. "Le Théâtre de J. M. Synge." La Revue
     du Mois, 12 (October), 456-468.
          The audacity of Synge's treatment of the Irish peasant
     is justified by "les exigences de l'art...."

38   CONNOLLY, JAMES B. "Sincere in His Art." The Boston Daily
     Globe (17 October), p. 9.
          Stresses Synge's sincerity and his deep knowledge of
     the Irish people. For example, Synge did not intend Martin
     Doul to be a "type of the Irish people, but rather a vil-
     lain, who knocks holy water from the hands of a Catholic
     priest" [sic]. The Playboy of the Western World reflects
     Synge's poetic nature: he sees life through a mist of fan-
     tasy. See 1911.27.

39   D., E. K. "The Irish Theatre Society." The Dial, 51 (16 De-
     cember), 521.
          Praises Synge's "masterpieces" and the work of the Irish
     players generally despite the "unappreciative public."

40   DUNSANY, [LORD]. "Romance and the Modern Stage." The Na-
          tional Review, 57, Part 2 (July), 827-835.
              Briefly, praises Yeats and Synge as providing a "res-
          pite" from a materialistic age which has banished fancy
          and romance.

41   EGERTON, GEORGE. "Irish National Drama Real Says Noted Eng-
          lish Writer." Boston The Christian Science Monitor
          (23 September), p. 25.
              Finds much worth in the developing Irish Players: "One
          need only compare the ordinary Boucicault stage hero with,
          for instance, Chrysty [sic] Mahon...to see what a distance
          has been traversed since the Irish players first took the
          stage."

42   FIGGIS, DARRELL. "The Art of J. M. Synge." The Fortnightly
          Review, 110 NS (December), 1056-1068.
              Comments on the earthiness of Synge's works (a quality
          learned on the Aran Islands) and their sense of fatality
          and on Synge's dialect. About the plays: "If Riders to
          the Sea is Synge's loftiest achievement, The Well of the
          Saints is the most human." The Playboy of the Western
          World is his "greatest," and Deirdre of the Sorrows, "de-
          spite some strange faults, his most beautiful." The Play-
          boy of the Western World "chances to be the play in which
          Synge most fully found himself." Structural faults of
          Deirdre of the Sorrows come from Synge's early death--
          before he had a chance to correct the contradictory moti-
          vations of the heroine's character. Reprinted with slight
          revisions: 1912.16, 17.

43   [FORD], FORD MADOX [FORD MADOX HUEFFER]. The Critical Atti-
          tude. London: Duckworth, pp. 82-83.
              Speaking of Shaw and his stress on ideas, writes, "Not
          one of his plays will leave as much mark upon the emotions
          as, let us say, 'The Playboy of the Western World'...."

44   FULLER, EUNICE. "The Abbey Theatre." Boston Evening Tran-
          script (7 October), Part 3, p. 4.
              About the early Synge: "'He had written a book of folk-
          lore on the Aran Islands, which I [Lady Gregory] myself
          took around to all the London publishers, only to have it
          rejected; and he had written some poems and plays of no
          value.'" Reprinted: 1913.9.

23

1911

45   [GREGORY, LADY.] "Isabella Augusta, Lady Gregory, 'The Comedy
     Spirit of Ireland': A Grand-mother Author and Says She Has
     a Right to Laugh." Boston The Sunday Herald (1 October),
     Magazine Section, p. 4.
        Lady Gregory quoted as saying about The Playboy of the
     Western World: "I will admit that I have some sympathy
     for the honest objectors to it." To the charge of pagan-
     ism in the Irish Theatre movement, Lady Gregory answers,
     "humbug." Article contains Lady Gregory's curious state-
     ment that she and Yeats "often" accepted scenarios of
     plays from contributors and then wrote the dialogue for
     them themselves. (One wonders which dramatists and which
     plays.)

46   _____. "Lady Gregory Here with Irish Players." The New York
     Times (20 November), p. 11.
        On the day of the Irish Players' first appearance in New
     York, Lady Gregory avers that opposition to The Playboy of
     the Western World is due in part to "'race sensitiveness.'"
     Also, Lady Gregory "told of the Police Chief in one city,
     who recommended that certain lines in the play be omitted
     under the impression that he was seeing" The Playboy of the
     Western World. Actually, he had been witnessing Shaw's
     Blanco Posnet.

47   HALE, PHILIP. "Dramatic and Musical Review: Mr. W. B. Yeats
     and J. M. Synge." Boston The Sunday Herald (1 October),
     p. 24.
        The relationship between Yeats and Synge shows how "one
     genius found another...." Hale thinks that Synge's "low
     vitality" helped him to become "observant and contempla-
     tive."

48   _____. "Dramatic and Musical Review: The Origin of 'The
     Playboy.'" Boston The Sunday Herald (15 October), p. 24.
        Based upon remarks by Yeats, article contains good mate-
     rial on the etymology of "playboy"; it explains Yeats's
     decision not to restage The Playboy of the Western World
     at the Abbey during Synge's lifetime on the basis of his
     "very delicate constitution" (the excitement of even a suc-
     cessful performance in London, Yeats maintains, made him
     ill); and describes the success of the play in London's
     Great Queen Street Theatre on June 10, 1907, where the au-
     dience was "nearly entirely Irish...."

49 HOARE, JOHN EDWARD. "Ireland's National Drama." The North
American Review, 194 (October), 566-575.
Compares the artistic unity of Riders to the Sea to
Poe's The Fall of the House of Usher, and The Well of the
Saints to Ibsen's The Wild Duck. Alludes to Synge's learn-
ing his dramatic language in Wicklow and on the Aran Is-
lands. Regards The Tinker's Wedding as of not much worth.

50 _____. "John Synge." The University Magazine, 10 (February),
91-109.
In In the Shadow of the Glen one feels from the beginning
"a sense of oppression...almost fatalism...." Discusses the
tragic effect of Riders to the Sea and compares The Well of
the Saints to Ibsen's The Wild Duck.

51 JORDAN, MICHAEL J. "Vulgar, Brutalizing." The Boston Daily
Globe (17 October), p. 9.
The Playboy of the Western World is depraved and a gross
libel. Flatly states, "The Playboy is a glorification of
murder." Synge is a symptom of the "diseases of the age."
See 1911.27.

52 KENNY, M., S.J. "The Irish Pagans." America, 6, no. 2
(21 October), 31-32.
"The statement of the Irish Ecclesiastical Record, that
what has been termed the 'Yeats and Synge boom,' is 'part
and parcel of a pagan renaissance,' has been again con-
firmed in a letter of Mr. Yeats to the New York Sun of
October 8...." Attacks Yeats for defending Synge's view
of the peasant and contrasts both with the worthy Douglas
Hyde.

53 _____. "The 'Irish' Players and Playwrights." America, 5
(30 September), 581-582.
"In all his plays ugly sneers at the people's morals and
religious practices are frequent, but in 'The Playboy' his
anti-Catholic animosity is openly revealed."

54 _____. "The Plays of the 'Irish' Players." America, 6,
no. 4 (4 November), 78-79.
Denounces Synge's vile anti-clericism: Riders to the
Sea is an un-Irish adaptation to Connacht fishermen of
Loti's Pêcheur d'Islande, but this play alone of Synge's
work "is fit for a decent audience." Contrasts Synge to a
"Protestant gentleman," Sir Samuel Ferguson, a man of
"cleanly mind." Argues that Yeats is even more dangerous
than Synge. Debates the position of Yeats and Synge that
tinkers were never converted to Catholicism.

1911

55   LARKIN, P. O'NEIL. "Declared Untrue." The Boston Daily Globe
     (17 October), p. 9.
          About the girls who adore Christy Mahon: "All are...
     beslavering him.... It is animalism under the guise of
     realism." Objects to Flaherty's profane statements in the
     presence of his daughter. See 1911.27.

56   M., K. "Dublin and 'The Playboy.'" Boston Evening Transcript
     (14 October), Part 3, p. 4.
          "A New York society is already out with a bull, both
     papal...and Irish in its humorous mistakes against, G. N.
     Synge's 'Plowboy of the Western World.'" This Gaelic-
     American society avers that Irish do not make a hero of a
     "parasite." Provides lengthy material about the riots over
     The Playboy of the Western World in Dublin four years pre-
     vious.

57   _____. "Synge's Posthumous Play." Boston Evening Transcript
     (27 September), p. 19.
          Deirdre of the Sorrows is a "tragedy of the mind, not of
     the dagger. It is an epic humanized." Detailed plot sum-
     mary.

58   _____. "'The Tinker's Wedding.'" Boston Evening Transcript
     (18 October), p. 23.
          Although The Tinker's Wedding is not dramatically ef-
     fective--even if the censors would allow its production--
     and "must remain on the library shelves," it is "the very
     breath of a wild, roaming, open life."

59   [MacMANUS, SEUMAS.] "Seumas M'Manus Raps 'The Playboy.'"
     The New York Times (27 November), p. 11.
          MacManus apparently said that "...Yeats has accepted a
     pension from the British Government and...is lost to Ire-
     land." MacManus maintains that he knows the islanders and
     country people and is not an outsider as is Synge. He
     never found among the faults of these people two vices,
     "vulgarity and immodesty." Castigates the vile language
     which Synge has imposed upon Pegeen and her throwing her-
     self at a man who supposedly murdered his father. About
     Yeats' bringing the play to London to get a disinterested
     hearing: "'The case of the Lamb was brought for an impar-
     tial verdict to the court of the Wolf.'" See 1911.28.

60   MASEFIELD, JOHN. "John M. Synge." ContempR, 99 (April),
     470-478.
          Discusses Synge's physical appearance, his taciturnity
     except when speaking to women, his Bloomsbury lodgings, his

habit of composing directly on a typewriter, the influence
of Pierre Loti on Synge, Synge's habits of revising his
works many times, and the background of Synge's poem "Danny." "Those who want to know what he was in himself should
read the poems." Reprinted: 1915.4; 1924.5; 1950.5;
1977.7.

61 MENCKEN, H. L. "The New Dramatic Literature." The Smart Set,
34, no. 4 (August), 151-158.
Although finding Synge's prose pedestrian, lavishes
praise on Synge's plays. Finds Synge to be "the one undoubted genius of the Neo-Celtic movement--not a fantastic,
pale green mystic like W. B. Yeats...."

62 MONTAGUE, C. E. "The Plays of J. M. Synge," in Dramatic Values. London: Methuen, pp. 1-15.
Praises Synge's tragic effects, realized in part through
his speech rhythms, which give "...English people a glimpse
of a strange place where English is not much worn or
faded...." Synge's humor is "harsh, sane, earthen...biting
as carbolic acid to slight minds...."

63 MONTGOMERY, K. L. "Some Writers of the Celtic Renaissance."
The Fortnightly Review, 96, NS 110 (1 September), 545-561.
Passing mention of Synge in connection with William
Boyle as writers of peasant plays.

64 MOORE, GEORGE. "George Moore on the Irish Theatre." Boston
Evening Transcript (23 September), p. 8.
Provides good information on the beginnings of the Irish
Theatre, praises the Anglo-Irish dialect for redeeming the
Abbey from the "conventional play" and from lifeless newspaper idiom, maintains that Synge's "strange" manner of
life was what probably appealed most to Yeats, says that
Yeats cried "'Euripides!'" when he first read In the Shadow
of the Glen, and calls The Playboy of the Western World
"the most original piece of stage literature that has been
written since Elizabethan times...."

65 MULLEN, THOMAS A. "Shocking Travesty." The Boston Daily
Globe (17 October), p. 9.
The Playboy of the Western World has not "a single line
that is truly Irish." Play revives the stage Irishman.
The "disgusting burlesque" will confirm beliefs about Ire-
land which her enemies hold. See 1911.27.

1911

66 O'BRIEN, EDWARD J. "Introduction," in <u>J. M. Synge, Riders to</u>
    <u>the Sea</u>. Boston: J. W. Luce, pp. 1-11.
        Sees <u>Riders to the Sea</u> as "the greatest modern tragedy
    in the English tongue," emphasizing Synge's depiction of
    elemental passions far removed from the debilitating super-
    ficialities of modern civilization.

67 P., H. T. "The Embattled 'Playboy.'" <u>Boston Evening Tran-</u>
    <u>script</u> (17 October), p. 12.
        Contains a description of the relatively mild protests
    at the Plymouth Theatre and gives a summary of Synge's
    dramatic talents in <u>The Playboy of the Western World</u>, in-
    cluding a comparison between Synge and Rostand.

68 _____. "The Irish Players: An Evening of New and Rare Im-
    pressions." <u>Boston Evening Transcript</u> (25 September),
    p. 12.
        Calls <u>In the Shadow of the Glen</u> an "eery Tragic-Comedy
    of Isolation," praises Synge's mastery of dialogue and
    technique in the play, and deplores the fact that the au-
    dience, guffawing deliberately at the wrong times, made
    Synge into a "fun-maker," much to the "surprise and annoy-
    ance of the players...."

69 _____. "Plays and Players: The Debate Over the Irish Plays."
    <u>Boston Evening Transcript</u> (9 October), p. 13.
        Maintains that those who oppose <u>The Playboy of the West-</u>
    <u>ern World</u> are both lacking in humor and defensive; praises
    the Irish Players' "genius" and demands to know just how
    the opposition will "suppress" the Irish Players' presenta-
    tions--a stated aim of Synge's enemies.

70 _____. "Two More Irish Plays: One Puzzling and One Pungent
    Comedy." <u>Boston Evening Transcript</u> (27 September), p. 19.
        Finds <u>The Well of the Saints</u> "Baffling" and tries to
    trace autobiographical significance in it.

71 PHILPOTT, A. J. "Taken Too Seriously." <u>The Boston Daily</u>
    <u>Globe</u> (17 October), p. 9.
        Says that Synge is a "clever writer" but that <u>The Play-</u>
    <u>boy of the Western World</u> is merely a "farce," though a
    good one. <u>See</u> 1911.27.

72 QUINN, JOHN. "Lady Gregory and the Abbey Theatre." New York
    <u>The Outlook</u> (16 December), pp. 916-919.
        Mentions that Quinn offered to pay the publication ex-
    penses of <u>The Aran Islands</u>, but that Yeats "said that he
    wanted the book taken on its merits, even if Synge had to

wait some years for a publisher." Holds that Synge's chief concern about the Dublin attack on The Playboy of the Western World was that it might "hurt the theater or endanger the cause of his friends."

73 ROOSEVELT, THEODORE. "The Irish Players: Introduction by Theodore Roosevelt." New York The Outlook (16 December), p. 915.
    Included in Roosevelt's hectoring of Americans who ape foreign ways is his praise of Lady Gregory and the Irish playwrights. Their works "spring from the soil...."

74 SCOTT-JAMES, R. A. "A Book of the Day: The Dramatist of Ireland." London The Daily News (1 February), p. 3.
    Synge's "common sense" balances the "gruesomeness" of his tragic and of his comic imagination. Reprinted: 1913.16; 1932.9.

75 SHAW, BERNARD. "Bernard Shaw's Greatest Masterpiece." New York The Gaelic American (16 December), pp. 2, 7.
    Interviewing himself, Shaw says that Synge's satire has a "joyousness and a wild wealth of poetic imagery that Swift never achieved."

76 TENNYSON, CHARLES. "Irish Plays and Playwrights." The Quarterly Review, 215 (July), 219-243.
    Synge's conversion to a belief in the worthiness of his peasant subjects' emotions was sincere--a reaction against the decorative and lifeless writing of his day.

77 _____. "The Rise of the Irish Theatre." ContempR, 100 (August), 240-247.
    Rehearses Nationalist opposition to In the Shadow of the Glen and The Playboy of the Western World: "the wind of the storm...reached as far as London and gave the Irish movement that suggestion of a succès de scandale which seems the only chance of prosperity for any genuinely artistic enterprise in our pedestrian Metropolis."

78 WALBROOK, H. M. "'The Playboy of the Western World,'" in Nights at the Play. London: W. J. Ham-Smith, pp. 107-110.
    Calls The Playboy of the Western World "remarkable" but "ghastly" in its picture of the evils of Irish emigration.

1911

79   YEATS, JOHN B. "Synge and the Irish." Harper's Weekly, 55
         (25 November), 17.
            Mentions Synge's inability to perform any morally "un-
         worthy" act. Reprinted in part: 1918.5 and 1977.7.

80   YEATS, W. B. "J. M. Synge and the Ireland of His Time." The
         Forum, 46 (August), 179-200.
            See 1911.83. Reprinted: 1912.36; 1924.9; 1961.14;
         1969.25; 1977.7.

81   _____ . "Opened with the New Irish Drama." The Boston Sunday
         Globe (24 September), p. 9.
            Yeats says in a speech from the stage of the Plymouth
         Theatre that he sent a circular to Abbey dramatists telling
         them to avoid the "love interest" and instead to think of
         the life they have "grown up amongst...." About Synge
         and The Playboy of the Western World: "I don't think it is
         the partiality born of friendship that makes me see in him
         one born with an imagination like that of Swift."

82   _____ . "Plays and Players: Mr. Yeats Explains." Boston
         Evening Transcript (13 October), p. 14.
            Yeats maintains that priests in Ireland are not opposed
         to the Abbey and that they have often attended the plays.
         Argues, again, that Synge was not influenced by decadent
         European writers. Reprinted: 1977.10.

83   _____ . Synge and the Ireland of His Time by William Butler
         Yeats with a Note Concerning a Walk through Connemara with
         Him by Jack Butler Yeats. Churchtown, Dundrum: Cuala
         Press, 48 pp.
            Yeats begins this famous essay by describing the "pa-
         triotic journalism," started by Thomas Davis and the Young
         Ireland school of poets; Synge "unfitted to think a polit-
         ical thought," was doomed from the beginning to draw only
         the wrath of the jingoistic Dubliners. Yeats maintains
         that Synge "had no life outside his imagination," that he
         was a "drifting silent man full of hidden passion," who
         "loved wild islands...." Yeats raises the possibility that
         "low vitality helped him to be observant and contempla-
         tive...." In sum: "Synge...sought for the race...in the
         depths of the mind...." Reprinted: 1911.80; 1912.36;
         1924.9; 1961.14; 1969.25; 1977.7. See 1966.18.

84   _____ . "The Theatre of Beauty." Harper's Weekly, 55 (11 No-
         vember), 11.
            In an address at Harvard, Yeats points out that Synge
         "gave up his intention of showing upon the stage a fight in

a plowed field between 'The Playboy' and his father, because he would not have six large trees, three on each
side, growing in the middle of a plowed field." Reprinted:
1976. 30.

85 _____. "Yeats Upon Irish Drama: His Speech before the Drama
League." Boston Evening Transcript (29 September), p. 14.
     Dublin rejected Synge but "repented sooner than most
countries.... The six days rioting was his laurel wreath."
Compares Synge with Cervantes.

1912

1   ANON. "Editorial Notes." The Forum, 47 (March), 380-381.
         About the rioting over The Playboy of the Western World:
    "once again, a poet and a prophet is found not without
    honor, except in his own country and amongst his own peo-
    ple." Makes a prophecy, also: "The next generation will
    have its new abuses to remedy: but it will certainly not
    tolerate the abuse of Synge."

2   ANON. "Fight Irish Plays." Chicago The Sunday Record-Herald
    (28 January), Part 1, p. 8.
         The Playboy of the Western World was opposed by the
    Irish clubs and also by the Anti-Cruelty Society, which
    arranged to "take over the entire ticket sale" for the
    production of the play, scheduled to begin in Chicago on
    February 6.

3   ANON. "Irish Actors Freed by Order of Court." Philadelphia
    The Evening Bulletin (23 January), p. 1.
         Dismissal of the charges of immorality brought against
    the Irish Players by Joseph McGarrity, "wholesale liquor
    dealer." Actors had been defended by John Quinn.

4   ANON. "Irish Play Halted by More Disorder." Philadelphia
    The Evening Bulletin (17 January), p. 1.
         Describes the constant tumult in the Adelphi Theatre
    complete with egg, pie, and rolled-program throwing,
    coughing, an abbreviated speech by an incensed man from
    Connaught, and an "amusing incident" of a man who had his
    own rotten eggs crushed in his pockets in a scuffle with
    police.

5   ANON. "Irish Play Row in Philadelphia." The New York Times
    (16 January), p. 8.
         Another view of the disturbances at the Adelphi Theatre
    in Philadelphia. Ten minutes into the performance the

1912

(supposed) vice president of the Ancient Order of Hiberni-
ans rose to protest The Playboy of the Western World; audience was fashionable; about thirty hecklers were ejected.

6   ANON. "Irish Players and Their Most Famous Dramatists."
    Chicago The Sunday Record-Herald (4 February), Part 7,
    p. 1.
        Besides several important letters and articles, contains
    photographs of Yeats, Synge, Máire Nic Shiubhlaigh, and
    Arthur Sinclair.

7   ANON. "John Synge and His Critics." The Independent, 73
    (7 November), 1071-1073.
        Agrees with Synge exegetes that the city is antithetical
    to great drama and that Synge's strength comes from the
    still rustic nature of Western Ireland.

8   ANON. "'Playboy' Actors Held for Court." Philadelphia The
    Evening Bulletin (19 January), p. 1.
        The Irish Players were held on a recent Pennsylvania law
    prohibiting plays "against public morals." Witnesses for
    the prosecution included two priests, one of whom objected
    that The Playboy of the Western World "exalts a parricide,"
    the other that the work was "lascivious in innuendo." In-
    cludes a picture of the "Irish Players as They Appeared at
    Their Hearing Today."

9   BENNETT, CHARLES A. "The Plays of John M. Synge." YR, NS 1,
    no. 2 (January), 192-205.
        Synge avoids Naturalism and the preaching of the problem
    play, but "There is nothing wan and exquisite in Synge; he
    is too close to life." Synge succeeds artistically in cap-
    turing the brutality and the sinister, dark natures of the
    characters in his plays; and his "laughter...leaps out like
    a red stab in the darkness and by contrast makes the dark-
    ness more terrifying." Examines Synge's use of startling
    contrasts in The Playboy of the Western World, The Tinker's
    Wedding, and in The Well of the Saints. About Deirdre of
    the Sorrows: "In none of his work was Synge master of
    such a spell of breathless beauty." Riders to the Sea is
    Synge's "greatest achievement," capturing the loneliness
    of the Irish.

10 BICKLEY, FRANCIS. J. M. Synge and the Irish Dramatic Move-
    ment. London: Constable; Boston and New York: Houghton
    Mifflin, 96 pp.
        Devoted half to Synge and half to modern Irish litera-
    ture and the Irish theater generally, begins by discussing

Synge's objectivity in observation, which stemmed in part
from his readings in French writers. Of the plays, finds
that Riders to the Sea is "one of those achievements before
which the voice of criticism is dumb"; believes that The
Well of the Saints "is not so interesting as any of the
others"; maintains that the ending of The Playboy of the
Western World reveals the peasants to be "as sound morally
as aesthetically" (but that the last act of the play moves
too slowly); and feels that Deirdre of the Sorrows is dramatic, as opposed to the merely poetic renderings of the
legend by Yeats and by George Russell. And about Synge's
poems: "There is a touch of temper about them, which makes
one feel that they were written in reaction rather than in
a normal mood."

11   BRAITHWAITE, WILLIAM STANLEY. "A Study of Synge, the Irish
     Author Whose Work Evades Definitions." The New York Times
     (15 September), p. 501.
          Says that Synge's ability to create intense characteri-
     zation is the heart of his achievement, though we are not
     yet able to define Synge in relation to the great modern
     dramatists.

12   BROWN, STEPHEN J. (S.J.), ed. A Guide to Books on Ireland:
     Part I, Prose Literature, Poetry, Music and Plays. Dublin:
     Hodges, Figgis; London: Longmans Green, pp. 10, 105, 244-
     246, 267-268.
          Features an attack on Synge by the editor, with quota-
     tions from hostile newspapers. Also provides an individual
     summary for each play.

13   DUKES, ASHLEY. Modern Dramatists. London: Frank Palmer,
     pp. 95, 97, 275.
          Brief comparison of Christy Mahon to Frank Wedekind.
     The Playboy of the Western World delineates "the effect of
     even a self-styled giant upon a race of pigmies," drained
     of blood by emigration.

14   EATON, WALTER PRICHARD. "The Theatre: The Literary Drama."
     American Magazine, 73 (March), 617-626.
          The Irish Theatre produced "one genius, J. M. Synge...."

15   _____. "The Theatre: Some Plays Worth While." American
     Magazine, 73 (February), 487-496.
          The works of Synge "are perhaps as genuinely and unaf-
     fectedly poetic as anything in the whole range of modern
     drama...." Complains about those who opposed The Playboy
     of the Western World: "It would seem that the Irishman,
     like the Jew, finds it hard to see a joke upon himself."

1912

16   FIGGIS, DARRELL. "The Art of J. M. Synge." The Forum, 47
      (January), 55-70.
           Reprint, with slight revision, of 1911.42.

17   _____. "The Art of J. M. Synge," in Studies and Appreciations.
      London: J. M. Dent, pp. 34-59.
           Reprint, in slightly revised form, of 1911.42 and
      1912.16.

18   GALSWORTHY, JOHN. The Inn of Tranquillity: Studies and Es-
      says. London: Heinemann, p. 207.
           Reprint of 1912.19.

19   _____. "Meditation on Finality." EngRev, 11 (July), 537-541.
           The attacks on The Playboy of the Western World, Synge's
      "masterpiece," are part of the audiences' demand for fac-
      tual finality," for "mankind at large has little patience
      with puzzling fellows." Reprinted: 1912.18.

20   GREGORY, LADY. "The Irish Theatre and the People." YR, NS 1,
      no. 2 (January), 188-191.
           About Synge: "In his return to Ireland just at that
      time of imaginative awakening [the Irish Renaissance] he
      found fable, emotion, style." And about the islanders in
      Riders to the Sea and their unequal fight against the sea:
      "he has shaped it so that there are now many who cannot
      hear Aran spoken of without a pulling at the heartstrings."

21   GUNNELL, DORIS. "Le Nouveau théâtre irlandais." La Revue,
      94, no. 1 (January), 91-106.
           Comments on the poetic strengths of The Playboy of the
      Western World and of Deirdre of the Sorrows.

22   HAMILTON, CLAYTON. "The Irish National Theatre." The Book-
      man, 34 (January), 508-516.
           Comments on The Well of the Saints, Riders to the Sea,
      In the Shadow of the Glen, and The Playboy of the Western
      World, "that uproarious and splendid comedy...." Contains
      photographs of Bartley's body being keened and of the re-
      turn of Old Mahon. Concludes: "Let us then be riders to
      the sea, and wander till we meet a playboy, talking deep
      love in the shadow of a glen."

23   HARRISON, AUSTIN. "Strindberg's Plays." EngRev, 13 (Decem-
      ber), 80-97.
           Brief comparison of Riders to the Sea to The Crown
      Bride: "Both savour of the earth, of hemp, and both

reflect that spirit of mediaeval mysticism...." Both Synge
and Strindberg delineate the "subconscious self" in their
plays.

24 HOWE, P. P. J. M. Synge: A Critical Study. London: Martin
    Secker, 215 pp.
       Just under one half of this book deals with Synge's
    plays considered individually; the rest discusses his prose
    (and poems) as source materials for the plays, argues that
    the intensity of the plays comes from their attention to
    craftsmanship and their being rooted in reality, dwells at
    some length on Synge's heroines, especially Pegeen Mike,
    and concludes with a brief discussion of the Prefaces as
    reactions against the tired European drama of Synge's day.
    Howe describes the compression in The Well of the Saints;
    finds that Riders to the Sea, though a fine play, violates
    unity of time, so much happening within a half hour; main-
    tains that with The Playboy of the Western World, Synge
    "placed himself amongst the masters" through the play's
    depiction of Christy's increasingly poetic nature, its
    skilled blending of comedy and tragedy, and the beauty of
    its love poetry passages; judges The Tinker's Wedding the
    "smallest" of Synge's plays; and traces the theme of in-
    evitability in Deirdre of the Sorrows, excusing the play's
    lapses into trite diction on the ground that Synge died
    before he could impress his distinctive idiom onto the
    play. Regards Synge's prose as a refutation of his enemies'
    allegation that he was influenced by French decadents.
    Synge's difficulties over the reception of his poetic dic-
    tion resembled those "confronting the authors of Lyrical
    Ballads a century earlier in England...." In general,
    Synge "brought the theatre back to its first concern, with
    words; and he made it plain that there can be no fine drama
    without an unfailing care for form."

25 JACKSON, HOLBROOK. "John M. Synge," in All Manner of Folk:
    Interpretations and Studies. London: Grant Richards; New
    York: Mitchell Kennerley, pp. 61-77.
       Because of its brevity, Riders to the Sea is "almost a
    tragic epigram, but it contains the whole of the direct
    tragedy of life...." Sees the main conflict in Synge's
    plays as "the clash between vision and actuality...." Con-
    trasts Synge's protagonists with past Stage Irishmen.
    Synge's plays show that each man can become a hero--at
    least to himself.

1912

26 JOYCE, JAMES. "Gas from a Burner," in <u>The Critical Writings of James Joyce</u>. Edited by Ellsworth Mason and Richard Ellmann. New York: The Viking Press, pp. 242-245.
    Speaking through the persona of George Roberts, the publisher, and John Falconer, the printer, Joyce says of Synge's works, "I printed the great John Milicent Synge/Who soars above on an angel's wing/ In the playboy shift that he pinched as swag/ From Maunsel's manager's travelling-bag...." As Mason and Ellmann point out, "Roberts was a traveller in ladies' underwear." <u>See</u> 1964.9.

27 MASEFIELD, JOHN. "Glimpses of the Author of 'The Playboy.'" Chicago <u>The Sunday Record-Herald</u> (11 February), Part 7, p. 3.
    Synge's somber expression gave people the impression that he was "forever listening to life's case before passing judgment...."

28 _____. "Synge, John Millington (1871-1909)," in <u>The Dictionary of National Biography</u>, Second Supplement, vol. 3. New York: Macmillan; London: Smith, Elder, 468-471.
    Sketch of Synge's life and works, including a physical description and a listing of portraits of Synge. Masefield sees Synge's best plays as "ironic visions of himself...."

29 NEWELL, MARY O'CONNOR. "The First Lady of Ireland." Chicago <u>The Sunday Record-Herald</u> (4 February), Womans [sic] Section, p. 1.
    An important article in which Lady Gregory spells out her opinion of <u>The Playboy of the Western World</u> in answer to Ms. Newell's direct question: "'It is a masterpiece of literature...full of poetry and imagery.... The question is not whether you like it or not. I do not ask people to like it. As a matter of fact, there are other plays in our repertory I much prefer, but it has been made necessary for us now to give "The Playboy" in order to show that it is not what it has been called, indecent, unfit for presentation.'"

30 O'DONOGHUE, DAVID JAMES. <u>The Poets of Ireland: A Biographical and Bibliographical Dictionary of Irish Writers in English Verse</u>. Dublin: Hodges, Figgis; London: Oxford University Press, p. 448.
    Finds that Douglas Hyde used peasant speech with "more reticence and effect" than Synge and speaks (apparently, with conscious ambiguity) of Synge's "peculiar qualities."

31 O'NEILL, GEORGE (S.J.). "Irish Drama and Irish Views." The
    American Catholic Quarterly Review, 37, no. 146 (April),
    322-332.
        "I will...not...dispute the general value of the high
    commendations passed on each other's work by various repre-
    sentatives of this new Irish movement--for example, by Mr.
    Yeats on Mr. Synge's...." "I wish to inquire how far Ire-
    land...may have justly refused, to recognize in the new
    drama a fair portrait of herself...." Calls the produc-
    tions of the Abbey Theatre "a systematic propaganda of
    calumny." Traces what the author feels are Yeats's speci-
    ous attempts to pass off the Irish Theatre Movement as
    truly Irish, finding that Yeats is simply presenting new
    types of Stage Irishmen, and quarrels with Lady Gregory's
    view that The Playboy of the Western World is a prophecy
    of Ireland's future--with all the solid people emigrating.
    Charges that the Abbey rejected the works of able young
    dramatists who were not sufficiently pessimistic and gloomy
    to suit the Directors' tastes. Expands the concept of for-
    eign influences on Synge, especially Baudelaire's "freakish
    ways." In the Shadow of the Glen is not simply the old
    fable of the "Ephesian Matron"; it was also influenced by
    Voltaire's "Zadig."

32 ROLLESTON, T. W. "Thanking God for Synge." Chicago The Sun-
    day Record-Herald (4 February), Part 7, p. 1.
        Argues that Synge's place in European literature is
    assured, praises the "alive" nature of Synge's peasants,
    and adds: "...I have never found a portrayal of the Irish
    peasant which gave one so much confidence in the future of
    the race as Synge's."

33 SHERMAN, STUART P. "John Synge." The Nation, 95, no. 2478
    (December), 608-611.
        "Within the last year or two he [Synge] has become one
    of the most conspicuous figures in the literary world."
    Explores the differing attitudes towards Synge's literary
    antecedents. Synge's poems are those of a "despondent
    young Bohemian," deeply influenced by nineteenth century
    predecessors and by Villon. The Aran Islands falls into a
    tired class of writing by such as Pierre Loti, Lafcadio
    Hearn, Chateaubriand, and Anatole le Braz. When Synge went
    to the Aran Islands, "he never desired to return to his own
    people...he wished to escape into a perfectly strange and
    virgin environment."

1912

34   VAN HAMEL, A. G. "On Anglo-Irish Syntax." Englische Studien,
      45 (September), 272-292.
         Focusing upon In the Shadow of the Glen, Riders to the
      Sea, The Well of the Saints, The Playboy of the Western
      World, and The Aran Islands, van Hamel points out the "very
      realistic and vigorous Western Anglo-Irish" which Synge
      employed in his work.

35   WATKINS, ANN. "The Irish Players in America: Their Purpose
      and Their Art." The Craftsman, 21, no. 4 (January), 352.
         Though sympathetic to Synge, finds that "this much-
      talked of play...seems less significant" than either The
      Well of the Saints or In the Shadow of the Glen.

36   YEATS, W. B. The Cutting of an Agate. New York: Macmillan,
      pp. 25-35, 111-122, 123-129, 130-176.
         Reprint of 1905.12; 1909.3; 1910.6; 1911.80, 83. Re-
      printed: 1924.9.

37   _____. "'The Playboy': A Stay in the Court Proceedings:
      Mr. Yeats Interviewed." Dublin The Irish Independent
      (20 January), p. 5.
         Yeats comments on the arrest of the Irish Players in
      Philadelphia, on the educated classes' appreciation of
      Synge, and on the fact that Synge did not intend The Play-
      boy of the Western World to be a literal picture of Irish
      life. Reprinted: 1977.10.

38   _____. "What We Try to Do." Chicago The Sunday Record-Herald
      (4 February), Part 7, p. 1.
         Speaks of the "two opposite types" of Irishmen, con-
      trasting Synge to Goldsmith: "It is true that he [Synge]
      had little or no Irish blood, but in bringing up he was an
      Irish product. And that type is terribly bitter, hostile,
      sarcastic." Synge's personality was healthy, but,
      strangely enough, he "gained his healthiness from living
      for years facing death." Reprinted: 1976.30; 1977.10.

<u>1913</u>

1   BEWLEY, CHARLES. "The Irish National Theatre." The Dublin
      Review, 152, nos. 304 and 305 (January and April), 132-144.
         Argues that The Playboy of the Western World and Macbeth
      cannot really be compared, even though Synge's work "has
      been accepted as a classic...." "In Shakespeare's hands...
      Macbeth would openly exult in his murder, and Banquo and
      Macduff vie with one another in an ecstasy of enthusiastic

loyalty to the murderer...." Brings up the old charge that
Synge's ideas came from London and Paris, not from Ireland.

2   BLAKE, WARREN BARTON. "Irish Plays and Players." The Independent, 74, no. 3353 (March), 515-519.
"Two years ago people were still undecided as to the
pronunciation of the name Synge--those of them, that is,
who had ever seen or heard it." Holds that Synge "remains
the greatest dramatist of the Irish literary movement...."
Praises the versatility of the Irish Players and the un-
selfish "sinking of individual reputations in a common effort...."

3   BOURGEOIS, MAURICE. John Millington Synge and the Irish
Theatre. London: Constable, 353 pp.
Despite some inaccuracies in bibliography entries, this
ardently researched book is an indispensable storehouse of
facts about Synge's works and for many years was the classic study of Synge. Besides analyses of Synge's works and
discussions of both the Irish and the French influences on
him, the volume contains lengthy appendices of both descriptive and primary bibliography, a detailed genealogy of
Synge's family, notes on first performances, a list of portraits of Synge, and an exhaustive index. Reprinted:
1966.2; abridged: 1970.1.

4   _____. "Synge and Loti." The Westminster Review, 179, no. 5
(May), 532-536.
Compares, generally, the personalities of Synge and
Pierre Loti, e.g. their underlying melancholy; discusses
Synge's reading Loti and other French writers while in
Paris; and cites specific parallels between Riders to the
Sea and "Pêcheur d'Islande," e.g. "the strange family like-
ness between the Breton grandmother and the old Aran fish-
erwoman...." Synge, however, cannot be accused of plagiary,
for the plot of Riders to the Sea is common to the folk
literature of many countries.

5   BOYD, ERNEST A. "Le Théâtre irlandais." Revue de Paris, 5
(September-October), 191-205.
Synge alone combined the "dons d'imagination et d'ob-
servation...." Yeats merely revived the theater "d'im-
agination et de rêve...." Several comparisons between
Synge's works and those of Europeans.

6   BRYANT, SOPHIE. The Genius of the Gael: A Study in Celtic
Psychology and Its Manifestations. London: T. Fisher Un-
win, pp. 188-193.

1913

Finds <u>Deirdre of the Sorrows</u> the "most beautiful" of the plays. And: "Having seen <u>The Playboy</u> acted once, I do not desire to see it again: but I have read and will read it many times for the delight I take in the splendour of its language...."

7   CANBY, HENRY SEIDEL. "The Works of John M. Synge." YR, NS 2, no. 4, 767-772.
Attacks the notion that the spirit and substance of Synge's work come from France; cites Synge's ability to treat his characters objectively; and examines Synge's people in the light of his Celticism, a preference for the ideal over the real. Synge's plays are great because they present universal human emotions that "require no annotation of philosophy or symbolism in order to leap to recognition in the heart." However, "Synge's gallery is small. His depth is greater than his breadth."

8   GALSWORTHY, JOHN. "The New Spirit in the Drama." <u>The Hibbert Journal</u>, 11, no. 3 (April), 508-520.
Brief comparison and contrast between Synge and St. John Hankin, praising their sincerity and opposing their qualities to the contemporary, would-be "serious" dramatists.

9   GREGORY, LADY. "The Fight over 'the Playboy,'" "Synge," "The 'Playboy' in America," in <u>Our Irish Theatre: A Chapter of Autobiography</u>. New York and London: G. P. Putnam's, pp. 33-35, 42-43, 76, 93-94, 99, 104, 108, 109-118, 119-139, 147-149, 156-157, 169-252, 280-309, 316.
In "The Fight over 'the Playboy'" provides important data on the origins of <u>In the Shadow of the Glen</u> in Irish "fireside" stories, comments on the forty men who organized the initial disturbances over <u>The Playboy of the Western World</u>, spells out her belief that the real issue at stake during the rioting was artistic freedom from the masses, and points to several contemporary instances where the mob forced the removal of plays from the stage. "Synge," reprinted from 1913.10, repeats the story of Lady Gregory's first meeting with Synge. "'The Playboy' in America" is a lengthy and crucial chapter which not only details Lady Gregory's fight for Synge's play but also provides data concerning her opponents' strategies and reprints several newspaper accounts of the conflicts. The book reprints 1911.6, 44; 1913.10.

10 _____. "Synge." EngRev, 13 (March), 556-566.
 Describes her first, unexpected meeting with Synge in
 the Aran Islands, the liberating effects that Synge's im-
 mersion in Irish dialect had on him, some of his revisions
 of The Playboy of the Western World and Deirdre of the
 Sorrows, and her view that The Playboy of the Western World
 contained too much "bad language." Reprinted: 1913.9.

11 HOWE, P. P. "England's New Dramatists." The North American
 Review, 198, no. 2 (August), 218-226.
 Praises Synge's insistence that the drama must provide
 joy as well as reality: "There is one writer of our time
 who, treading no path but his own, yet points more clearly
 than any other to a future for the English drama."

12 HUNEKER, JAMES. "John M. Synge," in The Pathos of Distance:
 A Book of a Thousand and One Moments. New York: Scribner's, pp. 228-235.
 Synge's "argument never leaves the earth, yet few dramatists evoke such a sense of the Beyond."

13 JACKSON, HOLBROOK. "Holbrook Jackson on Wilde as Dandy and
 Artist," in Oscar Wilde: The Critical Heritage. Edited by
 Karl Beckson. London: Routledge and Kegan Paul, p. 337
 [1970].
 Writing in 1913, Jackson said of Oscar Wilde, "he was
 the playboy of the Nineties; and, like the hero of John
 Millington Synge's drama, he was subject to the intimida-
 tion of flattery."

14 McGIRR, ALICE THURSTON. "Reading List on John Millington
 Synge." BB, 7, no. 5 (April), 114-115.
 Lists reviews of Synge's works (1910) and, under "Criticism," includes eighteen briefly annotated secondary
 sources.

15 ROY, JAMES A. "J. M. Synge and the Irish Literary Movement."
 Anglia, 37:129-145.
 An overall favorable commentary on Synge's work, but
 finds that Synge "deliberately restricted himself to the
 study of a small section of humanity.... It is impossible
 to include him in the first rank of dramatists." Roy holds
 that Pegeen Mike "is a more complex study than the Playboy
 himself...."

16 SCOTT-JAMES, R. A. "J. M. Synge," in Personality in Literature. London: Martin Secker, pp. 135-139.
 Reprint of 1911.74. Reprinted: 1932.9.

1913

17 TUPPER, JAMES W. "J. M. Synge and His Work." The Dial, 54
   (March), 233-235.
   Traces the transforming power of the imagination through
   Synge's plays; argues that Synge's splendid dramatic poetry
   is Elizabethan, not hampered by polemics; and calls for a
   detailed study of foreign influences upon Synge: one "not
   even unworthy of a doctor's dissertation, though, of course,
   repulsively modern."

18 WEYGANDT, CORNELIUS. "John Millington Synge," in Irish Plays
   and Playwrights. London: Constable; Boston and New York:
   Houghton Mifflin, pp. 160-197.
   Sees Synge in Deirdre of the Sorrows. Finds the theme
   of "joy" throughout the works and feels that Synge, in com-
   bining this exultation with "mordancy," resembles Donne and
   Hardy. Traces "extravagance" and "grotesquerie" in the
   plays to their antecedents in Irish literature. Finds an
   analogue with Villon in The Tinker's Wedding. Maintains
   that if there is symbolism in Synge, it is unintentional.
   Says that Hyde's peasant speech was only a beginning for
   Synge's. Examines Synge's "candor" in the plays, whose
   characters are very different from Synge himself. Comments at some length on the "travel" sketches. And finds
   that the structure of Synge's plays could have been im-
   proved.

19 YEATS, WILLIAM BUTLER. "'The Playboy': Action of the Liverpool Police." London The Times (1 December), p. 66.
   Protests the suggestion of the police that The Playboy
   of the Western World, "the master-work of the dramatic
   movement of Ireland," not be presented at the Saturday
   matinee. Reprinted: 1976.30.

20 _____. "The Playboy at Liverpool." London The Times (4 December), p. 12.
   Although protests over The Playboy of the Western World
   have been ubiquitous, "nowhere outside Liverpool have the
   police made 'suggestions' which are a precedent for mob
   law and a menace to all playwrights who would serve their
   art and not their purse...."

1914

1 CHANDLER, FRANK WADLEIGH. Aspects of Modern Drama. New York:
   Macmillan, pp. 269-275.
   Praises Synge's use of the folk element, the "dreamy
   cadence" of his language, the "noble" style of Riders to

the Sea, and the diction of The Playboy of the Western
World. The Tinker's Wedding is Synge's "least original"
comedy.

2   MONAHAN, MICHAEL. "Yeats and Synge," in Nova Hibernia: Irish
     Poets and Dramatists of Today and Yesterday. New York:
     Mitchell Kennerley, pp. 13-37.
         Emphasizes the fact that Synge truly understood the
     Irish peasant and that his comprehension goes "deep under
     the surface...." In the section "The Matter with the
     'Playboy,'" Monahan avers that the chief opposition to the
     work was religious: Synge's "plays do not flatter priestly
     sensibilities--they even wound ecclesiastical coquetry in a
     land where the priest is supreme."

3   MOORE, GEORGE. Hail and Farewell: A Trilogy: Vale. New
     York: Appleton; London: Heinemann, pp. 194-219.
         Reprint with slight revisions of 1914.4.

4   _____. "Yeats, Lady Gregory, and Synge, Part 2." EngRev,
     16 (February), 350-364.
         Despite mistakes in chronology such as the one that has
     Synge in the Aran Islands and having written his book on
     them before meeting Yeats for the first time, Moore pre-
     sents much indispensable biographical information. He
     discusses Synge's interest in things as opposed to ideas,
     the weaknesses of Synge's early essays, Synge's wandering
     with tinkers (wherein he appreciated the "fine flavour of
     some drunkard's oath or blasphemy"), the scene of the riots
     over The Playboy of the Western World as recounted by Ed-
     ward Martin (the bloody bandage on Old Mahon's head really
     caused the disturbances), the fact that Synge wrote Act 3
     of The Playboy of the Western World thirteen times, and
     Synge's death, which Moore movingly recalls. Reprinted
     with slight revisions: 1914.3.

5   STORER, EDWARD. "Dramatists of To-Day: J. M. Synge." The
     British Review, 5 (January), 73-80.
         Though maintaining that Synge is the most important of
     the playwrights who have "written for the English [sic]
     stage in the last twenty years," feels that The Playboy of
     the Western World is too fantastic to be believable. In
     Deirdre of the Sorrows the peasant language is not suit-
     able for the tragic theme and the work is "pagan" as op-
     posed to the strong Christian beliefs in The Well of the
     Saints, Riders to the Sea, and The Tinker's Wedding.
     Riders to the Sea is not on the same tragic plane as
     Deirdre of the Sorrows--in the former we are not struck by
     the same inevitability of the deaths. Reprinted: 1914.6.

1914

6 _____. "Dramatists of To-Day: V -- J. M. Synge." The Living
   Age, 280 (28 March), 777-781.
   Reprint of 1914.5.

1915

1 ANON. "Ireland's Playwright." The Independent, 83 (September), 433-434.
   About Synge: "it should become obvious enough...that
   this man was a poet and not a historian of the Irish nation
   or a generalizer about Irish types."

2 CLARK, JAMES M. "The Irish Literary Movement." Englische
   Studien, 49 (July), 50-98.
   Although Clark relates that The Playboy of the Western
   World first appeared "on the Dublin stage in 1897," the
   rest of his essay is more useful. Of the figures in the
   Irish Renaissance, Synge is the "most original and, as a
   dramatist at least, the greatest...."

3 COLUM, PADRAIC. "The Irish Literary Movement." The Forum, 53
   (January to June), 133-148.
   Maintains that Synge's Gaelic-English language came from
   Yeats's introducing him to Hyde's translations of the Con-
   naught songs; that the refusal of the Abbey directors to
   bow to local opposition in the matter of The Playboy of the
   Western World "had the effect of hardening the minds of the
   directors against Irish opinion..."; and that this play and
   Riders to the Sea reveal "the Irish mind in its integrity
   and its intensity."

4 MASEFIELD, JOHN. John M. Synge: A Few Personal Recollections
   with Biographical Notes. New York: Macmillan, 35 pp.
   Reprints and expands 1911.60. Book is the same as the
   1911 article except for the added biographical information
   which follows the main body of the text: "I have been
   asked to add to these memories a few notes, and the chief
   dates in Synge's life, as far as we know them." Adds:
   "...I should say that his favorite author, during the
   greater part of his life, was Racine."

5 NORDMAN, C. A. "J. M. Synge, Dramatikern." FT, 79 (July-
   December), 26-70.
   Provides an overview of Synge's plays. Examines The
   Well of the Saints in the light of Matthew Arnold's criti-
   cism and of Maeterlinck's plays and sees both Molière and
   Shakespeare in The Well of the Saints. Riders to the Sea

"är det populäraste af Synges dramer och det lättast
förstadda," and The Tinker's Wedding "är det minst betyd-
ande af Synges dramer." Compares Christy Mahon to Peer
Gynt.

1916

1   ALLEN, BEVERLY S. "John Synge: A Problem of His Genius."
    The Colonnade, 11, no. 1 (January), 5-15.
    Synge's "problem" is the charge that he is pessimistic,
    which allegation stems from unflinching confrontation of
    the "assurance of disillusionment...."

2   ANON. "Mr. Masefield's Recollections of John M. Synge." The
    Dial, 60 (March), 285.
    Calls Synge an "Ironic spirit seeking refuge from the
    embittered consciousness of self and century in the sim-
    plicity of the primitive...."

3   BOYD, ERNEST. "J. M. Synge," in Ireland's Literary Renais-
    sance. Dublin: Maunsel; London and New York: Knopf,
    pp. 316-335.
    Calls the "great 'event'" in the Irish theater the "dis-
    covery and universal recognition of the genius of J. M.
    Synge...." De-emphasizes the French influence upon Synge,
    while stressing his Irish sources; describes the antece-
    dents of the "cult of hostility" surrounding The Playboy of
    the Western World; details Synge's aversion to "ideas"
    about playwriting; traces similarities between Deirdre of
    the Sorrows and the other plays; and maintains that Synge
    "revealed Ireland to us, its beauty and its ugliness; but
    in so doing he enabled us to see beyond the limitations of
    place and time into the regions inhabited by the eternal
    spirit of mankind."

4   ERSKINE, JOHN. The Delight of Great Books. New York: Colum-
    bia University Press, pp. 310-313.
    Synge's genius is not typically Irish but universal:
    "Perhaps he might have written about Italian or German
    peasant life with the same kind of sympathy that he brought
    to the Aran Islands."

5   O'HAGAN, THOMAS. "The Irish Dramatic Movement," in Essays on
    Catholic Life. Baltimore: John Murphy, pp. 57-73.
    Complains of Synge's misrepresentation of the Irish
    people, especially seen in his portrayal of an unchaste

1916

woman. The Playboy of the Western World, an "enigma," is
"a very rioting of the abnormal." Even Riders to the Sea,
Synge's "masterpiece," depicts little of Irish spiritual-
ity.

6   TURQUET-MILNES, G. Some Modern Belgian Writers: A Critical
Study. London: H. Muirhead, pp. 29-30, 36.
     Says that Synge is Maeterlinck's superior and feels that
"presentiment is the real leit-motiv [sic]" in Riders to
the Sea and in Deirdre of the Sorrows.

1917

1   MORRIS, LLOYD R. The Celtic Dawn: A Survey of the Renascence
in Ireland, 1889-1916. New York: Macmillan, pp. 20, 76,
80-81, 107, 124-134, 136, 149-150, 156, 163, 165, 168, 170.
     Mentions the violent and bitter nature of Synge's poetry
and the attacks upon Yeats for advertising and advocating
In the Shadow of the Glen. Sketches Synge's life and work
and dramatic theories, compares Synge to Rabelais and to
Anatole France, and points out Synge's influence on Ruther-
ford Mayne and on George Fitzmaurice.

2   SHERMAN, STUART P. "The Exoticism of John Synge," in On Contemporary Literature. New York: Henry Holt, pp. 190-210.
     Analyzes the conflicting portraits of Synge drawn by
Yeats, Moore, and others; compares The Aran Islands to
Loti's work; points out that "the dramatist himself is in
secret heart a vagrant...." Riders to the Sea is "not a
tragedy at all, because it is not a drama." It has no
protagonist "in the proper sense of the word...."

1918

1   HACKETT, FRANCIS. "John Synge," in Horizons: A Book of
Criticism. New York: B. W. Huebsch, pp. 189-197.
     Writing in 1909, Hackett states, "The monosyllable Synge
will convey little to many American readers. In Dublin,
where the dramatist died last March, the name is known to
every one [sic]." Abridged: 1919.5.

2   JOYCE, JAMES. "Programme Notes for the English Players:
Riders to the Sea by John M. Synge," in The Critical Writ-
ings of James Joyce. Edited by Ellsworth Mason and Richard
Ellmann. New York: The Viking Press, p. 250.

Says that "<u>anagke</u>" or destiny is the "inexorable sea."
Maintains that "the ear and the heart mislead one gravely
if this brief scene from 'poor Aran' be not the work of a
tragic poet." <u>See</u> 1964.9.

3 PHELPS, WILLIAM LYON. "The Advance of English Poetry in the
    Twentieth Century: Part VI." <u>The Bookman</u>, 47 (March),
    58-72.
        Discusses Synge's musical training as an influence on
    the verbal harmonies of his writings; maintains that Synge
    "had the greatest mental endowment of all the Irish writers
    of his time," although he also had a "savage heart"; and
    feels that Synge wrote about himself so much because he
    "knew that much biography and criticism would follow his
    funeral." Reprinted with revisions: 1918.4.

4 _____. <u>The Advance of English Poetry in the Twentieth Century</u>.
    New York: Dodd, Mead, pp. 171-177.
        Revised version of 1918.3.

5 YEATS, JOHN BUTLER. "Synge and the Irish," in <u>Essays Irish
    and American</u>. Dublin: Talbot Press; London: T. F. Unwin;
    New York: Macmillan, pp. 51-61.
        Partially a reprint of 1911.79, partially includes new
    observations. Stresses Synge's delight in the "spectacle
    of life." "Those who object to Synge's plays are suffering
    from the delicate stomach of people who have lived effemi-
    nate lives." Of Christy Mahon: "he is neither a weakling
    nor a fool, but a young poet in the supreme difficulty of
    getting born...." Adds that no one really believes his
    story. Also, Pegeen "towers over every one [sic]...."
    And: "Some day people will recognize in this play Synge's
    tribute to the Irish peasant girl." Supplies brief but
    important autobiographical and biographical data, culmi-
    nating in a comparison of Synge to Michael Davitt.

                              1919

1 A., M. "After the Play." <u>The New Republic</u>, 18 (March), 153.
        "Of modern Irish dramatists there are two with pervading
    magic--Synge and Lord Dunsany." The two have little in
    common, but they do "share a predilection for minted
    phrases, and an air of remoteness from ordinary life...."

1919

2   BOYD, ERNEST A. "Dublin, March 6." The Dial, 66 (April),
    358-360.
        Comments on those who carp at Synge's peasant dialect
    "as if Synge had ever undertaken to compile a species of
    Congressional Record of the Aran Islands."

3   _____. "The Impulse to Folk Drama: J. M. Synge and Padraic
    Colum," in The Contemporary Drama of Ireland. The Contem-
    porary Drama Series, edited by Richard Burton. Boston:
    Little, Brown, pp. 88-109.
        "Innumerable studies in periodical and book form have so
    familiarized the public with the life and works of J. M.
    Synge that little remains to be said." Riders to the Sea
    approaches perfection, and The Tinker's Wedding is too
    slight for two acts. Synge's use of dialect contrasts with
    Lady Gregory's mechanical adaptation of peasant, Kiltartan
    speech. Deirdre of the Sorrows is "the greatest modern
    version of the Gaelic classic."

4   CARNEVALI, EMANUEL. "Synge's Playboy of the Western World:
    Variation." The Dial, 66 (April), 340.
        Short poem about an idealized New York, presumably one
    in which riots would not occur over plays.

5   HACKETT, FRANCIS. "A Fragment about Synge." Theatre Arts,
    3 (January), 1.
        Abridgement of 1918.1.

6   LYND, ROBERT. "The Fame of J. M. Synge," in Old and New Mas-
    ters. London: T. F. Unwin, pp. 94-97.
        Attacks the Synge cult, begun by Yeats, and maintains
    that Synge is merely "the peer, say, of Stevenson." Holds
    that Riders to the Sea and not The Playboy of the Western
    World is Synge's greatest achievement. In general, Synge's
    "genius was a genius of decoration, not of psychology," his
    strength lying in language, not in characterization.

7   WILLIAMS, HAROLD. "John Millington Synge, 1871-1909," in Mod-
    ern English Writers: Being a Study of Imaginative Litera-
    ture, 1890-1914. Vol. 1. New York: Knopf, pp. 206-216.
        Praises Synge's The Aran Islands and the shorter plays
    but complains of the adulation directed at Synge and says
    that the abilities of Padraic Colum are not far behind
    those of Synge. Important for the emphasis placed on
    Synge's non-dramatic prose. Also, traces the theme of
    "joy" in Synge's works.

1920

1   ERVINE, ST. JOHN. "Some Impressions of My Elders: Bernard
      Shaw and J. M. Synge." The North American Review, 211
      (May), 669-681.
         Basically an attack on Synge's personality. Ervine
      sees Synge as sharing the "sewer revelations of James
      Joyce." Without Yeats, "the world might never have heard
      of that singular man of twisted talent," who "may be said
      to have died of sheer inability to assert himself." Synge's
      work "smelt too strongly of the medicine bottle to be of
      supreme merit," and Ervine cannot convince himself of
      Synge's greatness. Reprinted: 1922.1.

2   FIRKINS, O. W. "Drama: Rostand and Synge." The Weekly Re-
      view, 3 (18 August), 155-156.
         About the performance of Riders to the Sea at the Bram-
      hall in August, 1920: "...motherhood and grief have turned
      prehistoric and cosmical beneath his [Synge's] touch."

3   _____. "Drama: Synge at the Bramhall Playhouse." The
      Weekly Review, 3 (6 October), 297-299.
         About Deirdre of the Sorrows: the theme is the "modern
      fear of living...it is hard to forgive Deirdre and Naisi
      for crossing the threshold of the lazarhouse."

4   JAMESON, STORM. "J. M. Synge," in Modern Drama in Europe.
      London: W. Collins & Sons, pp. 212-216.
         Maintains that "the drama of J. M. Synge is a very dif-
      ferent thing from the bemused babbling of Mr. Yeats's
      spooks."

1921

1   ANON. "Some Recent French Plays." TLS (30 June), p. 416.
         Maintains that "M. Martin du Gard's Testament du Père
      Leleu is an amusing little farce, rather recalling Synge's
      Shadow of the Glen from its macabre humour."

2   BLOXAM, R. N. "The Source of a Plot." TLS (28 July), p. 484.
         Says the source for In the Shadow of the Glen "is to be
      found, again with an Irish setting, in Charles Lever's
      'Con Cregan,' published in 1849."

1921

3   BLUNT, WILFRID SCAWEN. My Diaries: Being a Personal Narrative of Events: 1888-1914: Part Two [1900-1914]. New
York: Alfred A. Knopf, pp. 166, 172, 252.
Interesting comments about The Playboy of the Western
World: says that Lady Gregory "admits that it was a mistake to produce the play...," mentions a threat against her
by the editor of The Freeman's Journal, and tells of the
boycott at Coole because of Lady Gregory's insistence that
the play not be taken from the stage. Discusses the London
reception of the work in a half-filled theater, in which
the English missed much of the Irish dialect. Reprinted:
1977.7.

4   BRAWLEY, BENJAMIN. "John Millington Synge," in A Short History of the English Drama. New York: Harcourt, Brace,
pp. 233-234.
Finds that The Playboy of the Western World "is concerned with the real awakening of the Playboy, his performing of wonderful feats...."

5   BRIGHOUSE, HAROLD. "The Source of a Plot." TLS (14 July),
p. 453.
In the Shadow of the Glen was "anticipated by a story
appearing in Once a Week for September 29, 1860, called
'A Night Adventure in Ireland,' described anonymously as
'by a Soldier.'"

6   CLARK, BARRETT H. "John Millington Synge," in The British
and American Drama of To-Day: Outlines for Their Study.
Cincinnati: Stewart & Kidd, pp. 188-197.
Discusses Riders to the Sea as a one-act play and The
Playboy of the Western World as an astute creation of
"atmosphere."

7   _____. "Riders to the Sea: J. M. Synge," in Representative
One-Act Plays by British and Irish Authors. Boston: Little, Brown, pp. 391-393.
Riders to the Sea is "without doubt the dramatist's
best sustained effort."

8   COLUM, PADRAIC. "Memories of John M. Synge." The Literary
Review [of The New York Evening Post], 2 (4 June), Section
3, 1-2.
Gives important personal details about Synge, who was
a "made man in a city [Dublin] of men in the making."
Says that the opposition to Synge came from Yeats's earlier, grandiose claims for him. Contains data on the acting
of The Playboy of the Western World. Reprinted with slight
revisions: 1926.1; abridged: 1977.7.

9   ERVINE, ST. JOHN. "Some Impressions of My Elders: John
    Galsworthy." The North American Review, 213 (March), 371-
    384.
        Synge's works are his best biography: "It is impossible
    to rise from his books without an impression of intense
    loneliness and unachievable desires...." Reprinted:
    1922.1.

10 KERBY, PAUL. "The Source of a Plot." TLS (7 July), p. 437.
        Calls attention to a possible common source of Du Gard's
    work, Synge's In the Shadow of the Glen, and Puccini's one-
    act opera Gianni Schicchi.

11 RENWICK, W. L. "The Source of a Plot." TLS (21 July), p. 469.
        The plot of In the Shadow of the Glen "is evidently
    traditional. The essentials...appear in Du Parc's 'His-
    tore Comique de Francion,' towards the end of Livre VIII."

12 SCHOEPPERLE, GERTRUDE. "John Synge and His Old French Farce."
    The North American Review, 214, no. 791 (October), 503-513.
        Synge's source for The Well of the Saints is Andrieu
    de la Vigne's L'aveugle et le boiteux, a late fifteenth
    century "farce."

13 THORNING, JUST. J. M. Synge: En moderne irsk Dramatiker.
    Studier fra Sprog- of Oldtidsforskning, No. 121. London
    and Copenhagen: V. Pios, 64 pp.
        Play by play analyses with approximately thirty of the
    sixty-four pages spent on The Playboy of the Western World
    and on Deirdre of the Sorrows. First eight pages sketch
    Synge's life and works.

                            1922

1   ERVINE, ST. JOHN. Some Impressions of My Elders. New York:
    Macmillan, pp. 116-118, 129-132, 198-202.
        Reprint of 1920.1 and 1921.9.

2   HIND, C. LEWIS. "J. M. Synge," in More Authors and I. New
    York: Dodd, Mead, pp. 279-284.
        Perpetuates the legend of Synge as brooding and silent,
    a man whose life can be evenly divided into two clear
    parts: before his visit to the Aran Islands and after.
    Provides a brief glimpse of Synge and Yeats in the summer
    of 1907: "They were the quietest couple in the theatre."

1922

3   JOYCE, JAMES. <u>Ulysses</u>. Paris: Shakespeare and Company.
    Also in New York: Random House, Vintage Books, 1961, pp.
    pp. 185, 193, 198, 199, and 205.
        Several references to Synge; for example, Shakespeare is
    (ironically) the "chap that writes like Synge."

4   STRONG, L. A. G. "J. M. Synge." <u>Beacon</u>, 2 (July), 695-701.
        Important as a brief but early statement about Synge's
    greatness, which Strong later developed. Reprinted:
    1922.5.

5   _____. "J. M. Synge." <u>The Living Age</u>, 314 (September), 656-
    660.
        Reprint of 1922.4.

<u>1923</u>

1   ARCHER, WILLIAM. <u>The Old Drama and the New: An Essay in Re-</u>
    <u>Valuation</u>. Boston: Small, Maynard, p. 370.
        "Short comment on the "melancholy humour" of <u>The Playboy</u>
    <u>of the Western World</u> and <u>The Well of the Saints</u>. <u>Riders to</u>
    <u>the Sea</u> is of a "weird and tragic beauty." Finds that
    other Irish dramatists are too simplified in the structure
    of their plays but that Synge is "unique."

2   AUGUR, HELEN. "Pirandello's New Play for Duse." <u>The New York</u>
    <u>Times</u> (4 March), Magazine Section, pp. 1, 11.
        Quotes Pirandello as having said, "Of modern dramatists
    I know few--Synge is my favorite, and Shaw and Barrie are
    always a delight."

3   CARROLL, SYDNEY W. "'The Playboy of the Western World,'" in
    <u>Some Dramatic Opinions</u>. London: F. V. White, pp. 69-73.
        Argues that the work "was the product of a great brain
    soured by illness, made morbid by disease." <u>The Playboy of</u>
    <u>the Western World</u> is the kind of "enigmatic rollick in-
    dulged in by a doomed consumptive...."

<u>1924</u>

1   FAUSSET, HUGH I'A. "Synge and Tragedy." <u>The Fortnightly Re-</u>
    <u>view</u>, NS 115 (February), 258-273.
        The greatest influences on Synge were not France and
    formal study but Ireland and its earth and sea: "Our mod-
    ern critical values, our rational ideals, scarcely touched
    him."

2   GORKI, MAXIM. "Observations on the Theatre." EngRev, 38
    (April), 494-498.
        The Playboy of the Western World is characterized by an
    "inner harmony" in which artificiality is "replaced by
    art," as Synge describes with mild and sad irony the uni-
    versal need of people to create a hero and afterwards to
    ridicule him. In the play, "the comical side passes quite
    naturally into the terrible, while the terrible becomes
    comical just as easily. J. M. Synge, like a truly wise
    artist, does not inject his own point of view; he just ex-
    hibits the people: they are half gods and half beasts...."

3   H., H. C. [CHERRIE MATHESON HOUGHTON]. "John Synge as I Knew
    Him." Dublin The Irish Statesman (5 July), pp. 532-534.
        These remarks by Synge's former beloved one are disap-
    pointingly impersonal and provide mostly external data on
    Synge, such as his guttural speech, his frequent misspell-
    ings in letters and cramped writing style, and his often
    quoted statement that, although his family views him as
    unorthodox in his religion, his Parisian friends think of
    him as a saint. Reprinted: 1977.7. See 1931.6.

4   LYNCH, ARTHUR. My Life Story. London: John Long, pp. 121,
    148-150.
        Lynch mentions an allusion to himself in Act 1 of The
    Playboy of the Western World. Also, tells of Synge's
    living in Paris on "forty pounds" for a year. Gives a
    physical description of Synge and relates one harrowing
    episode, when Synge was knocked unconscious by a police
    club. Reprinted: 1977.7.

5   MASEFIELD, JOHN. "John M. Synge," in Recent Prose. London:
    Heinemann, pp. 163-187.
        Reprint of 1911.60.

6   MEYERFELD, MAX. "Letters of John Millington Synge." YR, 13
    no. 4 (July), 690-709.
        Opening note by Max Meyerfeld describes the beginning of
    his correspondence with Synge over translating The Well of
    the Saints into German, the play's failure in Berlin in
    1906, and the cooling of the two men's relationship after
    Meyerfeld decided not to translate The Playboy of the West-
    ern World into a play for Germany. The "new play" referred
    to in the letters is The Playboy of the Western World.

1924

7   MORGAN, ARTHUR EUSTACE. "Synge, 1871-1909," in <u>Tendencies of</u>
    <u>Modern English Drama</u>. London: Constable, pp. 158-173.
        Provides an overview of Synge's plays, seeing <u>Riders to</u>
    <u>the Sea</u> as an almost "perfect" play and placing <u>The Well of</u>
    <u>the Saints</u> in a category with <u>The Tinker's Wedding</u>: "be-
    lieving in the greatness of mankind, though fully conscious
    of its littleness, he created works of art which not only
    were clever and meritorious, but were in the real sense of
    great."

8   TÉRY, SIMONE. "J. M. Synge et son oeuvre." <u>Revue Anglo-</u>
    <u>Américaine</u>, 2:204-216.
        Discusses Synge's life on "les arides îles d'Aran"; men-
    tions that both Yeats and Synge were received with "l'hos-
    tilité marquéé d'une certaine partie du public" (finding it
    ironic that Synge's joyous <u>The Playboy of the Western World</u>
    should be greeted with such hatred by Nationalists); says
    that foreigners often find Synge boring; analyzes at length
    the plays, especially <u>The Playboy of the Western World</u> and
    <u>Deirdre of the Sorrows</u>.

9   YEATS, W. B. <u>Essays</u>. London and New York: Macmillan,
    pp. 294-296, 369-378, 379-384, 385-424, 488-489.
        Reprint of 1905.12; 1909.3; 1911.80, 83; 1912.36.

10 _____. "A Memory of Synge." Dublin <u>The Irish Statesman</u>
    (5 July), pp. 530-532.
        Provides brief but important information about Synge,
    including his plans for future playwriting, which were
    curtailed by his early death. Reprinted: 1976.30; 1977.7.

                              1925

1   NICOLL, ALLARDYCE. <u>British Drama: An Historical Survey from</u>
    <u>the Beginnings to the Present Time</u>. New York: T. Y. Crow-
    ell; London: G. G. Harrap, pp. 404-410, 449-451.
        Stresses the influence of the Aran Islands upon Synge.
    <u>Riders to the Sea</u> is "grand in its majestic simplicity."
    Calls <u>The Well of the Saints</u> and <u>In the Shadow of the Glen</u>
    "cynical."

2   TÉRY, SIMONE. "J. M. Synge," in <u>L'Île des Bardes: Notes sur</u>
    <u>la littérature irlandaise contemporaine</u>. Paris: Ernest
    Flammarion, pp. 140-166.
        A sympathetic sketch of Synge's works with the unfortu-
    nate conclusion that he is "presque intraduisible."

3   VAN DOREN, CARL and MARK VAN DOREN. "Synge: 1871-1909," in
     American and British Literature Since 1890. New York and
     London: Century, pp. 291-297.
         Synge "by general consent is one of the most powerful
     dramatic writers who have used the English language."

4   YEATS, W. B. The Bounty of Sweden: A Meditation, and a
     Lecture Delivered Before the Royal Swedish Academy and
     Certain Notes. Dublin: Cuala Press, pp. 1, 28, 40, 43-47,
     48-49.
         In his lecture before the Swedish Royal Academy, Yeats
     speaks of Lady Gregory and Synge as "an old woman sinking
     into the infirmity of age and a young man's ghost." Re-
     printed: 1955.10.

                              1926

1   COLUM, PADRAIC. The Road Round Ireland. New York: Macmillan,
     pp. 352-373.
         Reprint, with slight revisions, of 1921.8. Reprinted:
     1977.7.

2   LALOU, RENÉ. "Synge et le Théâtre," in Panorama de la lit-
     térature anglaise contemporaine. Paris: KRA, pp. 189-195.
         Stresses Synge's union of imagination with realism and
     sees him as Ireland's greatest dramatist: "Mais le maître
     de la scène irlandaise reste incontestablement Synge."

3   YEATS, W. B. "A Defence of the Abbey Theatre: Speech Deliv-
     ered at a Meeting of the Dublin Literary Society, on Feb-
     ruary 23rd." DM, 1, no. 2 (April-June), 8-12.
         Emphasizes Lady Gregory's and Synge's intimate knowledge
     of Irish dialect. Reprinted: 1976.30.

                              1927

1   BELLINGER, MARTHA FLETCHER. A Short History of the Drama.
     New York: Henry Holt, pp. 344-345.
         The Playboy of the Western World is "an extravaganza in
     which a bragging peasant boy is brought to book...."

2   CUNLIFFE, JOHN W. "The Irish Drama and J. M. Synge," in Mod-
     ern English Playwrights; A Short History of the English
     Drama from 1825. New York and London: Harper, pp. 131-
     142.

1927

Erroneously places Yeats's meeting with Synge in Paris in the year 1899; traces the sources of Synge's plays in his prose writings; denies that Synge was a "bitter" man; and says that the "curious detachment of the self-contained artist explains some of the difficulties that arose between him and his fellow countrymen...."

3 DICKINSON, THOMAS H. "J. M. Synge," in An Outline of Contemporary Drama. Boston and New York: Houghton Mifflin, pp. 227-228.
Cites Irish sources for Synge's works.

1928

1 CHISLETT, WILLIAM, JR. "The Irish Note in J. M. Synge's Translations," in Moderns and Near-Moderns: Essays on Henry James, Stockton, Shaw, and Others. London: Grafton Press, pp. 157-159.
Finds that "Hardly a paragraph in Synge's translations fails to yield an Irish turn of Speech." In sum: "Synge is "more Irish than Father Prout...."

2 CLARK, BARRETT H. "John M. Synge," in A Study of the Modern Drama. New York and London: Appleton, pp. 336-344.
Emphasizes the literary merit of Riders to the Sea.

3 CUNLIFFE, J. W. "John Millington Synge (1871-1909)," in English Literature During the Last Half-Century. Second edition. New York: Macmillan, pp. 257-263.
Includes a brief comparison between Synge's public and that of Arnold Bennett's Five Towns novels. Also, although Synge may have collaborated with the peasants, "his genius was predominant."

4 LEWIS, D. B. WYNDHAM. François Villon: A Documented Survey. New York: Coward-McCann; Hartford: Edwin V. Mitchell, pp. 276, 385.
Alludes to Synge's "free and lovely prose-paraphrase" of a Villon Lament and includes Synge's translation of "Prayer of the Old Woman, Villon's Mother."

5 YEATS, W. B. "The Death of Synge and Other Pages from an Old Diary." The Dial, 84 (April), 271-288.
Also appears in 1928.6, 7. Reprinted: 1955.9.

6 _____. The Death of Synge, and Other Passages from an Old
Diary. Dublin: Cuala Press, 35 pp.
These few fragments, more than any other writings about
Synge, established his legend. Yeats continues the Greek
metaphors that he had used to describe Synge's abilities
when Synge was alive: "Our Daimon is silent as was that
other before the death of Socrates." Yeats's description
of Synge's death is as effectively understated as his picture of the mourners is rancorous: "Synge is dead. In the
early morning he said to the nurse, 'It is no use fighting
death any longer' and he turned over and died." During
Synge's lifetime, the mourners, named by their initials,
had spoken his name "but to slander." Yeats sees the dead
Synge as an Adonais: "He has gone upward out of his ailing
body into the heroical fountains." Yeats's ruminations in
the essay provide much data for Synge critics. Yeats
speaks, for example, of Synge's indifference to other writers: "I have never heard him praise any writer, living or
dead, but some old French farce writer." Another ubiqui-
tously quoted passage recalls words that Synge once spoke
to Yeats: "'We should unite stoicism, asceticism and ecstasy. Two of them have often come together, but the
three never.'" The essay is interesting, also, for the
dreams and visions which Yeats describes around the time of
Synge's death. For example, "Molly Allgood...was looking
at Synge, and suddenly the flesh seemed to fall from his
face and she saw but a skull." Also appears: 1928.5, 7.
Reprinted: 1955.9.

7 _____. "The Death of Synge and Other Passages from an Old
Diary." The London Mercury, 17 (April), 637-651.
Also appears in 1928.5, 6. Reprinted: 1955.9.

1929

1 BYRNE, DAWSON. "The Playboy of the Western World," "From
the Parting of the Fays to the Death of Synge," "John Millington Synge: A Review," in The Story of Ireland's National Theatre: The Abbey Theatre, Dublin. Dublin:
Talbot Press, pp. 56-64, 65-74, 75-86.
Contains some information about the reception of The
Playboy of the Western World not found in better known
accounts of the play's history.

1929

2 DICKINSON, P. L. <u>The Dublin of Yesterday</u>. London: Methuen,
   pp. 85-87, 105-106, 111.
       Although Dickinson argues that the language in <u>The Play-</u>
   <u>boy of the Western World</u> is not realistic, he stresses the
   fact that the "love-scene between Christy and Pegeen" is a
   "wonderful piece of convincing writing." Also, provides
   information on "Pat," who came to the defense of <u>The Play-</u>
   <u>boy of the Western World</u> in 1907.

3 MALONE, ANDREW E. "The Folk Dramatists: John Millington
   Synge," in <u>The Irish Drama</u>. London: Constable; New York:
   Scribner's, pp. 147-156.
       Praises <u>Riders to the Sea</u> but says that it is "tragic
   in the current journalistic sense rather than in the Aris-
   totelian," and believes that <u>The Playboy of the Western</u>
   <u>World</u> "will not rank with the greatest, perhaps," but that
   Synge "is in no danger of being ranked with the mediocre."

4 MASEFIELD, JOHN. <u>The Story of a Round-House and Other Poems</u>.
   Revised edition. New York: Macmillan, p. 175.
       Provides a picture of Masefield's nightly walks with
   Synge: "now I miss/That lively mind and guttural laugh of
   his...."

1930

1 ATKINSON, J. BROOKS. "The Play: Playboying the Western
   World." <u>The New York Times</u> (3 January), p. 20.
       "No spuds were flung at the actors who revived" <u>The</u>
   <u>Playboy of the Western World</u> "last evening at the Irish
   Theatre in the Village, showing, no doubt, how wondrously
   fifteen or twenty years of civilization are after taming a
   man." In spite of the uneven acting, "the play is one of
   the most comical ever written...." Compares Synge to
   O'Casey: "The humors are much the same. Only the bitter-
   ness of a political point of view has made them caustic."

2 CRAIG, GORDON. <u>Henry Irving</u>. New York and Toronto: Longmans, Green, p. 31.
       Mentions Synge in connection with the "scenes in Irish
   theatres which seem to do no harm...."

3 EATON, WALTER PRICHARD. "'Local' Drama and the Irish Revival
   --Synge and O'Casey," in <u>The Drama in English</u>. New York:
   Scribner's, pp. 287-292.
       Points out the "direct influence" of Synge's speech
   patterns in <u>In the Shadow of the Glen</u> and in <u>Riders to the</u>

<u>Sea</u> on "Paddy's long speech about the glories of the old sailing days" in Scene 1 of O'Neill's <u>The Hairy Ape</u>.

4 MacMANUS, M. J. "Bibliographies of Irish Authors, No. 4: John Millington Synge." DM, NS 5 (October-December), 47-51.
A listing and bibliographical description of Synge's works from 1904 through 1910. Consists of twelve entries.

1931

1 CORKERY, DANIEL. <u>Synge and Anglo-Irish Literature: A Study</u>. Dublin and Cork: Cork University Press; London: Longmans, Green, 256 pp.
First chapter is a sketch of Anglo-Irish literature; second is a summary of Synge's life. Chapter Three discusses Synge's prose. Chapters Five through Ten examine the plays chronologically, a chapter being devoted to each one. Chapter Eleven deals with Synge's poems and translations. Chapter Twelve concludes the book with the admonition that a writer must "sink himself in the heart of his own people." Synge's Nora of <u>In the Shadow of the Glen</u> wears "her lusts upon her sleeve...." Placed beside <u>Riders to the Sea</u>, <u>The Playboy of the Western World</u> seems "flashy, overwrought yet unfinished, unachieved." <u>The Tinker's Wedding</u> does not have any of Synge's typical poetry and is "scarcely worth considering...." <u>The Well of the Saints</u> is a true Irish work, and Martin Doul is much more vivid and real than Christy Mahon. <u>The Playboy of the Western World</u> is simply too "fantastic" to be effective as art; <u>Deirdre of the Sorrows</u> reveals a "ripened artistry": "But then he [Synge] died." <u>See</u> 1931.4; 1932.8.

2 ELLEHAUGE, MARTIN. "J. M. Synge," in <u>Striking Figures Among Modern English Dramatists</u>. Copenhagen: Levin and Munksgaard, pp. 16-29.
Sees Maeterlinck in <u>Riders to the Sea</u>, Maeterlinck and George Clemenceau and Ibsen's "'Vildanden'" in <u>The Well of the Saints</u>. Sees <u>The Tinker's Wedding</u> as the "author's protest against the reception of" <u>The Playboy of the Western World</u> and finds Shakespearean imagery in <u>Deirdre of the Sorrows</u>.

3 MILLER, ANNA IRENE. "The National Theatre of Ireland," in <u>The Independent Theatre in Europe: 1887 to the Present</u>. New York: Ray Long and R. R. Smith, pp. 255-310.
Maintains that if <u>The Playboy of the Western World</u> had not been so realistically produced in 1907, the Dublin riots might have been prevented.

1931

4   O'FAOLAIN, SEAN. Review of Daniel Corkery, <u>Synge and Anglo-</u>
     <u>Irish Literature</u>. <u>The Criterion</u>, 11 (October), 140-142.
          Praises Corkery's book but complains about his preju-
     dices, e.g. Corkery's finding Synge "lacking in spiritual
     sensitiveness because he has not presented the religious
     life of the people in an orthodox light." <u>See</u> 1931.1.

5   STRONG, L. A. G. "John Millington Synge." <u>The Bookman</u>,
     73, no. 2 (April), 125-136.
          Points out a few facts about Synge's personal life.
     Finds that, while the poetry "has no startling intrinsic
     merit...it is of the utmost importance to...other poets."
     Also, the protagonist in <u>In the Shadow of the Glen</u> "is not
     man but nature." States flatly that <u>Riders to the Sea</u> "is
     a Greek tragedy...." About <u>The Playboy of the Western</u>
     <u>World</u>: "in no play outside of Shakespeare [are] such rich-
     ness of language and variety to be found," but "Synge's
     was a narrow genius...." The unfinished <u>Deirdre of the</u>
     <u>Sorrows</u> is "little more than a lyric." Reprinted: 1932.10;
     1953.11.

6   SYNGE, SAMUEL, REV. <u>Letters to My Daughter: Memories of John</u>
     <u>Millington Synge</u>. Dublin and Cork: Talbot Press, 287 pp.
          Consists of letters written by Synge's brother which
     point out what the Reverend Synge thinks are positive as-
     pects of John's character. Samuel discusses John's soli-
     citude for hurt birds and his abhorrence of using worms
     for bait, his wide reading despite a weak pass at Trinity,
     his abstaining from alcohol and tobacco, and his refusal
     to pursue the affectation of using his hands when speaking.
     John felt saddened by the accidental death of pet hens and
     never fished merely for sport, but ate the catch. Nor did
     John use bad language--at least in front of Samuel--his
     largest oath being "Holy Moses!" Samuel feels certain
     that his renowned sibling died a Christian: after all,
     his writings are based largely upon the Scriptures, and
     his temporary straying from the flock was the result of
     depression caused by poor health. Pages 152-268 consist
     of extracts from diaries and letters of the Synges' mother.
     Samuel's more interesting points in this section take up
     the religious readings of the young Synges, and one sec-
     tion of the letters, pp. 270-272, answers statements made
     by Cherrie Matheson in her letter to <u>The Irish Statesman</u>
     (5 July, 1924). The diary and letter extracts of materi-
     als written by Mrs. Synge are taken up mainly with descrip-
     tions of her son's health and sicknesses and his bicycle
     trips, though once in a while she makes an interesting en-
     try such as that of 28 February, 1893: "John canvassed for
     Anti-Home Rule petition in the evening." <u>See</u> 1924.3; 1932.1.

7 WILSON, EDMUND. <u>Axel's Castle: A Study in the Imaginative</u>
   <u>Literature of 1870-1930</u>. New York and London: Scribner's,
   p. 43.
   Contains an important, brief comment on Synge's "poetic
   drama."

1932

1 ANON. "Recollections of Synge." TLS (10 March), p. 171.
   Review of Samuel Synge's <u>Letters to My Daughter</u> (1931.6).
   Maintains that Synge "has remained an enigmatic figure, and
   the scant reminiscences of his literary friends have all
   contributed to the picturesque legend of his silence and
   solitude." Notes that Samuel Synge left out the coarser
   elements in his letters to his daughter: he avoids "many
   questions of interest to adult readers."

2 ATKINSON, BROOKS. "Synge and Lady Gregory in the Abbey Theatre Bill." <u>The New York Times</u> (21 October), p. 25.
   Provides casts of <u>The Playboy of the Western World</u> and
   of Lady Gregory's <u>The Rising of the Moon</u>. The plot of the
   former is "familiar to most hardened theatregoers, and
   apparently it was thrice familiar to last evening's audience. They caught every line directly it was spoken."
   Through his poetic language, a contrast to the arid indus-
   trialism of the thirties, Synge's peasants transmute "the
   common events of the day into a troubadour's magic...."

3 BROOKE, STOPFORD and T. W. ROLLESTON, eds. <u>A Treasury of</u>
   <u>Irish Poetry in the English Tongue</u>. Revised and enlarged.
   New York: Macmillan, pp. 596-599.
   Sketches Synge's life and includes two poems: "The
   Passing of the Shee, After Looking at One of A. E.'s Pic-
   tures" and "Queens."

4 FARJEON, HERBERT. "The Birth of the Playboy." <u>Theatre Arts</u>
   <u>Monthly</u>, 16, no. 3 (March), 228-236.
   A summary of events surrounding <u>The Playboy of the West-</u>
   <u>ern World</u> during its first week in Dublin, including
   Synge's comments to a reporter about his intentions in the
   play. The work "was brought successfully, though not without a stern application of the forceps, into the world."

1932

5   FRENZEL, HERBERT. <u>John Millington Synge's Work as a Contri-</u>
    <u>bution to Irish Folk-Lore and to the Psychology of Primi-</u>
    <u>tive Tribes</u>. Inaugural Dissertation. Düren-Rhld: Max
    Danielewski, 69 pp.
         Inspired by Nazism's stress upon the pure race, this
    book draws copiously upon Synge's own writings to make
    "a systematic valuation of Synge's observations on folk-
    lore in the last strongholds of pure Celticism in the West
    of Ireland."

6   HANIGHEN, FRANK C. "The Irish Players Present." <u>Commonweal</u>,
    17, no. 9 (December), 237-238.
         Accounts for the success of the Irish Players in New
    York in 1932: they brought "the salty aroma of real peas-
    ant drama, the authentic comedy of a green, unsophisticated
    land." Love scenes in <u>The Playboy of the Western World</u>
    are "as great dramatic art" as <u>Romeo and Juliet</u>.

7   HARDING, D. W. "A Note on Nostalgia." <u>Scrutiny</u>, 1, no. 1
    (May), 8-19.
         Brief explanation of how Synge's <u>The Aran Islands</u> il-
    lustrates the fact that "the frustrated desire for an
    adequate group...lies behind typically nostalgic writing."

8   O'HEGARTY, P. S. "Book Reviews: Synge and Irish Literature."
    DM, NS 7, no. 1 (January-March), 51-56.
         Review of Daniel Corkery's <u>Synge and Anglo-Irish Litera-</u>
    <u>ture</u>: "Christy and Pegeen, seriously treated, would have
    made a good play, but the <u>Widow Quins</u> and the <u>Shawneen</u>
    <u>Keoghs</u> are perilously like caricatures." <u>See</u> 1931.1.

9   SCOTT-JAMES, ROLFE ARNOLD. "J. M. Synge," in <u>Personality in</u>
    <u>Literature: 1913-1931</u>. New York: Henry Holt, pp. 135-
    139.
         Reprint of 1911.74 and 1913.16.

10 STRONG, L. A. G. "John Millington Synge." DM, NS 7, no. 2
    (April-June), 12-32.
         Reprint of 1931.5. Reprinted: 1953.11.

<u>1933</u>

1   BENNETT, ARNOLD. <u>The Journal of Arnold Bennett</u>. New York:
    The Literary Guild, p. 693.
         Provides brief but crucial information about the Fay
    Brothers and the riots over <u>The Playboy of the Western</u>
    <u>World</u>. In a diary entry of September 6, 1919 Bennett

reports W. G. Fay as having said at dinner on September 5
that the opposition to <u>The Playboy of the Western World</u>
came from Synge's vow after the attack on <u>The Well of the
Saints</u>: "I'll write something that will make 'em sit up."

2   CUNLIFFE, J. W. "John Millington Synge (1871-1909)," in <u>Eng-
     lish Literature in the Twentieth Century</u>. New York: Mac-
     millan, pp. 105-110.
         Sees the influence of Lady Gregory, Douglas Hyde, and
     the Irish peasant in the speech patterns of Synge's writ-
     ings. Admits that <u>The Playboy of the Western World</u> is art
     of a high quality but questions whether the Irish villager
     should be expected "to be proud to be the vehicle of
     it...."

3   YEATS, W. B. "The Great Blasket." London <u>The Spectator</u>
     (2 June), pp. 798-799.
         Provides background data about Synge, the Aran Islands,
     and the Great Blasket. Reprinted: 1976.30.

4   Z[ABEL], M[ORTON] D. "Synge and the Irish." <u>Poetry</u>, 42,
     no. 2 (May), 101-106.
         Discusses Synge's clear strictures about poetry in op-
     position to the aestheticism of his day, his "plain-spoken
     poetic fundamentalism."

                              <u>1934</u>

1   ANON. "Abbey Players Gain Free Choice of Bills." <u>The New
     York Times</u> (14 August), p. 15.
         "The directors of the Abbey Theatre have settled their
     differences with the Free State Government, with the result
     that the company may perform what plays it chooses when it
     visits the United States next Autumn. In April the govern-
     ment, which subsidizes the theatre, objected to certain
     plays on its program, particularly" <u>The Playboy of the
     Western World</u> and O'Casey's <u>The Plough and the Stars</u>. It
     was felt that these plays would give Americans a "too
     gloomy impression of Irish life."

2   SWINNERTON, FRANK. <u>The Georgian Scene: A Literary Panorama</u>.
     New York: Farrar & Rinehart, pp. 211, 217, 227, 267.
         "The great dramatist of the Dublin stage was Synge...."
     Mentions the influence of Synge on St. John Ervine's <u>John
     Ferguson</u>.

1935

1   ALSPACH, R. K. "Synge's 'Well of the Saints.'" TLS (28 De-
     cember), p. 899.
         A source for the Douls' second blindness may be "Patrick
     Kennedy's story of 'The Blind Nun' that appeared in his
     'Bardic Stories of Ireland' (1871)."

2   AUFHAUSER, ANNEMARIE. Sind die Dramen von John Millington
     Synge durch französische Vorbilder beeinflusst? Inaugural
     Dissertation. Würzburg: Richard Mayr, 66 pp.
         Includes comparisons of Synge with Martin du Gard, Vol-
     taire, Loti, and Clemenceau. Riders to the Sea is the
     "Meisterwerk Synges."

3   COLLIGAN, FRANCIS J. "The Playboy of the Abbey Theatre
     Players." San Francisco Quarterly, 1 (May), pp. 81-88.
         An important early statement about The Playboy of the
     Western World that tries to define its genre. Critics of
     the work made the mistake "of judging the play under the
     light of the reading lamp rather than in the darkness of
     the theatre." Christy is a "fainthearted lad with a poetic
     strain in his undeveloped soul...."

4   COLUM, MARY. "Shaw and Synge." Forum and Century, 94, no. 6
     (December), 357-358.
         With the exception of his two weaker plays, The Well of
     the Saints and The Tinker's Wedding, Synge's works have an
     enduring "life." His characters avoid "tameness," and
     Yeats's early comparison of Synge to the Greek dramatists
     (greeted with condescension at the time) has proved to be
     valid.

5   EGLINTON, JOHN [WILLIAM KIRKPATRICK MAGEE]. Irish Literary
     Portraits. London: Macmillan, pp. 7, 29, 133.
         "Synge's plays...were far more successful in providing
     'West Britons' with entertainment than in bringing Yeats
     and Synge 'nearer' to 'Irish Ireland.'" For Synge was not
     merely "an episode in Yeats's history: he was a disturbing
     event, which brought Yeats back from the abstract to the
     personal."

6   FAY, WILLIAM G. and CATHERINE CARSWELL. The Fays of the Abbey
     Theatre: An Autobiographical Record. New York: Harcourt,
     Brace; London: Rich and Cowan, pp. 136-141, 166-169, 211-
     222.
         Comments on several aspects of Synge's work, including
     the actors' difficulty in speaking his lines and the

64

1935

volatile nature of The Playboy of the Western World. Includes one misleading statement: "Synge always finished a
play in his mind to the last detail before he started writing it down, and once it was on paper he could not alter
it." Reprinted in parts: 1977.7.

7   GREENE, GRAHAM. "Stage and Screen: The Cinema: 'Riders to
    the Sea.'" London The Spectator (20 December), p. 1028.
        Comments on "an independent film version of Synge's
    Riders to the Sea, played by the Abbey Theatre players and
    produced for the most part in Connemara." Says that the
    film lacks an "awareness of an audience...." Admittedly
    not "an admirer of Synge's plays," Greene finds fault with
    the timing of the deaths in the film version of Riders to
    the Sea, caused partially by the absence of "act divi-
    sions." Greene feels, generally, that "style" is often
    simply a decoration in Synge's works.

8   MILLETT, FRED B. and GERALD EADES BENTLEY. The Art of the
    Drama. New York: Appleton-Century-Crofts, pp. 17, 70,
    112, 228.
        Compares Riders to the Sea to Oedipus Rex, The Playboy
    of the Western World to Jonson's social satires, and
    Synge's "good prose dialogue" with the "lighter passages
    in Shakespeare, Beaumont, and Fletcher...."

9   PAUL-DUBOIS, L. "Le Théâtre irlandais: Synge." RDM, 27
    (June), 631-657.
        Praises Synge as a writer with an artistic--as opposed
    to scientific--temperament, even though he is "une création
    de M. Yeats"; provides a summary of Synge's works and ar-
    tistic theories. It is "non sans raison," however, that
    one criticizes the sometime grossness of the language and
    the immoral crudity of certain scenes.

10 WOODS, ANTHONY S. "Synge Stayed at Home by the Fireside."
    CathW, 141, no. 841 (April), 46-52.
        Praises Synge's rendering of the Irish peasant's devo-
    tion to his country but maintains that Synge "could not
    overcome the innate deficiencies of his birth and upbring-
    ing." Though he wrote in a "beautiful and natural idiom,"
    Synge did not understand the peasants' "spiritual devotion
    to their religion." Synge's Ascendancy class has the
    "superficial gloss of the Celtic civilization, but they
    have not the essence of the true Celt."

1936

1   BARNES, T. R. "Yeats, Synge, Ibsen and Strindberg." Scrutiny,
    5, no. 3 (December), 257-262.
       Synge expressed the "permanent values": in presenting
    his country's real people, he did not become provincial.

2   GWYNN, STEPHEN. Irish Literature and Drama in the English
    Language: A Short History. London and New York: Thomas
    Nelson, pp. 134, 156, 161-163, 178-180, 184-187, 202, 216-
    217.
       Though praising Synge's dialogue, says that it is "never
    realistic...." Rahter, "All Synge's work is essentially
    fantastic."

3   MacKENNA, STEPHEN. Journal and Letters of Stephen MacKenna.
    Edited with a Memoir by E. R. Dodds and a preface by Pad-
    raic Colum. London: Constable, pp. 11-13, 36, 38-39, 114,
    122.
       Relates the incident of Synge's being "bludgeoned by a
    Paris policeman" and other details of the Synge-MacKenna
    relationship, including MacKenna's possible influence on
    Synge's work despite MacKenna's disclaimer.

1937

1   AE [GEORGE WILLIAM RUSSELL]. The Living Torch. Edited by
    Monk Gibbon. London: Macmillan, pp. 95, 136, 151, 257.
       Mentions Synge in the company of those who "turn from
    the hearth and...roam in uncharted regions of the psyche."
    Of The Playboy of the Western World: "how many playboys
    may yet come out of that lawless imagination!" The play is
    "history in the making rather than history dramatised."

2   FLETCHER, JOHN GOULD. Life Is My Song: The Autobiography of
    John Gould Fletcher. New York: Farrar & Rinehart, p. 68.
       Cites the inspiration that Synge's disdain for the mob
    gives to the modern poet.

3   GOGARTY, OLIVER ST. J. As I Was Going Down Sackville Street:
    A Phantasy in Fact. London: Rich and Cowan; New York:
    Reynal and Hitchcock, pp. 292-294, 299-300.
       Points out a hidden reference to Synge's dialect in a
    poem by James Joyce, tells how Yeats exclaimed "Aeschylus"
    while reading Synge's Riders to the Sea, and includes a
    brief comment on Synge's refusal to explain the "meaning"
    of The Playboy of the Western World. Abridged: 1977.7.

4   HOARE, DOROTHY M. The Works of Morris and of Yeats in Relation to Early Saga Literature. Cambridge (England): Cambridge University Press, pp. 105-110.
     Though praising The Playboy of the Western World, maintains that the rest of Synge's plays are harmed by his romanticizing of his subject, his interest "in the embroidery of a situation rather than the situation itself, in literature rather than life."

5   RIVA, SERAFINO. La tradizione celtica e la moderna letteratura irlandese, I. John Millington Synge. Rome: Religio, 319 pp.
     Provides a lengthy but competent introduction to Synge's works from a European viewpoint.

1938

1   CASEY, HELEN. "Synge's Use of the Anglo-Irish Idiom." EJ, 27 (November), 773-776.
     Analyzes Synge's use of Anglo-Celtic in Deirdre of the Sorrows, wherein he catches the "blue fire" of the Irish people.

2   CONACHER, W. M. "The Irish Literary Movement." QQ, 45, no. 1 (Spring), 56-65.
     Questions whether Synge's plays are really masterpieces at all. The Playboy of the Western World is merely a "flight of fancy"; and The Tinker's Wedding, a "foul offence."

3   FALLON, GABRIEL. "The Ageing Abbey--II." The Irish Monthly, 66 (May), 339-344.
     Contains important information about Synge's obdurate attitude towards his artistic integrity in spite of the hostility of the audience.

4   RABUSE, VON GEORG. "J. M. Synges Verhältnis zur französischen Literatur und besonders zu Maeterlinck." Archiv, 174, pp. 36-53.
     Interesting discussion of symbolism in Synge's work, e.g. what is the meaning of the "Schwein mit den schwarzen" feet?

1938

5   WILDE, PERCIVAL. The Craftsmanship of the One-Act Play. Bos-
     ton: Little Brown, pp. 12, 38, 64, 205, 256, 272, 288,
     324, 329, 330, 363.
          "What can be more admirable than the perfect restraint
     of 'Riders to the Sea?'" "For every word that is spoken,
     ten are left unsaid." Calls Riders to the Sea "the great-
     est one-act play in the English language...." Defends
     Maurya's reference to the "stinking fish" at the end of the
     play even though some say it lacks elegance.

1939

1   COLUM, MARY. "Memories of Yeats." The Saturday Review of
     Literature, 19, no. 18 (February), 3-4, 14.
          Mentions public and academic opposition to bringing a
     body onto the stage in Riders to the Sea, describes in de-
     tail Yeats's fight for The Playboy of the Western World in
     Dublin, and identifies the man who began the hissing of
     the play at the Abbey Theatre as Francis Sheehy-Skeffington.

2   ELLIS-FERMOR, UNA. "John Millington Synge," in The Irish
     Dramatic Movement. London: Methuen, pp. 163-186.
          Emphasizes Synge's unique blending of nature-mysticism
     and dramatic poetry, even though in The Playboy of the
     Western World nature becomes an "undertone," and not an
     actor in the piece. Traces Synge's nature poetry to the
     "ancient poetry of his own race." Stresses Synge's subor-
     dination of action to poetic effectiveness. And delineates
     the affinities of The Playboy of the Western World with
     Jacobean drama. Reprinted: 1967.6. Abridged: 1969.25.

3   ESTILL, ADELAIDE DUNCAN. The Sources of Synge. Philadelphia:
     University of Pennsylvania, 54 pp.
          This dissertation defends Synge's use of his sources,
     just as Shakespeare's critics defend his. A chapter is
     devoted to each of the plays.

4   MOSES, MONTROSE J., ed. "John Millington Synge (1871-1901
     [sic])," in Representative British Dramas: Victorian and
     Modern. Boston: Little, Brown, pp. 931-933.
          "To certain writers the task of recording the career of
     Synge is almost as consecrated as the task of the Stevenson
     lover who visits every shrine and locality with the hope
     of finding something new about his subject."

5   O'CONNOR, FRANK [MICHAEL FRANCIS O'DONOVAN]. "Synge," in The
    Irish Theatre. [Lectures Delivered during the Abbey Thea-
    tre Festival Held in Dublin in August, 1938.] Edited by
    Lennox Robinson. London: Macmillan, pp. 29-52.
        Begins by defining Synge's specific Irishness and his
    opposition to middle class values, then evaluates each of
    the plays.

6   PERRY, HENRY TEN EYCK. Masters of Dramatic Comedy and Their
    Social Themes. Cambridge (Massachusetts): Harvard Uni-
    versity Press, pp. 364-366.
        Traces the idea of the vital life versus rigid formalism
    in Synge's plays, then cites several contrasts between
    Synge and Shaw.

7   RIVOALLAN, ANATOLE. "J. M. Synge," in Littérature irlandaise
    contemporaine. Paris: Hachette, pp. 21-31.
        Contrasts Yeats with Synge, touches on the controversy
    over The Playboy of the Western World, and spends the rest
    of the time on Riders to the Sea and on Deirdre of the
    Sorrows.

8   ROWE, KENNETH THORPE. "Analysis of a Great Play," in Write
    That Play. New York and London: Funk and Wagnalls,
    pp. 90-122.
        Deals with Riders to the Sea. Follows sections of the
    play with sections of questions for discussion.

1940

1   ANON. "Forty Years of Irish Drama, Yeats, Synge and Lady
    Gregory, From the Visionaries to the Realists." TLS
    (13 April), pp. 182, 186.
        Comments that the "great trio, Yeats, Synge and Lady
    Gregory, are mighty yet," even though the "drama that they
    founded has not been continued on the lines they meant...."

2   FAY, W. G. "The Poet and the Actor," in Scattering Branches:
    Tributes to the Memory of W. B. Yeats. Edited by Stephen
    Gwynn. New York and London: Macmillan, pp. 115-134.
        Brief mention of a possible Yeats influence on The
    Tinker's Wedding.

3   GWYNN, STEPHEN. "Scattering Branches," in Scattering Branch-
    es: Tributes to the Memory of W. B. Yeats. Edited by
    Stephen Gwynn. New York and London: Macmillan, pp. 1-14.
        Comments on Yeats's defense of Synge.

1940

4   _____, ed. Scattering Branches: Tributes to the Memory of
     W. B. Yeats. New York and London: Macmillan, pp. 1-14,
     115-134, 183-229.
         See individual entries: 1940, 2, 3, 5.

5   STRONG, L. A. G. "William Butler Yeats," in Scattering
     Branches: Tributes to the Memory of W. B. Yeats. Edited
     by Stephen Gwynn. New York and London: Macmillan,
     pp. 183-229.
         Contrasts Yeats's impassioned speech over The Playboy
     of the Western World to his defense of O'Casey, which had
     "passed through a filter."

1941

1   LEVIN, HARRY. James Joyce: A Critical Introduction. New
     York: New Directions, pp. 3, 5, 6, 9, 15, 23, 33, 53,
     206, 233.
         Book begins with Synge's comment, "All art is a collab-
     oration," which, according to Levin, poses the "problem of
     the artist in the twentieth century...." "The reception of
     Synge's Playboy...has retroactively justified Joyce's ti-
     rade [against what Joyce felt to be the Irish Theatre's
     capitulation to the groundlings]." Compares Stephen Deda-
     lus to Christy Mahon: "Like Synge's Playboy, he must go
     through the motions of parricide to make good his revolt."

2   MacLIAMMÓIR, MICHEÁL. "Introduction," in J. M. Synge's
     Plays, Poems, and Prose. London: J. M. Dent; New York:
     E. P. Dutton, pp. v-xi.
         Synge "more than any other changed the shape of Irish
     dramatic writing...."

3   PRITCHETT, V. S. "Current Literature: Books in General."
     London The New Statesman and Nation (19 April), p. 413.
         Compares Joyce and Synge in regard to their similarities
     of their characters' language and their theme of time's
     passing, and discusses the affinities of Synge's humor with
     the Elizabethans and with the Russian writers of the 1870s.
     Revised: 1942.5.

4   STRONG, L. A. G. John Millington Synge. P. E. N. Books.
     London: Allen and Unwin, 44 pp.
         Though repeating his previous critical judgments on
     Synge, Strong does allot important space to Synge's poems
     and translations. See 1942.1.

1942

1 ANON. "The Tinker." TLS (14 February), p. 79.
Review of Strong, John Millington Synge (1941.4): com-
plains that there is so little in Strong's book about
Yeats and Lady Gregory.

2 ENRIGHT, D. J. "A Note on Irish Literature and the Irish
Tradition," Scrutiny, 10, no. 3 (January), 247-255.
Although Synge is the only dramatist of the peasant play
school to attain more than local interest, he portrays in
The Playboy of the Western World "not very much more than
a comedy of l'homme moyen sensuel": he resembles Jonson
in dialect but differs from him in not having a moral purpose. In his excesses, Synge is like Keats, but Riders to
the Sea is an exception, a true tragedy and "the great
event of Irish drama." Says that Synge's plays fail to
record his subjects' spiritual life.

3 HONE, JOSEPH. W. B. Yeats, 1865-1939. New York: Macmillan,
pp. 132, 138, 172, 175, 193, 206-207, 212-214, 221-222,
228-229, 237-238, 247, 248, 270, 293, 326, 344, 356, 388,
441.
Comments generally on many aspects of the Synge-Yeats
relationship. Especially interesting in describing Synge's
and Yeats's deifying of each other.

4 O'HEGARTY, P. S. "Some Notes on the Bibliography of J. M.
Synge: Supplemental to Bourgeois and MacManus." DM, 17,
no. 1 (January-March), 56-58.
Corrects and updates previous descriptive bibliographies
of Synge's works.

5 PRITCHETT, V. S. "The End of the Gael," in In My Good Books.
London: Chatto and Windus, pp. 155-160.
Revised version of 1941.3.

1943

1 BROMAGE, MARY COGAN. "Literature of Ireland Today." SAQ,
42, no. 1 (January), 27-37.
Realism and "melancholy fatalism" in modern Irish
writing were both "foreshadowed by John M. Synge."

2 DUKES, ASHLEY. "Fashions in Comedy: Notes on London Summer
Season." Theatre Arts, 27, no. 10 (October), 584-590.
[Title page mistakenly has XXVIII.]

1943

"...Becque, Wilde and Synge are the modern writers in the classical comic tradition." Synge was "wholly free" from the need to please an audience.

3   STAMM, RUDOLF.   "Introduction," in Three Anglo-Irish Plays. Edited by Rudolf Stamm. Bibliotheca Anglicana, 5. Berne: A. Francke, pp. 3-18.
    Emphasizes the influences of peasant Ireland on Synge. Of Riders to the Sea: "The play has become a short one as no human conflicts, no by-interests are allowed to turn our attention from the main theme."

1944

1   YEATS, JOHN BUTLER. J. B. Yeats: Letters to His Son W. B. Yeats and Others, 1869-1922. Edited by Joseph Hone. London: Faber and Faber, pp. 23, 106, 109, 163, 169.
    Author's letter of July 1, 1908 records John Quinn's reaction to word of Synge's illness: "he was like a raging lunatic.... He seemed to think that no one cared whether Synge lived or died." Riders to the Sea records a "perfect grief...." Also, Synge may have been considering writing a play on the subject of a "workman's marriage."

1945

1   BROOKS, CLEANTH and ROBERT B. HEILMAN. Understanding Drama: Twelve Plays. New York: Henry Holt, pp. 26-27.
    In "Appendix A," gives a critique of Riders to the Sea and provides questions for students.

1946

1   BABLER, O. F. "John Millington Synge in Czech Translations." N&Q, 191 (September), 123-124.
    Besides providing data about the Czech translations of Synge's work, quotes from the translator, Karel Musek, in his Foreword to The Playboy of the Western World. Musek found Synge to be "large, a mighty figure," but "not as full of health as he seemed."

2   CLARK, WILLIAM SMITH, ed. "Introduction to The Playboy of the Western World, The Rise of the Irish Theater and Drama: Synge and Folk-Comedy," in Chief Patterns of World Drama: Aeschylus to Anderson. Boston: Houghton Mifflin, pp. 887-891.

Synge was "the first dramatist to set down truthfully
the passion and the splendor in folk life."

3   GIBBS, WOLCOTT. "The Theatre: Gaels and Gagmen." NY, 22
    (2 November), 57-58.
        A review of The Playboy of the Western World production
    by Theatre Incorporated, with Burgess Meredith as Christy.
    Finds the play "tiresome," with artificial diction and
    imagery and "overly whimsical invention."

4   GREENE, DAVID H. "An Adequate Text of J. M. Synge." MLN, 61,
    no. 7 (November), 466-467.
        Points out lacunae in the four editions of Synge's works
    published up to 1946. For example, "Both the London and
    the New York publishers claim to have assembled their edi-
    tions from texts submitted to them by the Synge estate, but
    apparently no check was made to determine their accuracy or
    completeness."

5   KRUTCH, JOSEPH WOOD. "Drama." The Nation, 163 (9 November),
    536.
        States that The Playboy of the Western World was written
    as a protest against modern drama, but underestimates the
    play's complexity.

6   PEACOCK, RONALD. "Synge," in The Poet in the Theatre. Lon-
    don: Routledge and Kegan Paul; New York: Harcourt, Brace,
    pp. 105-116.
        Discusses Synge's romanticism, his cynicism, and his
    "delicate self-mockery" in The Playboy of the Western
    World. Maintains that Synge's "most ambitious work has for
    its very theme the imagination, the fine idea and the fine
    word." Reprinted: 1969.25.

7   WYATT, EUPHEMIA VAN RENSSELAER. "The Drama: 'The Playboy of
    the Western World.'" CathW, 164 (December), 262-263.
        Review of the production of the play at the Booth.
    About the riots in 1911-12 over Synge's picture of Irish
    peasants: "since the characters happen to be three old
    soaks and the Mayo equivalent of bobby-soxers, it would
    seem as unfair to denounce The Iceman Cometh as a libel on
    New Yorkers."

1947

1 CLARK, BARRETT H. and GEORGE FREEDLEY, eds. A History of
   Modern Drama. New York and London: D. Appleton-Century,
   pp. 217-222, 225, 226, 227, 568.
   Calls Synge "the greatest Irish dramatist who has ever
   lived.... Shaw is certainly to be considered non-Irish as
   far as drama movements are concerned." The Tinker's Wedding is a "crude, Hans Sachs kind of farce...."

2 COLLINS, R. L. "The Distinction of Riders to the Sea." The
   University of Kansas City Review, 13 (Summer), 278-284.
   Develops at length the reasons that Riders to the Sea
   is unlike the rest of Synge's plays, that the characters
   are "a race apart." Reprinted: 1970.1.

3 COLUM, MARY. Life and the Dream. Garden City, New Jersey:
   Doubleday, pp. 90, 105, 108, 112, 119, 134, 136-139, 140,
   158, 185, 229, 286, 301-302.
   Contrasts the shy and affable Synge to Lady Gregory,
   who "behaved as if she were a grand duchess...." Provides
   an important summary of the motivations behind the protests over The Playboy of the Western World, e.g. "that a
   drunken man was on the stage and drunken men did not appear
   in American plays...."

4 EMPSON, WILLIAM. Seven Types of Ambiguity. New York: New
   Directions, pp. 38-42.
   A lengthy comment on how the storm scene in Deirdre of
   the Sorrows is effective dramatically.

5 FARREN, ROBERT. The Course of Irish Verse in English. New
   York: Sheed and Ward, pp. 123-128.
   "This poetry of bitch and ditch and rotten queens was
   part of Synge; a true part; but not all of him." Compares
   Synge (favorably) to Hopkins.

6 GILDER, ROSAMOND. "New Year, New Plays: Broadway in Review,
   The Playboy of the Western World." Theatre Arts, 31 (January), 21-22.
   Pictures Burgess Meredith as Christy in the Theatre Incorporated offering of the play as "Dancing along the
   hilltops of high sounding words, singing a song of revolt
   against the humdrum, the obvious, the real[;] the Playboy
   is one with the young Peer Gynt, with Paul Bunyan and all
   the bold heroes of legend who lay about them with fine
   phrases and tall tales."

7   GREENE, DAVID H. "The Playboy and Irish Nationalism." JEGP,
       46, no. 2 (April), 199-204.
           Traces several structural and verbal revisions through
       the drafts of The Playboy of the Western World in the
       light of Synge's sources, such as the case of James Lynch-
       ehaun. For instance, "It is hair-raising to think of how
       the indignant audiences would have received the deleted
       phrase of one of the early drafts which reads, 'To hell
       with the Pope.'" "It was merely Synge's fate to be caught
       up in the nationalistic movement.... The audiences were
       not incapable of appreciating satire: they were just not
       in a mood for it." Reprinted: 1969.25.

8   _____. "The Shadow of the Glen and The Widow of Ephesus."
       PMLA, 62, no. 1, part 1 (March), 233-238.
           The ending of In the Shadow of the Glen swings the play
       "from its logical and somber conclusion into the realm of
       romantic symbolism. To do that it was necessary that the
       entire emphasis be withdrawn from the guilty lovers and re-
       focused on the tramp and the lonely girl who finds release
       from her bondage in his company." Takes issue with critics
       who say that Synge's plot could not have come from Ireland
       by citing the Irish folklore commission and other sources:
       "There can be no doubt that Synge modelled The Shadow of
       the Glen on an authentic Irish folk tale which is still
       current in the west of Ireland."

9   _____. "The Tinker's Wedding: A Revaluation." PMLA, 62,
       no. 3 (September), 824-827.
           Brief description of the manuscript versions of The
       Tinker's Wedding, which, though "not a good play," is an
       "important connecting link between the one-act plays of
       Synge's apprenticeship and the three-act plays of his ma-
       turity." Greene feels that the play's weaknesses arise
       because Synge did not revise the work as diligently as he
       did his others. In summary: "A fair estimate of The
       Tinker's Wedding is that it contains a crude farcical ele-
       ment which is typical of Synge, little or no deftness of
       characterization, perhaps one good scene at the end where
       the tinkers rush off in confusion with the priest's curses
       ringing in their ears, and a few passages of lyric vigor
       such as one associates with Synge's best writing."

10 GREGORY, LADY. Lady Gregory's Journals, 1916-1930. Edited
       by Lennox Robinson. New York: Macmillan, pp. 52, 74, 80,
       119, 146, 217, 220-221, 272.
           Points out that "when these journals start the Playboy
       quarrel is almost forgotten." Lady Gregory's entry for 13

1947

November, 1923, alludes to a production of In the Shadow of the Glen in Gaelic; another, for 24 December, 1920, recalls the English demand to cut the expression "loosèd kharki cut-throats": "It is likely those forces are being spoken of this Christmas Eve in Aran in yet more loaded words than even Synge's fancy could create." Records Emily Lawless' complaint that Synge's writing is not Irish enough.

11 O'HEGARTY, P. S. "Bibliographical Notes: The Abbey Theatre (Wolfhound) Series of Plays." DM, NS 22 (April-June), 41-42.
Contains an important note on the first edition of The Well of the Saints.

12 TINDALL, WILLIAM YORK. Forces in Modern British Literature, New York: Knopf, pp. 63, 64, 67-71, 81, 304.
Sees The Well of the Saints as rising to the "plane of myth." About The Playboy of the Western World: "the word 'shifts'...bothered some who did not understand the shifts of Synge."

1948

1 CHEW, SAMUEL C. "Synge," in A Literary History of England. Edited by Albert C. Baugh. New York: Appleton-Century-Crofts, pp. 1513-1514.
Deirdre of the Sorrows is Synge's "greatest work." The Tinker's Wedding (unnamed in the article on Synge) is a "negligible farce." In the Shadow of the Glen is "no more than a sketch," and The Playboy of the Western World is a comedy which is "too exceptional in its subject...."

2 FREYER, GRATTAN. "The Little World of J. M. Synge." Politics and Letters, 1, no. 4 (Summer), 5-12.
Places Synge's Aran work in the context of writings by previous folklorists, examines the simplistic notion that Synge was apolitical, sees the "tramp" as a projection of Synge's personality, explains Synge's theme of the "triumphant power of the imagination," and compares Synge to D. H. Lawrence.

3 GREENE, DAVID H. "Synge's Unfinished Deirdre." PMLA, 63, no. 4 (December), 1314-1321.
Notes how Synge's Deirdre of the Sorrows differs from its probable source, comments on Synge's manuscripts of the play, and concludes that it is a much underrated work which

merits much future attention. Synge's "sense of theater
[is] nowhere so sound" as in Deirdre of the Sorrows.

4   TREWIN, J. C. "The World of the Theatre: Lovers' Meeting."
    The Illustrated London News (3 April), p. 386.
        Passing reference to The Playboy of the Western World
    with a photograph of the "torture scene." Trewin writes,
    "Much of the finest love-passage we have had in the London
    theatre of late is one more than forty years old. It is
    that between the Playboy...and the country girl, Pegeen
    Mike...." The play still has a "rapture unexampled in our
    time."

1949

1   GREBANIER, BERNARD D. N., SAMUEL MIDDLEBROOK, STITH THOMPSON,
    and WILLIAM WATT, eds. "John Millington Synge (1871-
    1909)," in English Literature and Its Backgrounds: From
    the Forerunners of Romanticism to the Present. Vol. 2.
    Revised edition. New York, Chicago, and San Francisco:
    Holt, Rinehart, and Winston, pp. 1056-1057.
        The Playboy of the Western World is "Synge's masterpiece
    in comedy." Calls Riders to the Sea "a bleak, lyrical...
    play about the pathetic resignation of an old fisher-
    woman...."

2   JEFFARES, A. NORMAN. W. B. Yeats: Man and Poet. London:
    Routledge and Kegan Paul, pp. 107-108, 147, 152, 155, 156,
    159, 163, 170, 176-178, 226, 248, 292, 320, 322, 333.
        Comments generally on several aspects of the Synge--
    Yeats relationship, including the effect of The Playboy of
    the Western World on Yeats's own career.

3   MacNAMARA, BRINSLEY [A. E. WELDON]. Abbey Plays 1899-1948,
    Including the Productions of the Irish Literary Theatre.
    Dublin: at the Sign of the Three Candles, pp. 8, 10, 12,
    17, 28-30, 33.
        Gives dates of first productions of Synge's plays through
    1910. Says that O'Neill "had his first urge to write from
    seeing the work of Synge in the repertoire of the Company
    during...first Abbey tours...."

4   NEWLIN, NICHOLAS. The Language of Synge's Plays: The Irish
    Element. Philadelphia: University of Pennsylvania,
    198 pp.
        This typewritten doctoral dissertation contains a useful
    four page bibliography.

1949

5 RAHILLY, SEAN O'MAHONY. "Synge and the Early Days of the
   Abbey." Dublin The Irish Press (21 April), p. 4.
      Includes comments by Molly Allgood about her relation-
   ship with Synge. Reprinted: 1977.7.

6 WHITE, H. O. "John Millington Synge." Irish Writing, 9
   (October), 57-61.
      Based upon a "talk broadcast by the B.B.C. on the North-
   ern Ireland Home Service and later re-broadcast on the
   Third Programme." General discussion of Synge's work, in
   which White sees Synge as "certainly the greatest dramatist"
   of the Abbey Theatre movement. Contains some mistakes in
   biographical data, e.g. Synge's birth date is not 1875,
   and he did not meet Yeats for the first time in 1899.

1950

1 BROWN, ALAN L. "John Millington Synge (1871-1909)." The
   London Quarterly and Holborn Review, 175, no. 1 (January),
   44-49.
      Sees Synge as "the first dramatist writing in English
   since the end of the Jacobean Period in whose work dramatic
   and poetic elements achieved true union...."

2 COLUM, PADRAIC. "Early Days of the Irish Theatre." DM, NS
   25 (January-March), 18-25.
      Describes the chilly reception afforded In the Shadow
   of the Glen, seen by John Butler Yeats as a "satire on the
   arranged marriage," but by the Dublin audience and by some
   actors, as the "Big House against the Cabin."

3 KAVANAGH, PETER. The Story of the Abbey Theatre: From Its
   Origins in 1899 to the Present. New York: Devin-Adair,
   pp. 35-42, 47-52, 55-66, 91-95.
      Delineates the opposition to Synge, "the most hated of
   all the Abbey dramatists."

4 KELLEHER, JOHN V. "Matthew Arnold and the Celtic Revival,"
   in Perspectives of Criticism. Edited by Harry Levin.
   Cambridge, Massachusetts: Harvard University Press,
   pp. 197-221.
      Passing reference to Synge's "reserve," which precluded
   his being part of any movement.

5 MASEFIELD, JOHN. A Book of Prose Selections. London and New
   York: Macmillan, pp. 77-78.
      Reprint of 1911.60.

6   NICOLL, ALLARDYCE. <u>World Drama from Aeschylus to Anouilh</u>.
New York: Harcourt, Brace & World, pp. 661, 663, 690-
696, 698, 729, 922, 928.
      Compares Synge with Chekhov in exploring a world apart
from the metropolitan centers of Western Europe and emphasizes the delightful cynicism of Synge's plays.

7   QUINN, OWEN. "No Garland for John Synge." <u>Envoy</u>, 3, no. 11
(October), 44-51.
      A literate enumeration of Synge's faults as a play-
wright. While praising <u>Riders to the Sea</u>, attacks the
other works. Synge "was totally unfitted for the task of
collaborating with Irish Catholic life...." With <u>In the
Shadow of the Glen</u>, Nora's moods "are too fleeting...."
Denies the Oedipal implications of <u>The Playboy of the
Western World</u> and maintains that those who call it "vulgar
are probably doing it the least injustice." Concludes,
however, by averring that Synge's "technical competence,
his highly developed sense of humour, his quaintness alone
would seem to ensure him a permanent, if not very high,
place in the history of drama."

<u>1951</u>

1   ELIOT, T. S. <u>Poetry and Drama</u>. London: Faber and Faber;
Cambridge (Massachusetts): Harvard University Press,
pp. 21-22.
      Contains a short reference to Synge's diction.

2   KAVANAGH, PATRICK. "Diary." <u>Envoy</u>, 4, no. 16 (March), 67-72.
      An attack on Synge, which finds "hate" everywhere in his
works.

3   PRICE, ALAN F. "A Consideration of Synge's 'The Shadow of the
Glen.'" DM, NS 26, no. 4 (October-December), 15-24.
      Shows how Synge turned into an effective and artistic
play the tale told to him by Pat Dirane on the Aran Islands.
Synge emphasizes the humanity of the character instead of
the "stark account of a cuckold's swift vengeance" and
situates his human creations in a countryside that is "one
of the most active forces" in the play.

4   ROBINSON, LENNOX. <u>Ireland's Abbey Theatre: A History, 1899-
1951</u>. London: Sidgwick and Jackson, pp. 34-37, 52-55, 65,
95, 100.
      Provides much useful background, with many scattered
references to Synge. Includes data on such items as letters and casts of players.

1951

5   SETTERQUIST, JAN. Ibsen and the Beginnings of Anglo-Irish
     Drama: I. John Millington Synge. Upsala Irish Studies.
     Vol. 2. Edited by S. B. Liljegren. Upsala: Lundequistka;
     Dublin: Hodges, Figgis; Copenhagen: Munksgaard; Cam-
     bridge, Massachusetts: Harvard University Press, 94 pp.
        This monograph, which admittedly draws parallels between
     Synge's and Ibsen's plays throughout the essay, devotes a
     chapter to each of Synge's plays and includes two other
     sections: one commenting on dialogue in Ibsen and Synge,
     the other discussing Synge and the problem play. Point is
     that Synge "may be said to take interest in situations that
     involve the same questions as those dealt with by his Nor-
     wegian forerunner. He also maps out these problems in much
     the same way, and the conclusions, if any, are those al-
     ready arrived at by Ibsen." Abridged: 1970.1.

                              1952

1   BAKER, BLANCHE M. "Synge, Edmund John Millington, 1871-1909,"
     in Theatre and Allied Arts: A Guide to Books Dealing with
     the History, Criticism, and Technic of the Drama and Thea-
     tre and Related Arts and Crafts. New York: H. W. Wilson,
     p. 118.
        Lists twenty-five books devoted in whole or in part to
     Synge, briefly annotating five of these.

2   DAVIE, DONALD A. "On the Poetic Diction of John M. Synge."
     DM, NS 27, no. 1 (January-March), 32-38.
        "Synge had the novel idea of seeing human dignity not in
     what distinguished man from the brute, but in what he and
     the brute had in common...." Like T. S. Eliot's, Synge's
     poetic strictures were a reaction against the "inhumanly
     exalted poetry of his time...." For Davie, Synge "remains
     one of the very few poets, writing in English since the end
     of the eighteenth century, who have talked sense about the
     question of diction in poetry."

3   KRONENBERGER, LOUIS. "Synge," in The Thread of Laughter:
     Chapters on English Stage Comedy from Jonson to Maugham.
     New York: Knopf, pp. 284-288.
        Contrasts Synge with Shaw and emphasizes Synge's robust-
     ness and his unsparing but comic view of his peasant char-
     acters.

4 SUSS, IRVING D. "The 'Playboy' Riots." Irish Writing, 18
   (March), 39-42.
        Accounts for opposition to Synge's play by Irish poli-
   tics and other specifically Irish forces: "Participation
   in the riots became a kind of touchstone of patriotism."

5 WILLIAMS, RAYMOND. "J. M. Synge," in Drama: From Ibsen to
   Eliot. London: Chatto and Windus, pp. 154-174.
        "Synge is undoubtedly the most remarkable English-
   speaking prose dramatist of the century...." Sees the
   early Second Shepherds' Play in In the Shadow of the Glen;
   finds The Tinker's Wedding "very good" though inferior to
   In the Shadow of the Glen; thinks Riders to the Sea pa-
   thetic rather than tragic"; compares The Well of the Saints
   with The Wild Duck; sees Molière and Cervantes in The Playboy of the Western World; and thinks Deirdre of the Sorrows
   "slight." Includes a lengthy comment on Synge's speech.

1953

1 BEERBOHM, MAX. Around Theatres. London: R. Hart-Davis,
   pp. 314-319.
        Reprint of 1904.2.

2 BENTLEY, ERIC. In Search of Theater. New York: Knopf,
   pp. 11, 43, 103-106, 227, 231, 290, 321, 327, 333, 334-341.
        Synge did indeed reflect the Irish people, for one must
   remember that "the mirror the artist holds up to nature is
   not always a simple, flat one."

3 BROWN, E. K. Willa Cather: A Critical Biography. Completed
   by Leon Edel. New York: Knopf, p. 147.
        Willa Cather found the first London performance of The
   Playboy of the Western World puzzling, i.e. "interesting
   but lacking in the dramatic."

4 DUNSANY, LORD. "Irish Writers I Have Known." Atlantic Month-
   ly, 192 (September), 66-68.
        Contrasts Synge's method of using peasant materials with
   Lady Gregory's and cites the influence of Kipling's "The
   Gift of the Sea" in Riders to the Sea.

5 ENGEL, EDWIN A. The Haunted House of Eugene O'Neill. Cambridge,
   Massachusetts: Harvard University Press, pp. 42, 45.
        Compares the language of The Playboy of the Western World
   to Mat Burke's "exuberance" in Anna Christie and says that
   this play and Riders to the Sea have an "identical" theme.

1953

6 JANOUCH, GUSTAV. <u>Conversations with Kafka: Notes and Remi-
niscences</u>. Translated by Goronwy Rees. Introduction by
Max Brod. New York: Frederick A. Praeger, p. 41.
Says that Synge was "right" in <u>The Playboy of the Western World</u> to see the revolt of the son against the father
as essentially comic.

7 KETTLE, ARNOLD. <u>An Introduction to the English Novel</u>. Vol 2:
<u>Henry James to the Present Day</u>. London: Hutchinson,
p. 183.
"The theme of <u>The Playboy</u> is that of the un-heroic victim who has heroism thrust upon him through the needs of
the people for a myth to enrich their barren lives." Also,
compares Synge to Joyce Cary.

8 LAMM, MARTIN. "Irish Drama," in <u>Modern Drama</u>. Translated by
Karin Elliott. New York: Philosophical Library, pp. 293-
314.
Places Synge after Yeats as an Irish dramatist. Speaks
of Synge's "grotesque humour" and maintains that <u>Riders to
the Sea</u> is a "confusing medley of comic and tragic elements." Prefers Synge's short plays because, in the longer
ones, he "tended to be whimsical and unsymmetrical in his
construction of plots."

9 LEVENTHAL, A. J. "Dramatic Commentary." DM, NS 29, no. 4
(October-December), 39-41.
"In some fifty years <u>The Playboy of the Western World</u>
has become a classic in the best sense." Praises Siobhan
McKenna's "individual interpretation of the part of Pegeen
Mike...."

10 PODHORETZ, NORMAN. "Synge's <u>Playboy</u>: Morality and the Hero."
EIC, 3 (July), 337-344.
<u>The Playboy of the Western World</u> develops the paradox
that "individual achievement and communal progress depend
on murder"--albeit in this instance symbolic murder. Reprinted: 1969.25.

11 STRONG, L. A. G. "John Millington Synge," in <u>Personal Remarks</u>.
London: P. Nevill, pp. 34-37.
Reprint of 1931.5; 1932.10.

12 USSHER, ARLAND. <u>Three Great Irishmen: Shaw, Yeats, Joyce</u>.
New York: Devin-Adair, pp. 79, 85-88.
The troubles over <u>The Playboy of the Western World</u>
turned Yeats "inwards upon himself...."

1954

13   WARNOCK, ROBERT, ed. "Riders to the Sea," in <u>Representative</u>
     <u>Modern Plays: British</u>. Glenview, Illinois: Scott, Fores-
     man, pp. 341-345.
          <u>The Playboy of the Western World</u> is "whimsical" and
     <u>Riders to the Sea</u> is "more typical of this essentially
     serious writer." Refers to the influence of Maeterlinck in
     <u>Riders to the Sea</u>.

<u>1954</u>

1   GASSNER, JOHN. "The Genius of Synge," in <u>Masters of the</u>
    <u>Drama</u>. New York: Dover, pp. 553-562.
         Shows how Synge's "genius" manifests itself in all of
    his plays. Even <u>The Tinker's Wedding</u> is praised as "the
    most joyous, pungent modern low comedy in the English
    language...."

2   _____. "John Millington Synge: Synthesis in Folk Drama" and
    "<u>The Playboy of the Western World</u>, 1946," in <u>The Theatre in</u>
    <u>Our Times: A Survey of the Men, Materials and Movements in</u>
    <u>the Modern Theatre</u>. New York: Crown Publishers, pp. 217-
    224, 537-541.
         Compares Synge to Lorca, analyzes <u>Deirdre of the Sorrows</u>
    at some length. Finds <u>Riders to the Sea</u> "static" drama but
    successful. Thinks it dubious that Synge would have
    achieved "larger range" had he lived and maintains that
    "...Synge is not a world figure in the theatre, because he
    made himself a national playwright." Reviews the Theatre
    Incorporated production of <u>The Playboy of the Western World</u>,
    calling the protagonist "Chris" and saying that the play
    reveals a "sophisticated" artist delineating unsophisticat-
    ed people, an esthete influenced by the "art for art's sake"
    philosophy.

3   HABART, MICHEL. "Le Théâtre irlandais." <u>Théâtre Populaire</u>,
    9 (September-October), 24-43.
         Says that <u>The Tinker's Wedding</u> remained "interdite" be-
    cause Synge "osait y exposer la vénalité d'un prêtre." <u>The</u>
    <u>Playboy of the Western World</u> is a virulent satire on the
    complacent attitude which sought to recover "'idéalisme
    celtique.'" Synge possessed the ability to mold Titans
    out of earthy buffoons.

4   MacLEAN, HUGH H. "The Hero as Playboy." <u>The University of</u>
    <u>Kansas City Review</u>, 21 (Autumn), 9-19.
         Cites a number of highly specific parallels between
    Christ's mission and Christy's. In Synge's parody the

1954

villagers learn that their salvation cannot come from an
outside force (Christy) but must originate in themselves.

5   O'CONNOR, BROTHER ANTHONY CYRIL. "Synge and National Drama."
     Unitas, 27, no. 2 (April), 294-346.
          A broad survey of Synge's life and works, divided into
     such areas as "Significance of the Term, National Drama",
     and "John Millington Synge: The Formative Years." See
     1954.6.

6   _____. "Synge and National Drama." Unitas, 27, no. 3 (July),
     430-464.
          Comments generally on Synge's works. See 1954.5.

7   SAUL, GEORGE BRANDON. "An Introductory Bibliography in Anglo-
     Irish Literature." BNYPL, 58, no. 9 (September), 429-435.
          Lists a few standard works on Synge and several on the
     Irish Renaissance generally under the heading "The Yeatsian
     Era."

8   STEPHENS, EDWARD M. "Synge's Last Play." ContempR (November),
     pp. 288-293.
          Stressing the view that Synge's works reflect the events
     of his life, sketches several factors that helped form the
     basis of Deirdre of the Sorrows: Synge's union in external
     nature with Molly Allgood, the departure of Willie Fay from
     the Abbey, and Synge's final illness. For example: "The
     days he spent there [Glen Cree] with her...inspired the
     dramatization of Naisi in the woods with Deirdre."

9   TAYLOR, ESTELLA RUTH. The Modern Irish Writers: Cross Cur-
     rents of Criticism. Lawrence: University of Kansas Press,
     pp. 8, 20, 28, 30, 42-43, 58, 62-63, 68, 101, 114-115,
     117-119, 122, 135, 137-138, 141, 164.
          Comments on many aspects of the interrelationship be-
     tween Synge and the Irish Theatre movement.

1955

1   ALBRIGHT, H. D., WILLIAM P. HALSTEAD, and LEE MITCHELL.
     Principles of Theatre Art. Cambridge, Massachusetts: Riv-
     erside, p. 336.
          In giving advice to directors, writes, "To conceal the
     rhythm or to speak against it in the plays of Synge would
     be to ignore one of the chief elements of their aesthetic
     pattern...."

84

2   DONOGHUE, DENIS. "Synge: <u>Riders to the Sea</u>, A Study." <u>Uni-</u>
     <u>versity Review</u>, 1 (Summer), 52-58.
          Though <u>Riders to the Sea</u> is not tragedy in a classical
     sense, it effectively expresses the pathos of the charac-
     ters' battle against the sea. Reprinted: 1970.1.

3   _____. "'Too Immoral for Dublin': Synge's 'The Tinker's
     Wedding,'" <u>Irish Writing</u>, 30 (March), 56-62.
          Discusses comic and ironic reversals in the play: "the
     comedy of <u>The Tinker's Wedding</u> depends on the mock-conflict
     between certain attitudes in the tinkers themselves and all
     those other conventions which are covered by the word 'or-
     thodoxy.'"

4   FOX, R. M. "Same Program...Fifty Years Later." <u>American Mer-</u>
     <u>cury</u>, 81 (July), 43-44.
          Summarizes Golden Jubilee celebration of the Abbey Thea-
     tre held at the Queen's Theatre, Dublin: "Plays by
     Synge...left the golden mist behind, though we had to wait
     for the full realistic approach until Sean O'Casey...."

5   JACOBS, WILLIS D. "A Silent Sinner." <u>American Mercury</u>, 81
     (August), 159-160.
          Summary of the hostile reaction to <u>The Playboy of the</u>
     <u>Western World</u> seen against a romanticized picture of the
     dying Synge, whom the obtuse audiences helped to kill.
     <u>Deirdre of the Sorrows</u> is the "most intense and human play
     of our century."

6   MACGOWAN, KENNETH and WILLIAM MELNITZ. <u>The Living Stage: A</u>
     <u>History of the World Theater</u>. Englewood Cliffs, New Jersey:
     Prentice-Hall, pp. 421-422, 424.
          <u>The Playboy of the Western World</u> is the "peak" of Synge's
     work, "highly original and brilliant...."

7   NIC SHIUBHLAIGH, MAIRE [MARY WALKER]. <u>The Splendid Years:</u>
     <u>Recollections of Maire Nic Shiubhlaigh as Told to Edward</u>
     <u>Kenny</u>. Foreword by Padraic Colum. Dublin: James Duffy,
     pp. xv, 16, 18, 27, 39-47, 52-56, 59, 62, 63, 71, 79-88,
     111-122, 124-138, 201-203.
          A fulsome and indispensable account of the acting in and
     reception of Synge's plays by the original Nora Burke of <u>In</u>
     <u>the Shadow of the Glen</u>. Details, for example, the back-
     ground of the <u>caoine</u> in <u>Riders to the Sea</u> and the staging
     of <u>The Playboy of the Western World</u> at the Abbey. Abridged:
     1977.7.

1955

8   O'CASEY, SEAN. "Song of a Shift," in Drums Under the Windows.
    New York: Macmillan, pp. 168-190.
        A lengthy satirical picture of the tumult occasioned in
    Dublin by The Playboy of the Western World: "Some blasted
    little theatre or other has put on a play by a fellow named
    Singe or Sinje or something, a terrible play...."

9   YEATS, W. B. Autobiographies. London: Macmillan, pp. 497-
    527, 529-572.
        Reprints 1925.4; 1928.5, 6, 7.

10 _____. The Letters of W. B. Yeats, Edited by Allan Wade.
    New York: Macmillan, pp. 14, 436, 441, 447-448, 453, 459,
    461-463, 466, 468, 495-496, 510-511, 526-529, 534-538, 553,
    563, 587, 618, 711, 838-839, 860.
        Although this lengthy volume does not contain any of the
    few letters that Yeats wrote to Synge, Synge is mentioned
    in a significant way in several of them. For example, a
    letter to John Quinn dated 15 February 1905 comments on the
    reception of The Well of the Saints and speaks of Yeats's
    "squabble with Arthur Griffith" over Synge's works.

                                1956

1   BLACK, HESTER M. "A Check-List of First Editions of Works by
    John Millington Synge and George William Russell." T. C. D.
    Annual Bulletin (Trinity College Dublin), pp. 4-9.
        Though superseded by more complete analyses of primary
    bibliography, does provide important information. Synge
    section (three and one half pages) divides into "Plays,"
    "Other Writings," "Collected Works," and "Miscellaneous
    Prose." Items not held by Trinity are marked with aster-
    isks. Important brief descriptions, including number of
    copies, are devoted to the entries. The unexpurgated ver-
    sion of The Playboy of the Western World, which Trinity
    does have, is cited under "Plays." Though authored by
    Trinity College, the list was compiled by Hester M. Black.

2   YEATS, W. B. The Collected Poems of W. B. Yeats. Definitive
    Edition, with the Author's Final Revisions. New York:
    Macmillan, pp. 109, 130-133, 300, 316-318.
        "On Those That Hated 'The Playboy of the Western World,'
    1907" compares the mob to lecherous eunuchs and Synge to
    Don Juan. In "In Memory of Major Robert Gregory," Synge
    appears as "that inquiring man.../ That dying chose the
    living world for text...." In "Beautiful Lofty Things,"
    Yeats's father was one of the "Olympians" on the stage

during the rioting over The Playboy of the Western World; said, "'This Land of Saints,'" then added "'Of plaster Saints.'" "The Municipal Gallery Revisited" calls Synge "that rooted man."

1957

1 ANON. "John Millington Synge at Colby." CLQ, Series 4, no. 9 (February), 157-158.
   Announces "the arrival at Colby of Mr. James A. Healy's collection of John Millington Synge."

2 DONOGHUE, DENIS. "Flowers and Timber: A Note on Synge's Poems." Threshold, 1, no. 3 (Autumn), 40-47.
   Though Synge's poems do not have great merit, whatever value they do possess comes from their embodying two opposite principles, the "romantic" and the "earthy."

3 DYBOSKI, ROMAN. "Dramat: John Millington Synge (1871-1909)," in Sto Lat Literatury Angielskiej. Warszawa: Instytut Wydawniczy, "Pax," pp. 825-836.
   Devotes approximately equal time to each of Synge's plays and closes with a comparison between Synge and O'Neill in Anna Christie.

4 DYSINGER, ROBERT E. "Additions to the John Millington Synge Collection." CLQ, Series 4, no. 11 (August), 192-194.
   Adds eight items to 1957.5. Also, the "collection includes a miscellaneous lot of newspaper and magazine clippings about Synge and his work, but these clippings have not been itemized."

5 _____. "The John Millington Synge Collection at Colby College." CLQ, Series 4, no. 9 (February), 166-172.
   Divides into three parts: "Single works of Synge," "Autograph letters," and "Biographical and critical material." Many of the entries in the third section are available elsewhere. All three parts describe the collection given to Colby by James A. Healy. See 1957.4.

6 ELIOT, T. S. On Poetry and Poets. London: Faber and Faber, p. 82.
   Has a comment on the poetic nature of Synge's prose in the plays.

1957

7   FECHTER, PAUL. Das europäische Drama. Geist und Kultur im
     Spiegel des Theaters. II. Vom Naturalismus zum Expression-
     ismus. Mannheim: Bibliographisches Institut, pp. 257-259.
         Sees The Playboy of the Western World as half symbolic
     and half naturalistic, while discussing Synge in the com-
     pany of Yeats, Shaw, and Chesterton.

8   FRYE, NORTHROP. Anatomy of Criticism: Four Essays. Prince-
     ton: Princeton University Press, pp. 40, 168, 269.
         If Riders to the Sea "had been a full-length tragedy...
     the audience would have been helpless with unsympathetic
     laughter long before it was over." Relates Synge's playboy
     to the miles gloriosus tradition.

9   GREENE, DAVID H. "Synge and the Irish." CLQ, Series 4, no. 9
     (February), 158-166.
         Synge did not "foresee that the Ascendancy writer...
     would fall a casual but inevitable victim of the new na-
     tionalism with which Ireland was aflame. He was actually
     taking his life into his hands when he wrote the way he
     did about Irish peasants." Discusses the attack upon the
     Anglo-Irish Ascendancy class, Arthur Griffith's antipathy
     towards Synge, and opposition to The Playboy of the Western
     World in America.

10   McHUGH, ROGER. "Literary Treatment of the Deirdre Legend."
     Threshold, 1 (February), 36-49.
         Discusses several ways in which Synge humanized Deirdre
     and accounts for her motivation in the return to Ireland.

11   MELCHINGER, SIEGFRIED. "Synge, John Millington, 1871-1909,"
     in Drama zwischen Shaw und Brecht. Bremen: Carl Schüne-
     mann, pp. 431-432.
         Brief sketch of Synge's works.

1958

1   BROWNING, D. C. Everyman's Dictionary of Literary Biography,
     English and American. Compiled after John W. Cousin by
     D. C. Browning. London: J. M. Dent; New York: E. P.
     Dutton, p. 649.
         Calls Synge the "leading Irish dramatist of his time...."
     Synge "showed great power and range in his portrayal of
     Irish peasant life."

2   FAY, GERARD. "'Playboy' Battle," in The Abbey Theatre: Cra-
    dle of Genius. New York: Macmillan, pp. 112-124.
       Entire book contains over fifty references to Synge.
    Sketches the background of controversy about Synge's plays
    and situates him in the midst of the infighting among both
    the Abbey Company and the newspapers. Fay believes that
    Synge, like O'Casey, would have chosen to leave Ireland
    eventually because of its lack of appreciation of his work.

3   HAYES, RICHARD. "The Stage: The Road to the Isles." Common-
    weal, 68 (20 June), 303-304.
       Review of the Seven Arts Center revival of The Playboy
    of the Western World. Complains of the difficulty of
    Synge's language and his refusal to portray the dignity of
    the Irish. "...Synge recklessly commits the total burden
    of his theater to tone. His sense of character...was neg-
    ligible." Synge's world is too exotic, and it has had
    little influence on dramatists after him.

4   LEYBURN, ELLEN DOUGLASS. "The Theme of Loneliness in the
    Plays of Synge." MD, 1, no. 2 (September), 84-90.
       Maintains that the theme of loneliness not only "causes
    the actual sufferings which make the plots," but that the
    "characters conceive suffering in terms of loneliness."
    This thesis is illustrated most poignantly in The Playboy
    of the Western World "for all its gusty humor and reckless
    abandon."

5   TREWIN, J. C. "The World of the Theatre: Words and Music."
    The Illustrated London News (4 October), p. 578.
       A review of "The Heart's a Wonder" at the Westminster,
    which is The Playboy of the Western World set to music.
    Praises Synge's rich dialogue and expresses gratitude that
    the play has been revived even though with the additional
    music it is too long.

6   WYATT, EUPHEMIA VAN RENSSELAER. "Theater: The Playboy of the
    Western World." CathW, 187 (July), 312-313.
       Provides background on previous productions of the play
    in New York. In 1946, for example, "two of the Mayo girls
    were played by Julie Harris and Maureen Stapleton!"

1959

1959

1   COSMAN, MAX. "The Life and World of J. M. Synge." Common-
    weal, 70, no. 15 (17 July), 380–382.
        Review of 1959.5. Scores the limitations of the "objec-
    tive" approach to biography, which makes no attempt to look
    beyond the facts of a writer's life. For instance, how can
    we explain Synge's paradoxical attitude towards his mother?

2   CROSBY, ROBERT R. Review of David H. Greene and Edward M.
    Stephens, J. M. Synge, 1871-1909 (1959.5). QJS, 45, no. 3
    (October), 337–338.
        Provides background on the Greene-Stephens biography.

3   DREISER, THEODORE. Letters of Theodore Dreiser: A Selection.
    Vol. 3. Edited by Robert H. Elias. Philadelphia: Univer-
    sity of Pennsylvania Press, p. 774.
        In a letter of 14 April 1936 to Donald P. McCord, Dreis-
    er says that Synge had the "same approach" as a man "who
    would plant himself in front of any insect trapped by any-
    thing—a wasp dragging a grub across a field, a moth beat-
    ing itself free from a spider's web—and half chortling and
    half sighing over the cold and seemingly enforced mechanism
    of it all, proceed to talk."

4   ELLMANN, RICHARD. James Joyce. New York: Oxford University
    Press, pp. 128–129.
        Contains twenty references to such matters as Joyce's
    meetings with Synge and his disdain (mingled with respect)
    for Synge's work. At one point (1907), Joyce remarked that
    Synge's art "is more original than my own." Ellmann quotes
    Gertrude Stein as having said about Joyce, "Like Synge,
    another Irish writer, he has had his day." Abridged:
    1970.1.

5   GREENE, DAVID H. and EDWARD M. STEPHENS. J. M. Synge, 1871-
    1909. New York: Macmillan, 334 pp.
        This is the standard biography of Synge. It includes
    not only biographical information but also criticism of
    Synge's works integrated with background materials. Chap-
    ter 13, for example, provides a readable summary of the
    riots over The Playboy of the Western World. The book has
    been received favorably, with reviewers praising its ob-
    jectivity, even though complaining about Greene's unwill-
    ingness to "interpret" Synge's life. See 1959.1, 2, 12;
    1960.5, 7; 1963.7.

6 HOWARTH, HERBERT. "Edmund John Millington Synge, 1871-1909,"
    in The Irish Writers: 1880-1940; Literature Under Parnell's
    Star. New York: Hill and Wang, pp. 212-244.
        A remarkably thoughtful exegesis of Synge's work, ranging
    from a discussion of archetypal figures in The Playboy of
    the Western World to the history of the "shift" as an anti-
    Parnell emblem: "Synge offered the spectacle of fantasy
    boiling and no crust to contain it." Posits some possible
    influences of Synge on Joyce. Abridged: 1969.25.

7 LEWIS, THEOPHILUS. "Deirdre of the Sorrows." America, 102,
    no. 7 (14 November), 217.
        Brief mention of the production of Deirdre of the Sor-
    rows at the Gate. Sees Synge as "a playwright in whose art
    drama and poetry were engaged in perpetual struggle...."
    In The Playboy of the Western World, "drama won." In
    Deirdre of the Sorrows, "poetry came out on top." The last
    is a "moving play when read," but "it is not too impressive
    on the stage."

8 MacPHAIL, IAN. "John Millington Synge: Some Bibliographical
    Notes." Irish Book, 1, no. 1 (Spring), 3-10.
        Comments on translations of Synge's work, on various
    English editions of his writings, and although not present-
    ing "any startling discoveries," does lay to rest a 1910
    "ghost edition" of Synge's works.

9 MacPHAIL, IAN and M. POLLARD, comps. John Millington Synge,
    1871-1909: A Catalogue of an Exhibition Held at Trinity
    College Library Dublin on the Occasion of the Fiftieth An-
    niversary of His Death. Dublin: Dolmen Press for the
    Friends of the Library of Trinity College, Dublin, 38 pp.
        An indispensable tool for anyone wishing to do primary
    research in Synge materials. Divides into "Books," "Con-
    tributions to Periodicals," "Manuscripts," and "Miscella-
    neous" items. The catalogue attempts to include "every
    known edition of Synge's works"--including several in for-
    eign languages. Part One, "Books," begins with the 1904
    edition of In the Shadow of the Glen, privately printed in
    New York by John Quinn.

10 MALCOLM, DONALD. "Off Broadway, Near Myth." NY (24 October),
    pp. 91-92.
        About Deirdre of the Sorrows at the Gate: the "operatic
    implausibility" mars the plot. Criticizes the heroine's
    motive for returning to Ireland to her certain death.

1959

11 O'DONNELL, DONAT [O'BRIEN, CONOR CRUISE]. "Mother's Tongue."
London The Spectator (14 August), p. 201.
Calls controversy over The Playboy of the Western World
an "intellectual blind man's bluff...." Says that Synge's
early death deprived the Irish Theatre "of one who was prepared to argue about what the function of such a theatre
should be and to admit that that function might change with
time." Reprinted: 1965.18.

12 STARKIE, WALTER. "Everything Irish Was Sacred." Saturday Review, 42 (18 April), 19-20.
Says that "Synge's plays were a deliberate attempt to
create an Irish literature by going back to the sources:
to myth, folktale, and primitive speech." Review of
1959.5.

13 WATSON, E. BRADLEE and BENFIELD PRESSEY, eds. "Riders to the
Sea by John Millington Synge," in Contemporary Drama, Fifteen Plays: American, English and Irish [and] European.
New York: Scribner's, pp. 240-242.
Takes issue with George Moore's judgment that Riders to
the Sea is "essentially undramatic" and stresses the play's
"presentation of a progressive spiritual reaction to an
inscrutable destiny, by means of perfectly conceived characters and dialogue truthfully colored...." Contains brief
but important notes on the physical makeup of the Abbey
Theatre and a short chronology.

14 [WILSON, LAWRENCE.] John Millington Synge: Some Unpublished
Letters and Documents of J. M. Synge Formerly in the Possession of Mr. Lawrence Wilson of Montreal and Now for the
First Time Published for Him by The Redpath Press. Montreal: Redpath Press, McGill University Library, 34 pp.
Besides including an early anonymous review of Synge's
work, this scant collection contains an important comment
by Synge on "P.B."--as he called The Playboy of the Western
World--about what it is "so impossible to get our Dublin
people to see, obvious as it is--that the wildness and, if
you will, vices of the Irish peasantry are due, like their
extraordinary good points of all kinds, to the richness of
their nature--a thing that is priceless beyond words."

15 WYATT, EUPHEMIA VAN RENSSELAER. "Theater: Early Stages."
CathW, 189, no. 1131 (June), 241-243.
Brief mention of Lady Gregory's The Workhouse Ward and
Synge's The Well of the Saints, produced at the Gate as
part of an enterprise "which will utilize the vacant hours
in a theater for educational purposes...." Both plays "are

based on much the same philosophy that it is hard for man to play the part of God in interfering with men's lives, for each of us enjoys himself in his own peculiar way."

1960

1   ATHERTON, JAMES S. The Books at the Wake: A Study of Lit-
    erary Allusions in James Joyce's Finnegans Wake. New York:
    Viking, pp. 284-285.
        Lists several possible references to Synge in Joyce's
    last work.

2   BARNET, SYLVAN, MORTON BERMAN, and WILLIAM BURTO, eds. "J. M.
    Synge: Deirdre of the Sorrows," in The Genius of the Irish
    Theater. New York: New American Library of World Litera-
    ture, Mentor Books, pp. 151-154.
        Discusses Synge's use of folk dialect and the ancient
    mythological cycles in Deirdre of the Sorrows.

3   BOURNIQUEL, CAMILLE. Ireland. Translated by John Fisher.
    London and New York: The Viking Press, Vista Books, pp. 13,
    93, 136, 159-163, 172, 179-180.
        Comments on the influence of the Aran Islands on Synge.
    The Playboy of the Western World is "one of those monstros-
    ities of the theatre that are immediately stamped with im-
    mortality." Contains a picture of Maria Casare in Deirdre
    of the Sorrows, with a short selection from the play.

4   FRASER, RUSSELL A. "Ireland Made Him." The Nation, 190,
    no. 8 (20 February), 171-173.
        Riders to the Sea is "perhaps the finest tragedy written
    in English since the Renaissance."

5   LEYBURN, ELLEN DOUGLASS. Review of David H. Greene and Edward
    M. Stephens, J. M. Synge: 1871-1909. MD, 3, no. 1 (May),
    93-95.
        Though finding the book's style "competent" and the work
    generally praiseworthy, complains that Greene makes "no at-
    tempt to analyze the springs of Synge's genius...." See
    1959.5.

6   LUNARI, GIGI. "Lady Gregory e Synge," in Il movimento dramma-
    tico irlandese (1899-1922). Documenti di teatro, 13.
    Bologna: Cappelli, pp. 85-107.
        Discusses Lady Gregory and Synge in relation to several
    non-literary figures active in the Irish Renaissance, e.g.

1960

Annie Horniman, Arthur Griffith, and "un architetto di nome Joseph Holloway...."

7   MacNEICE, LOUIS. Review of David H. Greene and Edward M. Stephens, J. M. Synge: 1871-1909. The London Magazine, 7, no. 8 (August), 70-73.
    Maintains that Synge is "one of the forerunners of those modern playwrights for whom the drama approximates to the lyric, i.e. who concern themselves with problems which cannot be solved like those of algebra." See 1959.5.

8   MERCER, CAROLINE G. "Stephen Dedalus's Vision and Synge's Peasant Girls." N&Q, 7, no. 12 (December), 473-474.
    Joyce's picture of the bird-girl towards the close of Book Four of A Portrait of the Artist as a Young Man was influenced by Synge's description of Inishmaan girls washing clothing, which Synge gives in Part 1 of The Aran Islands.

9   MURPHY, DANIEL J. "The Reception of Synge's Playboy in Ireland and America: 1907-1912." BNYPL, 64, no. 10 (October), 515-533.
    Traces the disturbances caused by The Playboy of the Western World by drawing upon contemporary newspaper accounts and accounts of Synge's acquaintances. Also, compares the protests over Synge's plays to protests over other plays considered detrimental to Irish causes.

10 NATHAN, GEORGE JEAN. The Magic Mirror: Selected Writings on the Theatre by George Jean Nathan. Edited with an Introduction by Thomas Quinn Curtiss. New York: Knopf, pp. 8, 35.
    Maintains that "Tolstoy, with a sound, intelligent, and technically perfect aim and point of view, composed second-rate drama. So, too, Maeterlinck. Synge, by his own admission adjudged critically and dramatically guilty on both counts, composed one of the truly first-rate dramas of the Anglo-Saxon stage."

11 PEACOCK, RONALD. The Art of Drama. Second Impression with Some Corrections. London: Routledge & Kegan Paul, pp. 102, 214, 218, 220.
    Mentions Synge in the company of other major writers in defining "poetic" drama.

12 STARKIE, ENID. From Gautier to Eliot: The Influence of France
    on English Literature, 1851-1939. London: Hutchinson Uni-
    versity Library, pp. 125-126.
        Says that a passage in The Aran Islands shows the influ-
    ence of Maeterlinck.

13 STEINBERG, M. W. "John M. Synge [1871-1909]," in Aspects of
    Modern Drama. New York: Holt, Rinehart, and Winston,
    pp. 445-446.
        Brief biographical note. Also, says that the riots over
    The Playboy of the Western World were occasioned by the
    long "history of resentment which the Irish Catholics bore
    against the Protestant Anglo-Irish...."

14 STYAN, J. L. The Elements of Drama. Cambridge (England): at
    the University Press, pp. 57-63, 126-129, 257-260.
        Analyzes the basis of audience reaction to The Playboy
    of the Western World and finds Deirdre of the Sorrows "a
    far more complex play than its surface simplicity suggests."
    Abridged: 1969.25.

                              1961

1   AE [GEORGE WILLIAM RUSSELL]. Letters from AE. Edited by
    Alan Denson. London and New York: Abelard-Schuman, pp. 23,
    229.
        Contains a letter to Synge dated Christmas, 1897 from
    Belmullet, County Mayo, in answer to Synge's request for
    information about Yeats. Russell supplies Synge with
    Yeats's London address. Denson quotes Professor David H.
    Greene as saying, "this is the only AE letter among Synge's
    papers...."

2   CHICA SALAS, SUSANA. "Synge y García Lorca: Approximación de
    dos mundos poéticos." RHM, 27, no. 2 (April), 128-137.
        Includes comparisons between Riders to the Sea and Blood
    Wedding (Bodas de Sangre) and between The Playboy of the
    Western World and The House of Bernarda Alba (La Casa de
    Bernarda Alba). In general, Synge "encarnó el genio ir-
    landés, del mismo modo que García Lorca representó el genio
    español...."

3   CUSACK, CYRIL. "A Player's Reflections on Playboy." MD, 4
    (December), 300-305.
        The Playboy of the Western World should not be staged in
    the mummy-like, naturalistic, and wooden fashion that the
    early Abbey Directors insisted on, but rather in a livelier

1961

manner, with a bit of extravaganza. Ending of the play is
anti-climactic, the fault of Synge, not of the players.
Reprinted: 1969.25.

4   GREENE, DAVID H. "Synge and the Celtic Revival." MD, 4,
no. 3 (December), 292-299.
Assesses Synge's knowledge of and interest in Gaelic
language and folklore from before his days at Trinity College until after his return from the Aran Islands: "It
was Synge's work, therefore, more than any of his contemporaries', which came closer to achieving that assimilation
of the Gaelic past which the Irish Renaissance represented."

5   KRAUSE, DAVID. "The 'Rageous Ossean': Patron-Hero of Synge
and O'Casey." MD, 4, no. 3 (December), 268-291.
Traces the pagan delight represented by the anti-clerical
Ossian in Synge's plays: "Patrick is Ireland's patron-
saint, but Oisin is the patron-hero of her two finest modern
dramatists, Synge and O'Casey."

6   McARTHUR, HERBERT. "Tragic and Comic Modes." Criticism, 3
(Winter), 36-45.
Compares Molière's L'École des Femmes and Synge's Deirdre of the Sorrows in the light of the "virgin-bride" plot
"in order to help define the modes of tragedy and comedy as
ways of experiencing life."

7   MANDEL, OSCAR. A Definition of Tragedy. New York: New York
University Press, pp. 57, 59, 66, 67, 68, 101, 159.
Describes how Riders to the Sea rises subtly "beyond its
own brief facts"; says that in Deirdre of the Sorrows the
theme is "neither joyous nor despairing" and compares the
play to Molière's Bérénice.

8   OREL, HAROLD. "Synge's Last Play: 'And a Story Will Be Told
For Ever,'" MD, 4, no. 3 (December), 306-313.
Takes issue with past critics who simplify or dismiss
Deirdre of the Sorrows, which "For all its faults...suc-
ceeds in being compassionate, in charging the text with
life, and in moving outward from the emotion of Lavarcham's
final speech...to a final meaning, uniting stoicism, asceticism, and ecstasy."

9   PRICE, ALAN. Synge and Anglo-Irish Drama. London: Methuen,
247 pp.
Price's Introduction provides a crucial summary and
analysis of Synge criticism. The rest of the work (apart
from a separate chapter for the Conclusion) divides into

the following sections: "Literary Ideas and Craft," "Prose
Works," "Poems and Translations," "Early Shorter Pieces,"
"Longer Plays," and "Tragedies." The absence of religious
and metaphysical implications in Synge's work "suggests
that he is not among the greatest and that there may be
limitations in his outlook as a man...." The conclusion of
Deirdre of the Sorrows is "perhaps the finest thing Synge
ever wrote." The Well of the Saints is "perhaps Synge's
most profound and sombre work...." See 1962.5. Abridged:
1970.1.

10   REID, B. L. William Butler Yeats: The Lyric of Tragedy.
      Norman: University of Oklahoma Press, pp. 50-51, 57, 63,
      74, 88-90, 103, 108, 112, 224, 256, 257.
         Several scattered comments provide background for Yeats's
      written statements about Synge. Maintains, though, that
      Yeats "no doubt overvalued him [Synge] somewhat as an art-
      ist." Synge influenced Yeats's concept of tragedy and the
      "passionate-simple archetype."

11   SPACKS, PATRICIA MEYER. "The Making of the Playboy." MD, 4,
      no. 3 (December), 314-323.
         Traces fairy tale elements in The Playboy of the Western
      World, especially those surrounding the ritual murders.
      All of these lead to Christy as a "constructed man." Re-
      printed: 1969.25.

12   TYNAN, KENNETH. Curtains: Selections from the Drama Crit-
      icism and Related Writings. New York: Atheneum, pp. 70,
      85, 95, 285, 450, 456.
         Sees Synge as one of the "glittering Irishmen" who walk
      through English stage history. Couples The Playboy of the
      Western World with Ghosts and with Troilus and Cressida
      as "great" works. Comments on the Berliner Ensemble pro-
      duction of the "Hero" of the Western World, "which is in-
      terpreted as a satire on the Western cult of violence."

13   ULANOV, BARRY, ed. "John Millington Synge: The Well of the
      Saints," in Makers of the Modern Theater. New York and
      Toronto: McGraw-Hill, pp. 233-237.
         The blindness in The Well of the Saints is "uncommonly
      sensitive to...the shadows of pride and hypocrisy that fall
      across the bright bodies of self-appointed holy men."

14   YEATS, WILLIAM BUTLER. Essays and Introductions. New York
      and London: Macmillan, pp. 238-239, 298-305, 306-310, 311-
      342, 515, 527, 528, 529.
         Reprints 1905.12; 1909.3; 1911.80, 83.

1962

1   ALEXANDER, DORIS. The Tempering of Eugene O'Neill. New York:
    Harcourt, Brace and World, pp. 154, 188, 280.
       Mentions O'Neill's fascination with the Irish plays
    presented at the Maxine Elliott Theater in 1911 written by
    Synge and others. O'Neill had learned from Synge "that no
    more need happen in a one-act play than is necessary to re-
    veal the meaning of a way of life."

2   ANON. "Art of Collaboration." TLS, no. 3165 (26 October),
    p. 824.
       Synge's "collaboration" is with the people of the glens
    and the islands and with Douglas Hyde. In The Playboy of
    the Western World, the finest passages are inspired by the
    "passionate love songs of the west, most of them carried
    down from the seventeenth and eighteenth centuries...."

3   BLOCK, HASKELL M. and ROBERT G. SHEDD, eds. "John Millington
    Synge (1871-1909)" and "The Playboy of the Western World,"
    in Masters of Modern Drama. New York: Random House,
    pp. 397-398, 404.
       Sketches the background of Riders to the Sea and The
    Playboy of the Western World by drawing upon scattered
    opinions of the late 1950s. Also, points out that, "while
    Robert Flaherty was making...Man of Aran, he credited
    Synge with teaching him what to photograph on those sea-
    swept islands."

4   COXHEAD, ELIZABETH. J. M. Synge and Lady Gregory. Writers
    and Their Work, No. 149. London: Longmans, Green, 35 pp.
       Sketches points of comparison and contrast between
    Synge and Lady Gregory, including important comments on
    their use of dialect. "Today especially, when much serious
    drama either consists still of 'pallid and joyless words'
    or is downright inarticulate, there is refreshment of the
    spirit to be found" in their plays, "allying Irish charm
    and a rich flow of language to a universal applicability."

5   EDWARDS, PHILIP. Review of Alan Price, Synge and Anglo-Irish
    Drama. RES, NS 13, no. 51 (August), 320-322.
       Though finding Price's book generally helpful as an in-
    troduction to Synge, takes issue with some points and adds
    a few personal opinions. For example, when speaking of The
    Playboy of the Western World: "Just as in The Well of the
    Saints the crisis is the result of the interweaving of the
    fantasies of Martin and of the Saint, so the plot of The
    Playboy depends upon the crossing of the dramas of Pegeen
    and Christy." See 1961.9.

6   GRIGSON, GEOFFREY. "Synge." London The New Statesman (19 Oc-
     tober), pp. 528-529.
         Synge's good poems are such "hard, separate, thoroughly
     enjoyable objects" that Grigson wonders why Synge adopted
     the "Lady Gregorian chant" in his plays and translations.

7   KAIN, RICHARD M. Dublin in the Age of William Butler Yeats
     and James Joyce. Norman: University of Oklahoma Press,
     pp. 39, 55-56, 59-60, 95-96, 164-167.
         Numerous passing references to Synge throughout the
     book situate him in the vortex of the Irish Renaissance.
     Comments on Synge's "Beg-Innish." Also, The Playboy of the
     Western World is a "gem of humorous insights."

8   KNIGHT, G. W. The Golden Labyrinth: A Study of British Drama.
     New York: Norton, pp. 332-335, 336, 355.
         About The Well of the Saints: "The inward imagination
     [is] built on the Dionysian, the numinous, the sound values
     of nature rather than its Apollonian sights...." And of
     Riders to the Sea: Synge's people "have superstitious
     fears, but the dramatic guidance is agnostic."

9   KRAUSE, DAVID. Sean O'Casey: The Man and His Work. New York:
     Collier Books, a Division of the Crowell-Collier Publishing
     Company, pp. 88-93.
         Over fifty references to Synge are scattered throughout
     the book. Especially interesting are explanations of the
     opposition to Synge and O'Casey by Dublin forces.

10   KRUTCH, JOSEPH WOOD. "Synge and the Irish Protest," in "Mod-
     ernism" in Modern Drama: A Definition and an Estimate.
     New York: Russell & Russell, pp. 88-103.
         Discusses The Playboy of the Western World as an anti-
     modernist drama. Contrasts Synge to O'Casey: "the shock-
     ing blather of O'Casey's characters is Synge's 'Irish
     poetry' gone rancid."

11   LUCAS, F. L. The Drama of Ibsen and Strindberg. New York:
     Macmillan, pp. 271-272.
         Draws a parallel between the suicide of Synge's Deirdre
     before old age can ravish her and the fate of Ibsen's Mas-
     ter Builder.

12   MARTIN, JAY. Conrad Aiken: A Life of His Art. Princeton,
     New Jersey: Princeton University Press, p. 222.
         Briefly cites the possible influence on Aiken of the
     type of literary criticism expressed by Yeats and Synge in
     their Prefaces.

1962

13   MELCHINGER, SIEGFRIED and HENNING RISCHBIETER, eds. "John
     Millington Synge (1871-1909)," in Welttheater: Bühnen,
     Autoren, Inszenierungen. Braunschweig: Georg Westermann,
     pp. 357-358.
       Spends a paragraph on five plays (none on Deirdre of the
     Sorrows). Keeps the English title for The Playboy of the
     Western World, presumably finding it impossible to trans-
     late. Includes photos from German productions of the lat-
     ter.

14   MERCIER, VIVIAN. The Irish Comic Tradition. London and New
     York: Oxford University Press, Clarendon, pp. 35, 68-71,
     105, 161, 186, 212, 239-241, 246-247.
       Sees in The Playboy of the Western World the "effort to
     revive the [Irish] past, coupled with the world-wide twen-
     tieth century affinity for the macabre and grotesque...."
     Briefly compares and contrasts Synge with other writers in
     the long Gaelic tradition.

15   Ó SÍOCHÁIN, P. A. "Synge and the Aran Islands" and "Synge's
     Life on the Islands," in Aran: Islands of Legend.
     New York: Devin-Adair, pp. 159-166, 167-176.
       Synge's attitude towards the Aran Islands was that of
     the "literary dilettante and aspirant." He was never one
     with the islanders, and they are indifferent to the fame
     that Synge has brought them. Yet Synge's "intellectual
     sensitiveness" made him aware of the islanders' "unique
     historical continuity of race and race-thought...." Also,
     Synge accepted their "stories" as true beliefs in the super-
     natural.

16   SKELTON, ROBIN, ed. J. M. Synge: Collected Works. Vol. 1.
     Poems. Edited by Robin Skelton. London: Oxford Univer-
     sity Press, 164 pp.
       Contains an Introduction by Skelton (18 pp.), which
     sketches the development of Synge's poems and describes
     problems in dating some of them. The four appendices
     consist of worksheets for "Is It a Month" and "In Kerry,"
     the beginnings of "The Lady O'Conor," and a variant version
     of "Danny." See 1966.18; 1968.25, 26, for Volume 2 and
     Volumes 3 and 4.

17   _____. "The Poetry of J. M. Synge." Poetry Ireland, 1 (Au-
     tumn), 32-44.
       Concludes that Synge "left behind him a couple of dozen
     poems that will last out centuries, and that will always
     keep his name in mind as one of the great renewers of tradi-
     tion."

18   TRACY, ROBERT, ed. "General Introduction," "Important Dates
      in Synge's Life," "Introduction" to The Aran Islands, "In-
      troduction" to In Wicklow, "Introduction" to In West Kerry,
      "Introduction" to In the Congested Districts, and "Intro-
      duction" to Essays and Reviews, in The Aran Islands and
      Other Writings [by] John M. Synge. New York: Random
      House, Vintage, pp. vii-xx, xxi-xxiii, 3-5, 159-160, 213-
      214, 271-272, 337-338.
         Synge's prose writings "stand by themselves," forming a
      "unique and separate achievement, perhaps the only work of
      the Irish revival which tries to see the peasant plain and
      to portray him without bias."

                              1963

1   AUGHTRY, CHARLES EDWARD, ed. "John Millington Synge (1871-
      1909)," in Landmarks in Modern Drama: From Ibsen to Iones-
      co. Boston: Houghton, Mifflin, pp. 418-419.
         Notes that Synge's folk plays helped to inspire an "ex-
      tremely large number of regional plays in America...."

2   AYLING, RONALD. "Synge's First Love: Some South African As-
      pects." ESA, 6 (September), 173-185.
         Taking issue with David Greene's picture of Cherrie
      Matheson, who rejected Synge's offer of marriage, presents
      a sympathetic portrait of Ms. Matheson by discussing her
      true reasons for refusing Synge (differences in religion,
      unreciprocated love), her marriage to Kenneth Hobart
      Houghton in 1902, and their life together in South Africa.
      Reprinted: 1964.1.

3   BAUMAN, RICHARD. "John Millington Synge and Irish Folklore."
      SFQ, 27, no. 4 (December), 267-279.
         Analyzes traditional elements of folklore in The Aran
      Islands, such as riddles, superstitions, and the nature of
      the story-teller.

4   DIETRICH, MARGRET. Das Moderne Drama: Strömungen--Gestalten
      --Motive. Stuttgart: Alfred Kröner, pp. 9, 18, 20, 203,
      346, 370, 557, 606, 632, 684.
         Brief comments on Synge's plays, including comparisons
      with O'Neill, Lorca, and Maeterlinck. "Die Kräfte des
      Landes, der See, der Natur, sind Protagonisten in Synges
      Dramen...."

5   ERZGRÄBER, WILLI. "John Millington Synge: The Playboy of the
      Western World," in Das Moderne Englische Drama: Interpre-
      tationen. Edited by Horst Oppel. Berlin: Erich Schmidt,
      pp. 87-108.

1963

An overview of the play, touching on such matters as the
role of the father in The Playboy of the Western World and
the nature of Pegeen's attraction to the pagan Christy.
Ends with quotations from Dublin papers dealing with the
disturbances over the work.

6   GASKELL, RONALD. "The Realism of J. M. Synge." CritQ, 5,
     no. 3 (Autumn), 242-248.
     "The aim of this essay is to make clear what Synge un-
     derstood by reality, to consider how deeply in his plays he
     accepts it, and to enquire how far his vision of it is
     dramatic." Synge differs from Ibsen in bringing back
     "simplicity" and a "delight in the body" and in portraying
     the total reality of his characters. About The Playboy of
     the Western World: "The weakness of the play is, of course,
     the handling of Old Mahon." Also, "Synge's indifference to
     the will, though we may, with Yeats, welcome it as a cor-
     rective to Ibsen, makes a fully dramatic play virtually
     impossible."

7   GERSTENBERGER, DONNA. Review of David H. Greene and Edward M.
     Stephens, J. M. Synge: 1871-1909 (1959.5). WHR, 17
     (Spring), 193.
     Praises Greene-Stephens as a "coherent source" of new
     materials about Synge and contrasts this work with Eliza-
     beth Coxhead's "defense" of Synge in Lady Gregory: A Lit-
     erary Portrait (1966.6).

8   HENN, T. R., ed. The Plays and Poems of J. M. Synge. London:
     Methuen, 374 pp.
     Ninety pages are devoted to a general introduction to
     Synge; one to each of the plays; and one to the poems and
     translations. The last fifty-seven pages include appen-
     dices, bibliography, and forty-two pages of notes to Synge's
     works. Henn's close analyses of Synge's writings are in-
     dispensable. Abridged: 1969.25. See 1964.7.

9   O'NEILL, MICHAEL J. "Holloway on Synge's Last Days." MD, 6
     no. 2 (Fall), 126-130.
     Holloway, the Pepys of the Irish Renaissance, describes
     in his diaries Synge's final attitudes towards religion,
     related by the nurse who attended him at his death, and the
     small funeral and burial at Mount Jerome Cemetery.

10   STARKIE, WALTER. Scholars and Gypsies: An Autobiography.
     London: John Murray, pp. 37-39, 82-85.
     Discusses Synge's constant awareness of his own death.
     Also, the production of The Playboy of the Western World

was for Starkie "the most exciting experience of my youth...." Reprinted with revisions: 1972.71. Abridged: 1977.7.

11 TREWIN, J. C. "The World of the Theatre: Period Pieces." The Illustrated London News (10 August), p. 216.
     About a revival of "period pieces," in which category Trewin includes Synge's works: "it is a refreshment to hear again the caressing rhythms and cross-rhythms of Synge...."

12 VALENCY, MAURICE. The Flower and the Castle: An Introduction to Modern Drama. New York: Macmillan; London: Collier-Macmillan, pp. 8, 396.
     Brief mention of Yeats and Synge in connection with the development of a "new lyricism" and the "drama of the strangeness of familiar things...."

1964

1 AYLING, RONALD. "Synge's First Love: Some South African Aspects." MD, no. 4 (February), 450-460.
     Reprint of 1963.2.

2 CORRIGAN, ROBERT W. The Modern Theatre. New York: Macmillan, pp. xv, 878, 1286.
     Comparison of Synge with Lorca. Also, "The fusion of reality with fantasy is the dominant characteristic of all his work."

3 ELLIS-FERMOR, UNA. The Frontiers of Drama. Second edition. London: Methuen, pp. 80, 82-83, 140.
     Comments on Synge's use of nature imagery. In The Playboy of the Western World, Synge "has thrown upon the imagery and allusions the entire function of revealing a world outside..." of Flaherty's shebeen.

4 FALLON, GABRIEL. "Profiles of a Poet." MD, 7, no. 3 (December), 329-344.
     Mentions Yeats as saying about the protestors of The Playboy of the Western World: "...I fought them, Fallon; my father did a finer thing--he forgot them!" Comment was made just before the riots over The Plough and the Stars. Reprinted: 1977.10.

5 FREYER, GRATTAN. "The Irish Contribution," in The Pelican Guide to English Literature. Vol. 7. The Modern Age. Edited by Boris Ford. Revised Edition. Baltimore: Penguin Books, 196-208.

1964

Synge's power, like "that of Cervantes," resides in his "juxtaposition of the most earthy realism with the highest flights of fancy." Also, Synge's world is not that of contemporary life, "but a small pre-civilized world of the imagination." Briefly compares Synge with O'Casey.

6   FRICKER, ROBERT. "Synge, O'Casey und Johnston," in <u>Das moderne englische Drama</u>. Göttingen: Vandenhoeck & Ruprecht, pp. 45–68.
Comments on each of Synge's plays, including a comparison of <u>In the Shadow of the Glen</u> to Ibsen's <u>Puppenheim</u> (<u>The Doll's House</u>) and Shaw's <u>Mrs. Warren's Profession</u>.

7   GASKELL, ROBERT. Review of <u>The Plays and Poems of J. M. Synge</u>, edited by T. R. Henn (1963.8). CritQ, 6, no. 4 (Winter), 381–382.
Points out lacunae in Henn's commentary and adds two items to Henn's bibliography.

8   GERSTENBERGER, DONNA. <u>John Millington Synge</u>. TEAS, No. 12 New York: Twayne, 157 pp.
Chapter 1 deals with Synge's prose; Chapters 2, 3, 4, 5, 6, and 7 with (respectively) <u>In the Shadow of the Glen</u>, <u>Riders to the Sea</u>, <u>The Well of the Saints</u>, <u>The Tinker's Wedding</u>, <u>The Playboy of the Western World</u>, and <u>Deirdre</u>. Chapter 8 takes up Synge's poetry, verse plays, and translations; Chapter 9 provides an assessment of Synge's importance. As do all Twayne books in this series, Gerstenberger's contains a Preface, Chronology, an extensive Annotated Bibliography, and an Index. Gerstenberger concludes, "The permanence of Synge's place in the world of drama is well assured by the inclusion of one of his plays...in every major anthology of modern drama.... Synge's...voice, speaking of man's condition, is one which is heard with clarity and interest today." Abridged: 1970.1.

9   JOYCE, JAMES. <u>The Critical Writings of James Joyce.</u> Edited by Ellsworth Mason and Richard Ellmann. New York: Viking Compass, pp. 149–150, 242–245, 250.
Reprints 1904.6; 1912.26; 1918.2.

10 KRAUSE, DAVID. "Synge und das irische Melodram." <u>Theatre heute</u>, 5, no. 3 (March), 62–63.
Maintains: "Synge hatte es sehr viel schwerer mit den überempfindlichen Iren als O'Casey."

1964

11 LOFTUS, RICHARD J. <u>Nationalism in Modern Anglo-Irish Poetry</u>.
    Madison and Milwaukee: University of Wisconsin Press,
    pp. 4, 9, 14, 32, 134, 203-204, 212-213, 311.
        Discusses the attacks on Synge by the middle class, com-
    pares Synge to James Stephens, and includes passing com-
    ments on Synge's plays.

12 MacLIAMMÓIR, MICHEÁL. <u>Theatre in Ireland</u>. Irish Life and
    Culture, 1. Second edition. Dublin: at the Sign of the
    Three Candles, pp. 13, 15, 16, 37, 45.
        Synge had "the power of moulding out of the wild earth
    that had borne them, characters that seemed half human,
    half titanic...."

13 O'NEILL, MICHAEL J. <u>Lennox Robinson</u>. TEAS, No. 9. New York:
    Twayne, pp. 25, 39-40, 42, 46, 48, 61, 65, 114, 138-139,
    164, 166, 168.
        Included in references to Synge are a few comparisons
    with and contrasts between Robinson and Synge, for example
    in the matter of the Big House theme.

14 SADDLEMYER, ANN, ed. "Synge to MacKenna: The Mature Years."
    MR, 5, no. 2 (Winter), 279-295.
        Ms. Saddlemyer's running commentary provides background
    material and forms interstices between the letters. Also,
    this volume is devoted to Irish writers and prints several
    photos. Reprinted: 1965.25.

15 SAUL, GERORGE BRANDON, ed. "Synge, Edmund John Millington,"
    in <u>Age of Yeats: The Golden Age of Irish Literature</u>.
    Laurel Masterpieces of World Literature. New York: Dell,
    pp. 376-378.
        Feels that Yeats, not Synge, that "skeptically ironic
    poet," was "Ireland's greatest dramatist...."

16 SKELTON, ROBIN. "The Death of Synge." MR, 5, no. 2 (Winter),
    278.
        An eight-line poem commemorating Synge: "in his long
    dying/ he tested each bladed word upon his thumb/ against
    each other word...."

17 STEPHENS, JAMES. "Reminiscences of J. M. Synge," in <u>James,</u>
    <u>Seumas & Jacques: Unpublished Writings of James Stephens</u>.
    Chosen and edited with an introduction by Lloyd Frankenberg.
    London and New York: Macmillan, pp. 54-60.
        Broadcast over the BBC in 1928, discusses Synge's pains-
    taking methods of composition and "enchantment" with nature.
    Reprinted: 1977.7.

1964

18   VAN LAAN, THOMAS F. "Form as Agent in Synge's Riders to the
      Sea." Drama Survey, 3 (Winter), 352-366.
          Focuses upon the purposeful brevity of the play, e.g.
      examining in detail Maurya's speeches, to prove that all of
      the parts fit together to express the theme of human futil-
      ity. Reprinted: 1970.1.

19   WARD, A. C. Twentieth-Century English Literature: 1901-1960.
      New York: Barnes & Noble, pp. 113-115.
          Emphasizes Synge's economy in language, his "utmost de-
      gree of concentration," which becomes a fault in his plays.

20   WEISS, SAMUEL A. "John Millington Synge 1871-1909," in Drama
      in the Modern World: Plays and Essays. Lexington, Massa-
      chusetts: D. C. Heath, pp. 175, 177.
          Brief biographical sketch. Includes glossary with
      forty-nine entries.

                              1965

1   BRADBROOK, M. C. English Dramatic Form: A History of Its
      Development. London: Chatto & Windus; New York: Barnes &
      Noble, pp. 126, 128, 130, 141.
          Comments on The Playboy of the Western World and on
      Riders to the Sea. The second is "Synge's most formal
      play." In it, "the repetitive patterns and brilliant col-
      ours of ballad poetry lead up to Maurya's lament for her
      sons.... Maurya, like Yeats's characters, has crossed a
      boundary, and entered a new state of being, no less surely
      than her drowned sons."

2   BRUSTEIN, ROBERT. The Theatre of Revolt: An Approach to the
      Modern Drama. Boston and Toronto: Little, Brown, pp. 22,
      42, 273, 284, 325, 358.
          Sees Synge's work as part of the "Social revolt" in the
      modern theater. Points to the influence of Riders to the
      Sea on Brecht's Mother Courage and Her Children.

3   CHIARI, J. Landmarks of Contemporary Drama. London: Herbert
      Jenkins, pp. 29, 35, 70, 81-82, 108.
          Compares and contrasts Synge with other "major" drama-
      tists, such as Yeats, O'Casey, O'Neill, and Beckett.

4   COLDWELL, JOAN. "'The Art of Happy Desire': Yeats and the
      Little Magazine," in The World of W. B. Yeats: Essays in
      Perspective. Edited by Robin Skelton, David R. Clark, and
      Ann Saddlemyer. Revised edition. Seattle, University of
      Washington Press, pp. 24-37.

1965

Brief material on the defense of The Playboy of the Western World in The Arrow, and the backlash.

5   COMBS, WILLIAM W. "J. M. Synge's Riders to the Sea: A Read-
    ing and Some Generalizations." Papers of the Michigan
    Academy of Science, Arts, and Letters, 50:599-607.
        Focuses upon Maurya and sees the play as an expression
    of Synge's pessimism.

6   COXHEAD, ELIZABETH. Daughters of Erin: Five Women of the
    Irish Renascence. London: Secker & Warburg, pp. 54, 137,
    157, 170, 173, 174, 175, 177-180, 182, 183-194, 195-198,
    201, 203, 207-208, 215, 222.
        Comments on the pettiness shown by Synge in his "love"
    for Molly Allgood and portrays her love for him as dubious.
    Provides data concerning Molly's roles in Synge's plays.
    Molly is "the fatally fascinating creature who was to in-
    spire and devastate the last three years of John Millington
    Synge."

7   EDWARDS, A. C. "The Lady Gregory Letters to Sean O'Casey."
    MD, 8, no. 1 (May), 95-111.
        Contains a passing reference to the production of one of
    Synge's plays in Prague.

8   EVANS, SIR IFOR. A Short History of the English Drama. Sec-
    ond edition. Riverside Studies in Literature. Boston:
    Houghton Mifflin, pp. 177, 179-180.
        Cites the possible influence of Synge on John Masefield's
    The Tragedy of Nan (1908). About Synge and Yeats: "They
    met first in Paris in 1899 [sic], the year after [sic] Synge
    had visited the Aran Islands."

9   FRASER, G. S. The Modern Writer and His World: Continuity
    and Innovation in Twentieth-Century English Literature.
    New York and Washington: Frederick Praeger, pp. 53, 56,
    204-208, 211, 216, 253-254.
        Comments on the possibly artificial language of Synge's
    plays, comparing him to Joyce, and wonders if Synge is even
    part of a drama "tradition."

10 GARAB, ARRA M. "Times of Glory: Yeats's 'The Municipal Gal-
    lery Revisited.'" ArQ, 21 (Autumn), 243-254.
        Traces Synge in Yeats's poetry and prose. Important
    statement about the complexity of Arthur Griffith's atti-
    tude towards Synge and the other Irish dramatists.

1965

11   GERSTENBERGER, DONNA. "Yeats and Synge: 'A Young Man's
       Ghost,'" in W. B. Yeats, 1865-1965: Centenary Essays on
       the Art of W. B. Yeats. Edited by D. S. Maxwell and S. B.
       Bushrui. Ibadan, Nigeria: Ibadan University Press,
       pp. 79-87.
          Draws a number of parallels between Yeats and Synge,
       e.g. "The conflict between Crazy Jane and the Bishop is
       the conflict which is at the centre of all of Synge's
       art...." Basically, Yeats found in Synge "a symbolic
       figure...."

12   HAWKES, TERENCE. "Playboys of the Western World." London
       The Listener (16 December), pp. 991-993.
          Discusses Synge's language at length and cites several
       similarities between The Playboy of the Western World and
       Dylan Thomas's Under Milk Wood.

13   HENN, T. R. "Yeats and Synge," in The Lonely Tower: Studies
       in the Poetry of W. B. Yeats. Second edition. London:
       Methuen, pp. 72-87.
          While showing how Synge filled a lacuna in Yeats's
       understanding of the people, Henn feels that, even if
       Synge had lived, Yeats would have turned to other sources
       for stimulation. However, Yeats did see Synge's career in
       "retrospect" as "an image of his own journeying." Traces
       several examples of Synge's influence on Yeats's poetry.
       Synge was, to some extent, Yeats's "Anti-Self...." He
       accorded with Yeats's desire "for brutality and vio-
       lence...."

14   HENRY, P. L. "The Playboy of the Western World." PP, NS 8:
       189-204.
          Traces the heroic concept in The Playboy of the Western
       World and includes a detailed analysis of the "rhythmical
       structure of Synge's prose...."

15   JOHNSTON, DENIS. John Millington Synge. CEMW, No. 12. New
       York and London: Columbia University Press, 48 pp.
          Comments briefly on past Synge biographical information;
       contrasts Synge to Yeats in the way each thought the real
       Ireland to be; pens the now famous description of Synge's
       poetic language in In the Shadow of the Glen as a "depress-
       ing weather report"--and, incidentally, cites the charac-
       ters in Riders to the Sea for their "continuing disregard
       for the weather reports";--calls Riders to the Sea Orestean;
       judges The Well of the Saints too long; and finds the end-
       ing of The Tinker's Wedding unnecessarily violent, although
       the play does show an improvement in Synge's use of peasant

dialect. About Synge's use of dialogue generally states, "It is probably true that he had heard all the words he uses, though probably not in the same order." Traces Synge's relationship to Molly Allgood in The Playboy of the Western World and then writes about this play: "that he had any wish to denigrate the people of the boreens who were the love and target of his art--the friends and companions of his brief middle age--is simply absurd." Deirdre of the Sorrows is a failure, with the heroine "an earlier bard's woman--if indeed she is a woman at all and not a transvestite." Abridged: 1970.1.

16 MILLER, LIAM. "The Dun Emer and the Cuala Press," in The World of W. B. Yeats: Essays in Perspective. Edited by Robin Skelton, David R. Clark, and Ann Saddlemyer. Revised edition. Seattle: University of Washington Press, pp. 74-102.
    Refers to the "drawings by Jack Yeats...based upon Synge's Playboy of the Western World...in 1907."

17 O'CONNOR, FRANK [MICHAEL FRANCIS O'DONOVAN]. The Big Fellow: Michael Collins and the Irish Revolution. Revised edition. Dublin: Clonmore & Reynolds; London: Burns & Oates, pp. 3-4, 147.
    Comments on Collins's intimate knowledge of Synge and other Irish writers and maintains "the Ireland which had blackguarded Synge...believed it was all settled in the Penny Catechism."

18 O'DONNELL, DONAT [CONOR CRUISE O'BRIEN]. Writers and Politics. New York: Random House, pp. 110, 121-122.
    Reprints 1959.11.

19 PEARCE, HOWARD D. "Synge's Playboy as Mock-Christ." MD, 8 no. 3 (December), 303-310.
    Parallels with Christ such as the Epiphany and the Scapegoat concept are meant to be ironic in Synge's play when applied to Christy, who is a mock-hero. Reprinted: 1969.25.

20 PRICE, ALAN, ed. The Autobiography of J. M. Synge. Constructed from the manuscripts, with fourteen photographs by J. M. Synge and an essay on Synge and the photography of his time by P. J. Pocock. London: Oxford University Press, 47 pp.
    Price states, "The Autobiography crystallizes his [Synge's] impressions of the first twenty-two years of his

1965

life up to his decision to leave Ireland for Germany in the
hope of becoming a professional musician." Pocock comments
on the technical worthiness of Synge's photographs.

21 PYLE, HILARY. James Stephens: His Work and an Account of His
Life. New York: Barnes & Noble, 25, 31, 33, 45, 47, 89,
102.
AE's "finding" of Stephens stems from his rivalry of
Yeats, who had "found" Synge. Mentions Synge's possible
appearance in Stephens's novel The Charwoman's Daughter.
Stephens, in The Demi-Gods and in The Crock of Gold, "appears to have been parodying Synge's poetic lilt and cadence...."

22 SADDLEMYER, ANN. "'A Share in the Dignity of the World':
J. M. Synge's Aesthetic Theory," in The World of W. B.
Yeats: Essays in Perspective. Edited by Robin Skelton,
David R. Clark, and Ann Saddlemyer. Revised edition.
Seattle: University of Washington Press, pp. 111-133.
Addresses such topics as the musical quality of Synge's
work, Synge's interest in literary movements, and (exten-
sively) Synge's aesthetic theory--a concern that Synge had
long before he met Yeats.

23 _____. "'Worn Out With Dreams': Dublin's Abbey Theatre,"
in The World of W. B. Yeats: Essays in Perspective.
Edited by Robin Skelton, David R. Clark, and Ann Saddlemyer. Revised edition. Seattle: University of Washington
Press, pp. 207-219.
Several references to Synge's implacable attitude towards his artistic expression.

24 SIDNELL, M. J. "Synge's Playboy and the Champion of Ulster."
DR, 45 (Spring), 51-59.
Traces Synge's ironic use of the mythological "Champion-
ship of Ulster" from the Ultonian or Cuchulain Cycle.

25 SKELTON, ROBIN and DAVID R. CLARK, eds. Irish Renaissance:
A Gathering of Essays, Memoirs, and Letters from The Mass-
achusetts Review. Dublin: Dolmen, pp. 16, 18, 20, 65-79.
Reprints 1964.14.

26 SKELTON, ROBIN, DAVID R. CLARK, and ANN SADDLEMYER, eds. The
World of W. B. Yeats: Essays in Perspective. Revised
edition. Seattle: University of Washington Press,
pp. 24-37, 74-102, 111-133, 207-219.
See individual entries: 1965.4, 16, 22, 23.

27 STARKIE, WALTER. Luigi Pirandello, 1867-1936. Third Edition.
   Berkeley: University of California Press, p. 13.
      Compares Synge favorably with Chiarelli. And: "The
   fundamental notion of Synge's play [The Playboy of the
   Western World]--that reality counts for nothing beside
   illusion--is the central problem of modern drama in Europe."

28 TAIT, MICHAEL. "Drama and Theatre," in Literary History of
   Canada: Canadian Literature in English. Edited by Carl F.
   Klinck. Toronto: University of Toronto Press, pp. 641,
   653.
      Mentions the influence of Lady Gregory and (to a lesser
   extent) of Synge on John Coulter, a dramatist of the
   thirties.

1966

1 ARUNDELL, DENNIS. The Story of Sadler's Wells, 1683-1964.
   New York: Theatre Arts Books, p. 233.
      Reference to Clive Carey's "tense" production of Vaughan
   Williams' setting of Riders to the Sea during the 1952-53
   season at the Wells.

2 BOURGEOIS, MAURICE. John Millington Synge and the Irish
   Theatre. New York: Haskell House, 353 pp.
      Reprints 1913.3.

3 BURGESS, ANTHONY [JOHN ANTHONY BURGESS WILSON]. "Enemy of
   Twilight." London The Spectator (22 July), p. 124.
      While discounting Synge's poems, comments generously on
   his prose.

4 COHN, RUBY and BERNARD F. DUKORE, eds. "John Millington
   Synge, 1871-1909," in Twentieth Century Drama: England,
   Ireland, the United States. New York: Random House,
   pp. 91-95.
      Maintains that "Christy's maturation constitutes the
   spine of the play and recalls numerous mythic tales, from
   Oedipus...to the fairy-tale hero who vanquishes the mean
   giant and wins the princess."

5 COLEMAN, ARTHUR and GARY R. TYLER. "Synge, John," in Drama
   Criticism: A Checklist of Interpretation since 1940 of
   English and American Plays. Vol. 1. Denver: Alan Swallow,
   202-205.

1966

> Lists books and articles dealing at least in part with
> Synge. Arranged under <u>The Aran Islands</u> and then under the
> plays considered alphabetically.

6   COXHEAD, ELIZABETH. "'Collaboration'--Hyde and Synge," in
    <u>Lady Gregory: A Literary Portrait</u>. Second edition. Lon-
    don: Secker and Warburg, pp. 114-120.
        Approximately thirty references to Synge in the book
    describe such matters as Lady Gregory's defense of <u>The
    Playboy of the Western World</u> in America, although she hated
    the play; their knowledge of Irish; and their dealing with
    Annie Horniman. <u>See</u> 1963.7.

7   EVERSON, IDA G. "Young Lennox Robinson and the Abbey Thea-
    tre's First American Tour (1911-1912)." MD, 9, no. 1
    (May), 74-89.
        Summarizes some of the problems centering upon <u>The
    Playboy of the Western World</u> in America. Includes a val-
    uable Program of the Abbey Players for the 1911-1912 tour
    made from a "typescript copy in [the] Secretary's Office,
    Abbey Theatre Dublin."

8   GASCOIGNE, BAMBER. <u>Twentieth-Century Drama</u>. New York:
    Barnes & Noble, p. 69.
        Holds that Synge "developed an idiom in which each
    speech explodes with its own chaos of colours and then al-
    ways, like a good firework, has one extra and unexpected
    shower of sparks at the end."

9   GOODWIN, K. L. <u>The Influence of Ezra Pound</u>. London, New
    York, and Toronto: Oxford University Press, p. 88.
        Relates the background of a possible Synge reference in
    Yeats's "To a Child Dancing in the Wind."

10 HART, WILLIAM E., ed. "Introduction," in <u>John Millington
    Synge: The Playboy of the Western World and Riders to the
    Sea</u>. New York: Appleton-Century-Crofts, 26 pp.
        Besides a brief chronology and bibliography, contains
    introductions to the two plays, which sketch such matters
    as Synge's language and artistic purpose in <u>The Playboy of
    the Western World</u> and that play's enigmatic nature, that
    led to the riots. Also, comments on the powerful simpli-
    city of characterization in <u>Riders to the Sea.</u>

11 HENN, T. R. "The Irish Tragedy (Synge, Yeats, O'Casey)," in
    <u>The Harvest of Tragedy</u>. New York: Barnes & Noble,
    pp. 197-216.
        <u>Riders to the Sea</u> is a successful tragedy; <u>Deirdre</u>, less
    so. <u>The Playboy of the Western World</u> is a "deliberately

1966

distorted tragedy, all the joints wrenched out of place by
a comic vision that Synge imposed upon it, a comic vision
in the manner of Molière." Analyzes elements of classical
tragedy in The Playboy of the Western World.

12 JOYCE, JAMES. Letters of James Joyce. Edited by Stuart Gilbert. Vol. 1. New York: Viking, 66-67, 95, 98, 99, 117-
118, 121.
Comments about Joyce's translation of Riders to the Sea
and his 1902 meeting with Synge in Paris. Joyce says that
he is the first person to have read Riders to the Sea and
mentions how his wife, Nora, acted in the play.

13 KAIN, RICHARD M. "A Scrapbook of the 'Playboy Riots.'" The
Emory University Quarterly, 22, no. 1 (Spring), 5-17.
Kain summarizes a scrapbook in his possession that con-
sists of sixty news items dealing with the reception of
The Playboy of the Western World in Dublin in 1907.

14 KILROY, JAMES FRANCIS. "Dominant Themes and Ironic Techniques
in the Works of J. M. Synge." Dissertation Abstracts, 26
(March-April), 5438.
Analyzes Synge's use of irony in his works, Synge's goal
being "the expression of the essential balance of reality."

15 MALLINSON, VERNON. Modern Belgian Literature, 1830-1960.
New York: Barnes & Noble, p. 73.
Brief reference to the influence of Maeterlinck on
Synge, Yeats, and Masefield.

16 PINTO, VIVIAN DE SOLA. "Yeats and Synge," in Crisis in English Poetry: 1880-1940. The Academic Library, Harper
Torchbooks. New York: Harper & Row, pp. 85-111.
Contains a brief reference to Synge: "The fullest expression of Synge's genius is, of course, to be found in
his plays, but his handful of short poems must be reckoned
as an important contribution to the poetry of the modern
crisis." Mentions Synge's opposition to traditionally
poetic form and points out Synge's dictum that poetry must
be "brutal."

17 PRICE, ALAN, ed. "Introduction" and "Notes," in Emerald Apex:
A Selection from J. M. Synge's Studies of Irish People and
Places. London and Glasgow: Blackie, pp. vii-xx, 119-128.
Focuses on the prose but reprints ten poems. Book in-
cludes two pages of "Exercises" and a short chronology.
Synge's prose writings "possess an intrinsic worth that

1966

would remain even if he had written nothing else...." They
are "created things with a life of their own...."

18 _____. *J. M. Synge: Collected Works*. Vol. 2. <u>Prose</u>. London: Oxford University Press, 426 pp.
Besides Synge's prose, much previously unpublished, this
volume contains an Introduction, which sketches the publication history and problems of Synge's prose; plates and
thirty-five drawings by Jack B. Yeats; a 1909 letter concerning Synge written by Jack Yeats; citations from Synge's
notebooks and other sources that clarify much of the prose
published in the volume; and a seven page Index. A slight-
ly different form of the Yeats letter appeared in <u>Synge and
the Ireland of His Time</u> (<u>See</u> 1911.83.) Yeats comments on
Synge's love of nature and children, evidenced during his
walks and other journeys, on his ability to find delight in
simple things: "Synge was always ready to go anywhere with
one and when there to enjoy what came." <u>See</u> 1962.16 and
1968.25, 26.

19 ROLLINS, RONALD G. "Huckleberry Finn and Christy Mahon: the
<u>Playboy of the Western World</u>." MTJ, 13, no. 2 (Summer),
16-19.
"Perhaps the most manifest parallelism is that both
fictions focus on two young men...who desire to break away
from conformity and confinement...into a new existence offering greater morality and opportunity for adventure."

20 _____. "O'Casey and Synge: The Irish Hero as Playboy and
Gunman." ArQ, 22, no. 3 (Autumn), 217-222.
Both <u>The Shadow of a Gunman</u> and <u>The Playboy of the Western World</u> explore the Irish "tendency to mistake sham
heroes and false patriots for men of real conviction and
courage." Both protagonists, Donal and Christy, learn that
"it is one's character and conduct--not hasty estimates by
emotional associates--that reveal one's true essence."

21 SWANDER, HOMER. "Arthur Shields, the 'Playboy' Who Fought in
the Rising." <u>The National Catholic Reporter</u> 3 (20 July),
2-4.
For the occasion of the dedication of the new Abbey
Theatre in 1966, rehearses the tumult over <u>The Playboy of
the Western World</u>. Synge, Shields feels, wrote in true
collaboration with the Irish people. The part of Christy
Mahon is "the one that every Irish actor longs to play...."

22 TRIESCH, MANFRED. "Some Unpublished J. M. Synge Papers,"
ELN, 4 (September), 49-51.

Describes a "recent acquisition of the Rare Book Collection at the University of Texas," which centers upon
thirty-two letters written by Synge to Maire O'Neill
(Molly Allgood). The letters were composed from 1907 to
1909 and cast some light on his plays and much light on
his health during the last years. Other works in the collection, such as some of Synge's unpublished poems "are of
more general interest."

1967

1 ADELMAN, IRVING and RITA DWORKIN. "Synge, John Millington,
   1871-1909," in Modern Drama: A Checklist of Critical Literature on 20th Century Plays. Metuchen, New Jersey:
   Scarecrow Press, pp. 306-308.
   This "selective" list of articles and books about Synge
   divides into general studies concerning him and criticism
   devoted to the plays considered alphabetically.

2 BARNETT, PAT. "The Nature of Synge's Dialogue." ELT, 10,
   no. 3, 119-129.
   Synge's lyrical dialogue, frequently condemned as being
   overblown, actually is entirely functional. In In the
   Shadow of the Glen, lyrical speech mirrors the poetic nature of the Tramp and Nora, while Dan's limited personality
   is seen in his laconic and prosaic expression--as are the
   characters of Michael and the priest in The Tinker's Wedding.

3 BROWN, IVOR. "The High Froth." Drama, 87 (Winter), 32-34.
   Contrasts the lively dialogue of Synge and others with
   the deadness of language in contemporary playwrights.

4 COWELL, RAYMOND. "Synge: The Playboy of the Western World,"
   in Twelve Modern Dramatists. Oxford: The Pergamon Press,
   pp. 57-65.
   Reprints the conclusion of the play and supplies six
   "Questions and Discussion Points." Sees The Playboy of
   the Western World as a "celebration of one man's struggle
   to free himself from convention...."

5 COWLEY, MALCOLM. Think Back on Us...: A Contemporary Chron-
   icle of the 1930's by Malcolm Cowley. Edited by Henry Dan
   Piper. Carbondale and Edwardsville: Southern Illinois
   University Press; London and Amsterdam: Feffer & Simons,
   p. 325.

1967

Maintains that the Nationalists turning against Yeats in the matter of The Playboy of the Western World forced him to withdraw "almost completely from political life."

6   ELLIS-FERMOR, UNA. "John Millington Synge," in The Irish Dramatic Movement. University Paperbacks. London: Methuen, pp. 163-186.
     Reprint of 1939.2. Abridged: 1969.25.

7   _____. "Synge, (Edmund) John Millington (1871-1909)," in The Oxford Companion to the Theatre. Edited by Phyllis Hartnoll. Third edition. London: Oxford University Press, p. 931.
     Sketch of Synge's works: Riders to the Sea is "one of the finest, if not the finest, of all modern short plays...." The comedy of The Tinker's Wedding "is richer and more jovial than any other that Synge wrote."

8   GANZ, ARTHUR. "J. M. Synge and the Drama of Art." MD, 10, no. 1 (May), 57-68.
     Examines Synge's plays in the light of the alienated artist: Synge "desired to create an image of beauty that would stand against the sense of the absoluteness of death...." About The Tinker's Wedding, one of a group of plays that Ganz calls "wanderer plays": "even here the theme of the decay of beauty appears"--even though The Tinker's Wedding is basically a lighthearted farce. Ganz finds the theme of the "exile bard" in The Playboy of the Western World and feels that Deirdre of the Sorrows epitomizes Synge's themes: in it "the agony of life is transmuted into the perfect beauty of art."

9   HARMON, MAURICE. "J. M. Synge," in Modern Irish Literature, 1800-1967: A Reader's Guide. Dublin: Dolmen, pp. 33-34.
     Meant as an introduction to Irish literature, lists five critical works under "J. M. Synge." Other references to Synge are scattered throughout the seventy-one page monograph.

10   HOLLOWAY, JOSEPH. Joseph Holloway's Abbey Theatre: A Selection from His Unpublished Journal "Impressions of a Dublin Playgoer." Edited by Robert Hogan and Michael J. O'Neill. Carbondale and Edwardsville: Southern Illinois University Press; London and Amsterdam: Feffer & Simons, pp. 29, 71-72, 110, 124-125, 277-278.
     Over fifty references to Synge, starting with Holloway's "long chat" with him in 1903 and including Holloway's entry for 24 March 1909: "Poor Synge, he was a gentle and

lovable man personally, and not at all like his works."
Provides details about Synge's death. Abridged: 1977.7.

11 JOHNSON, WALLACE H. "The Pagan Setting of Synge's Playboy."
Renascence, 19, pp. 119-121, 150.
A brief statement to the effect that the locale is un-
important to the work: Synge simply transferred his pessimistic views of Aran to a new place.

12 O'CASEY, SEAN. "John Millington Synge (1946)," in Blasts and
Benedictions: Articles and Stories by Sean O'Casey.
Selected and introduced by Ronald Ayling. London: Macmillan; New York: St. Martin's Press, pp. 35-41.
The first appearance in English of an essay published
in Moscow in 1946: "The Playboy of the Western World has
not its match in Keltic satirical drama, and one would have
to search wide and deep for an equivalent of the melodious
pain in Riders to the Sea." Feels that the attacks on
Synge by hostile Dubliners hastened his death.

13 O'CONNOR, FRANK [O'DONOVAN, MICHAEL]. "All the Olympians,"
in The Backward Look: A Survey of Irish Literature. London: Macmillan; American title: A Short History of Irish
Literature: A Backward Look. New York: Putnam's,
pp. 183-193.
Shows how the worth of Synge's plays increases as he
draws farther away from Yeats's formulas and expresses his
own feelings more deeply.

14 OSBORN, MARGARET ELIZABETH. "The Concept of Imagination in
Edwardian Drama." Dissertation Abstracts, 28 (September--
October), 1443A.
Traces Shaw's concept of the "realistic imagination" in
The Well of the Saints and in The Playboy of the Western
World.

15 POPKIN, HENRY, ed. "Introduction" and "Commentaries," in
John Millington Synge, The Playboy of the Western World
and Riders to the Sea. The Avon Theatre Library. New
York: Avon Books, pp. 9-18, 123-189.
Christy Mahon "'kills' his father to escape another of
those loveless Irish marriages; at the same time, he is
participating in one of the most archetypal patterns of
all--the conflict between father and son." "Commentaries"
reprints several basic studies of Synge.

1967

16   POUND, EZRA. <u>Pound/Joyce: The Letters of Ezra Pound to James</u>
      <u>Joyce, with Pound's Essays on Joyce</u>. Edited by Forrest
      Read. New York: New Directions, pp. 32, 52, 209, 298.
            Sees Synge as the victim of Dublin's "stupidity." Also,
      includes a letter by John Quinn dated March 20, 1917, in
      which Quinn states: "In the old days I used to buy and
      give away Synge's and Yeats's things by the dozen."

17   PRITCHETT, V. S. <u>Dublin: A Portrait</u>. New York and Evanston:
      Harper & Row, pp. 5, 13, 76.
            Says that the "stage-Irishman...exists" in <u>The Playboy</u>
      <u>of the Western World</u>; and about the riots over the work:
      "People were sent in by the political clubs to make the
      play inaudible."

18   RYNNE, CATHERINE. "The Playwrights," in <u>The Story of the</u>
      <u>Abbey Theatre</u>. Edited by Sean McCann. A Four Square Book.
      London: New English Library, pp. 69-100.
            Describes the adverse reaction to <u>The Playboy of the</u>
      <u>Western World</u> and adds: "there is still an element among
      the Irish which cannot accept Synge."

19   SADDLEMYER, ANN. <u>J. M. Synge and Modern Comedy</u>. New Dolmen
      Chapbooks, 2. Dublin: Dolmen; London: Oxford University
      Press, 31 pp.
            Takes issue with Yeats's picture of Synge; examines such
      elements in Synge's work as nature and the dream or illu-
      sion; and guesses that Synge's penchant for experimentation
      would have led him away from the Abbey had he lived.

20   _____. "Rabelais <u>versus</u> A Kempis: The Art of J. M. Synge."
      <u>Komos</u>, 1, no. 3 (October), 85-96.
            Sketch of the relationship between Synge's life and
      work. Title refers to Synge's view that "the grotesque and
      the strong must answer the soft and the sweet."

21   SPANOS, WILLIAM V. <u>The Christian Tradition in Modern British</u>
      <u>Verse Drama: The Poetics of Sacramental Time</u>. New Bruns-
      wick, New Jersey: Rutgers University Press, pp. 17, 270,
      279.
            Cites possible influence of Synge on Norman Nicholson's
      <u>The Old Man of the Mountains</u>.

22   THOMPSON, WILLIAM IRWIN. <u>The Imagination of an Insurrection,</u>
      <u>Dublin, Easter 1916: A Study of an Ideological Movement</u>.
      New York: Oxford University Press, pp. 26, 27-28, 29, 57-
      58, 67-73, 115, 144, 150, 204, 205.

Says that Synge "had a sensibility that was more alive to the ironies and contradictions of human nature than to the historical conflations of Teutonic messianism."

23 VÖLKER, KLAUS. Irisches Theater I: William Butler Yeats [und] John Millington Synge. Friedrichs Dramatiker des Welttheaters, Band 29. Velber bei Hannover: Friedrich, 109 pp.
First section deals with the Irish Renaissance generally; second, with Yeats; third section devotes a part to each of Synge's plays considered individually; last several pages compare Yeats and Synge. Includes a seven-page chronology of the Irish Renaissance. Also, contains interesting photographs from scenes of Synge's plays, including four from foreign productions of The Playboy of the Western World.

1968

1 ASQUITH, LADY CYNTHIA. Diaries, 1915-1918. Foreword by L. P. Hartley. London: Hutchinson, p. 39.
In an entry for June 10, 1915, refers to Charles Whibley's view that among modern prose stylists "...Synge was the only one with a real sense of 'cadence.'"

2 BENTLEY, ERIC, ed. The Theory of the Modern Stage: An Introduction to Modern Theatre and Drama. Harmondsworth: Penguin, pp. 330-334, 343.
Reprints Yeats's letter to Lady Gregory, which contains a comment about acting in Riders to the Sea and several comments on why Synge was unpopular with the masses.

3 BESSAI, DIANE E. "Little Hound in Mayo: Synge's Playboy and the Comic Tradition in Irish Literature." DR, 48, no. 3 (Autumn), 372-383.
Discusses Synge's ironic use of materials from the ancient Irish sagas, especially the Cuchulain cycle. Synge himself resembles Bricrui, the mischievous archetypal Irish poet and satirist; Christy, Cuchulain, in his many exploits and in his relation to father figures; Pegeen, Emer, Cuchulain's wife; the Widow Quin, Scathach, Cuchulain's advisor; the Widow Casey, the Sheela-na-gig, the meanest hag of Ireland; and Old Mahon, the Dagda, the gross Irish giant.

1968

4   CALLAN, EDWARD. <u>Alan Paton</u>. TWAS, No. 40. New York: Twayne,
     pp. 54, 57.
          Compares <u>Riders to the Sea</u> to <u>Cry, the Beloved Country</u>.

5   CURRY, RYDER HECTOR and MARTIN BRYAN. "Riders to the Sea:
     Reappraised." TQ, 11, no. 4 (Winter), 139-146.
          Far from being a piece of mere reporting, <u>Riders to the
     Sea</u> is a deeply mysterious work which surges from Synge's
     repressed unconscious forces. It reflects, also, Synge's
     reading in the mystical, seen in the books that he brought
     with him to the Aran Islands. Maurya, for example, has
     affinities with the ancient Morrigan and with the Eddic
     Mara, the hag; and the play seems to be influenced by the
     rites of the Celtic feast of Samhain.

6   DAY, P. W. <u>John Mulgan</u>. TWAS, No. 58. New York: Twayne,
     p. 112.
          Points out a "slight" parallel between <u>The Playboy of
     the Western World</u> and Mulgan's <u>Man Alone</u>.

7   DONOGHUE, DENIS. <u>The Ordinary Universe: Soundings in Modern
     Literature</u>. London: Faber; New York: Macmillan, pp. 122,
     131, 139, 186, 238.
          Synge "went to the Aran Islands...to move in a world of
     sound."

8   DOW, MARGUERITE R. <u>The Magic Mask: A Basic Textbook of
     Theatre Arts</u>. New York: St. Martin's Press, p. 256.
          In <u>Riders to the Sea</u>, Synge "is said to have given the
     English-speaking theatre its greatest one-act tragedy..."

9   DREW, FRASER. "The Irish Allegiances of an English Laureate:
     John Masefield and Ireland." <u>Éire</u>, 3, no. 4 (Winter),
     24-34.
          Comments on Masefield's fast friendship with Synge.
     Synge inspired Masefield to look for similar folklore
     material in England.

10   _____. "Next Parish to Boston: The Blasket Islands and Their
     Literature." <u>Éire</u>, 3, no. 1 (Spring), 6-22.
          Details the doings of Synge in the Blaskets and briefly
     traces the influences in the work of "the most famous lit-
     erary visitor...."

11   FLOOD, JEANNE AGNES. "John Millington Synge: A Study of His
     Aesthetic Development." <u>Dissertation Abstracts</u>, 28 (May-
     June), 5052A.

In part by examining previously unavailable early prose of Synge, this study attempts "to define and understand the importance to Synge's creative aesthetic of the Aran experience."

12   _____. Review of J. M. Synge, Collected Works, Vols. 3 and 4, edited by Ann Saddlemyer (See 1968.25, 26). Éire, 3, no. 4 (Winter), 143-144.
      A brief statement that praises the laborious effort that went into the volumes and that points out uses which the source material might have as well as its possible pitfalls.

13   FRECHET, RENÉ. "Le Thème de la parole dans le théâtre de J. M. Synge." Etudes Anglaises, 21, no. 3 (July-September), 243-256.
      Traces the importance of the spoken word in Synge's plays. The Well of the Saints, for instance, develops the opposition between the ecclesiastical word and the pagan "parole."

14   HEILMAN, ROBERT BECHTOLD. Tragedy and Melodrama: Versions of Experience. Seattle and London: University of Washington Press, pp. 38-40, 47, 72, 80, 82, 137.
      Criticizes Riders to the Sea as being pathetic rather than tragic, with its participants merely "victims of disaster...."

15   HOLLOWAY, JOSEPH. Joseph Holloway's Irish Theatre. Vol. 1. 1926-1931. Edited by Robert Hogan and Michael J. O'Neill. Dixon, California: Proscenium Press, 11, 22, 31, 40, 49, 61, 67, 81.
      Contains, among other data, the surprising fact that William M. Boyle had not read or seen The Playboy of the Western World when he withdrew his own plays in protest over Synge's work in 1907. See 1969.5; 1970.7.

16   JEFFERS, ROBINSON. The Selected Letters of Robinson Jeffers, 1897-1962. Edited by Ann N. Ridgeway. Baltimore: The Johns Hopkins Press, p. 17.
      In a letter dated December 21, 1912, Jeffers puts Synge in a category with Ibsen, Strindberg, and Tolstoi, writers who, though they stick "a nasty tragedy under our noses we feel that there are principles at stake...."

17   KILROY, JAMES F. "The Playboy as Poet." PMLA, 83, no. 2 (May), 439-442.
      Sees the "growth of a poet" as a thematic unifying device in The Playboy of the Western World. Synge's play

1968

"dramatizes the gradual development of the poet's craft
from its first uncertain expression to the full display of
mature art...."

18   MIKHAIL, E. H. "French Influences on Synge." RLC, 42, no. 3
     (July-September), 429-431.
          Reviews past commentaries about French influences on
     Synge and then develops that of Anatole France.

19   MILLER, J. WILLIAM. Modern Playwrights at Work. Vol. 1.
     New York, Hollywood, London, and Toronto: Samuel French,
     pp. 238, 391, 395, 401, 406, 409-410, 433, 459, 461, 482.
          Discusses Synge and other playwrights in regard to such
     matters as their ages when they started their careers, the
     levels of education they attained, and their habits of
     keeping notebooks.

20   NAGARKAR, KIRAN. "Synge." Quest, 56 (Winter), 46-48.
          Sees Wordsworth in the language that Synge uses with his
     peasant characters.

21   PALMER, HELEN H. and ANNE JANE DYSON. "John Millington Synge,"
     in European Drama Criticism. Hamden, Connecticut: The
     Shoe String Press, pp. 407-410.
          Lists several books and articles pertaining to Synge's
     plays, which are treated alphabetically.

22   PRICE, ALAN. "Synge's Prose Writings: A First View of the
     Whole." MD, 11, no. 3 (December), 221-226.
          Synge's prose writings demonstrate that his work and
     his life form a continuum. For example, like Christy
     Mahon, Synge was "always interrupted and deflated" when he
     tried to communicate his deepest thoughts. Also, the
     prose demonstrates such other biographical data as the fact
     that Wicklow was as important to Synge as the Aran Islands.
     Finally, Price feels that Synge's prose should be examined
     in its own right—as writing with its own "intrinsic
     worth."

23   REID, B. L. The Man from New York: John Quinn and His
     Friends. New York: Oxford University Press, pp. 36, 46-
     49, 60, 65-68, 85, 115-118, 217, 357.
          Scattered references to Synge throughout the book pro-
     vide excellent background concerning Quinn's personal and
     business dealings with Synge's work. Quinn saw Synge "as
     a martyr, a kind of lay Christ-figure." Discusses the
     basis of opposition to Synge's plays in America, especially
     the hostility of John Devoy's newspaper, The Gaelic Ameri-
     can.

1968

24   RONSLEY, JOSEPH. <u>Yeats's Autobiography: Life as Symbolic</u>
      <u>Pattern</u>. Cambridge, Massachusetts: Harvard University
      Press, pp. 21, 36-39, 42, 72, 116, 120, 123-128, 134, 150,
      152, 161, 163.
          Analyzes Yeats's view of Synge in such issues as Synge's
      relationship to country and the attitude of Synge's "self"
      towards external reality.

25   SADDLEMYER, ANN, ed. <u>J. M. Synge: Collected Works</u>. Vol. 3
      <u>Plays</u>, Book 1. London: Oxford University Press, 316 pp.
          The three previously published plays in this volume
      (<u>Riders to the Sea</u>, <u>In the Shadow of the Glen</u>, and <u>The Well</u>
      <u>of the Saints</u>) are elucidated by copious references to the
      typescripts. "Unpublished Material, Part One" contains
      Synge's one-act play <u>When the Moon Has Set</u>. "Part Two"
      contains "Scenarios, Dialogues, and Fragments." The appen-
      dices to the three published plays and to the previously
      unpublished <u>When the Moon Has Set</u> consist of descriptions
      of textual sources, draft manuscripts, related passages
      from the notebooks, and notes on first productions. Ap-
      pendix to <u>The Well of the Saints</u> contains Synge's textual
      notes for Max Meyerfeld's translation. Volume also con-
      tains part of Yeats's memorandum to Synge's executors,
      1909, stating his reasons for rejecting <u>When the Moon Has</u>
      <u>Set</u>. Saddlemyer's Introduction (20 pp.) discusses Synge's
      insistence upon realistic presentations for his plays and
      his detailed explanations of his precise purposes in his
      works. See 1962.16; 1966.18; 1968.26. See also 1968.12.

26   _____ . <u>J. M. Synge: Collected Works</u>. Vol. 4 <u>Plays</u>, Book 2.
      London: Oxford University Press, 430 pp.
          Contains a twenty-two page Introduction and a short
      glossary. Extensive notes to the three plays in the vol-
      ume (<u>The Tinker's Wedding</u>, <u>The Playboy of the Western World</u>,
      and <u>Deirdre of the Sorrows</u>) explicate several passages in
      the works by citing in detail the many versions of parts of
      Synge's plays, contained in his typescripts and notebooks.
      The three appendices to the plays (123 pp.) contain de-
      scriptions of textual sources, draft manuscripts, related
      passages from the notebooks, notes on first productions,
      etc. Also, contains Synge's earlier drafts of his Preface
      to <u>The Tinker's Wedding</u>. See 1962.16; 1966.18; 1968.25.
      See also 1968.12.

27   SALERNO, HENRY F., ed. "John Millington Synge [1871-1909],"
      in <u>English Drama in Transition, 1880-1920</u>. New York:
      Pegasus, pp. 415-419.

1968

      Cites the close affinity of <u>The Playboy of the Western</u> <u>World</u> to tragedy. Also, "The play seems, among other things, a satire on the Irish themselves: their hero-worshipping, their blarney, is reduced to empty lies and self-deception...."

28   SANDERLIN, R. REED. "Synge's <u>Playboy</u> and the Ironic Hero." SoQ, 6 (April), 289-301.
      Says that Christy Mahon achieves no enlightenment in <u>The Playboy of the Western World</u>, but that Synge's purpose was to emphasize the delusion of the Irish villagers.

29   STYAN, J. L. "Synge and O'Casey," in <u>The Dark Comedy: The</u> <u>Development of Modern Comic Tragedy</u>. Second edition. Cambridge, England: at the University Press, pp. 130-132.
      Maintains that "Synge brought with him from Paris a sophisticated approach to life and a comic and ironic eye which mingled oddly with the peasant Ireland he wished to rediscover."

30   SULTAN, STANLEY. "The Gospel According to Synge." PLL, 4, no. 4 (Fall), 428-441.
      <u>The Playboy of the Western World</u> embodies a theme which runs throughout Irish literature, that of the rejected Messiah or Deliverer, and the play "presents a carefully developed analogue to the ministry and crucifixion of Jesus." Discusses several parallels, e.g. Palm Sunday events and the Good Samaritan Parable, between Christ and Christy.

31   TEMPLE, RUTH Z. and MARTIN TUCKER, eds. "John Millington Synge, 1871-1909," in <u>Twentieth Century British Literature:</u> <u>A Reference Guide and Bibliography</u>. New York: Ungar, pp. 239-240.
      Over twenty references to Synge throughout the book that provide a listing of his chief works, and scattered critical books that deal in part with Synge while being devoted to broader concerns.

32   TUBE, HENRY. "Books: It Goes Without Synge." London <u>The</u> <u>Spectator</u> (13 September), pp. 360-361.
      Reviews <u>The Best of Myles</u> by Flann O'Brien (also known as Brian O'Nolan and Myles na g Copaleen). Cites O'Brien's comment: "'it goes without Synge that many of my writings are very fine indeed.'" Tube calls the hero of O'Brien's <u>The Third Policeman</u> "a kind of successful playboy of the western world...." O'Brien, however, had himself once stated that there was "nothing in the whole galaxy of fake...comparable with Synge."

33 WELLS, HENRY W. "Poetic Imagination in Ireland and India."
     LHY, 9, no. 2, 37-48.
        Discusses a number of similarities between Indian and
     Irish tradition and applies them to Yeats and Synge.

1969

1 CONACHER, D. J. "Some Profane Variations on a Tragic Theme."
     PhoenixC, 23 (Spring), 26-38.
        Focuses on the Widow Quin as a figure of Jocasta to show
     that "...Synge had Sophocles' Oedipus in mind when he wrote
     The Playboy."

2 DAICHES, DAVID. The Present Age in British Literature.
     Bloomington and London: Indiana University Press, pp. 152,
     164, 177, 189.
        Contains a passing reference to the fact that Synge
     "first tried to restore a new kind of artistic vitality to
     modern English drama."

3 FACKLER, HERBERT V. "J. M. Synge's Deirdre of the Sorrows:
     Beauty Only." MD, 11, no. 4 (February), 404-409.
        Discusses the "dignified simplicity" of Synge's Deirdre
     of the Sorrows, his use of dialect to bring his personages
     to life, the "existential pantheism" that typifies the re-
     lationship of Synge's characters to external nature, the
     autobiographical source of Synge's view of death as a vic-
     tory, and Greek elements in the play, e.g. "The tragedy...
     is one in which all of Synge's characters share, through a
     common flaw--surrender to the will."

4 GORDON, JAN B. "The Imaginary Portrait: Fin-de-siècle Icon."
     UWR, 5, no. 1 (Fall), 81-104.
        Shows how Synge, among several others, used the "imag-
     inary portrait" technique of Walter Pater.

5 HOLLOWAY, JOSEPH. Joseph Holloway's Irish Theatre. Vol. 2
     1932-1937. Edited by Robert Hogan and Michael J. O'Neill.
     Dixon, California: Proscenium Press, pp. 17,20, 47, 56-
     57, 59, 68, 72, 74, 76, 77.
        Diary entry for July 27, 1936 contains a comment on
     Cyril Cusack as Christy Mahon: Cusack "over-brogued" his
     speeches. Cites possible influence of Hyde on language
     of Synge. See 1968.15; 1970.7.

1969

6   HOWARD-HILL, T. H.   Bibliography of British Literary Bibliog-
    raphies. Oxford: at the Clarendon Press, pp. 469-470.
    Lists eight sources of bibliography for Synge, anno-
    tates four.

7   KAVANAGH, PETER, ed.   Lapped Furrows, Correspondence 1933-
    1967 Between Patrick and Peter Kavanagh: With Other Docu-
    ments. New York: The Peter Kavanagh Hand Press, pp. 114,
    164.
        Patrick Kavanagh speaks of the "phoney Irish revival
    from Synge...," which was one of "two influences" present
    from the start of the movement and which "gave birth to
    much of Colum, Clarke, Higgins and even Stephens." Says
    that the "Yeats-Synge phoney Ireland was eminently suited
    for export to America."

8   KERNAN, ALVIN B.   "Riders to the Sea by John Millington
    Synge," in Character and Conflict: An Introduction to
    Drama. Second edition. New York: Harcourt, Brace and
    World, pp. 557-558.
        Synge's language in the plays is "unbelievably simple
    and direct and yet resonant and full of emotion and a sense
    of the powers of the world...."

9   LENGELER, RAINER.   "Phantasie und Komik in Synges The Playboy
    of the Western World." GRM, NS 19, no. 3 (July), 291-304.
        Includes several interesting analogues to the play from
    A Midsummer Night's Dream and Marlowe's Tamburlaine to
    Gay's Beggar's Opera.

10 LEVITT, PAUL M.   "The Structural Craftmanship of J. M. Synge's
    Riders to the Sea." Éire, 4, no. 1 (Spring), 53-61.
        Demonstrates that Riders to the Sea is unified by bib-
    lical references, especially those to Exodus and Revela-
    tions: Synge "compresses past and present action into the
    closing moments of a tragedy long unfolding. It is this
    organization, combined with the biblical imagery...which
    gives Riders its extraordinary compactness and intensity...."
    Reprinted: 1970.1.

11 MacNEICE, LOUIS.   The Poetry of W. B. Yeats. New York: Ox-
    ford University Press, Oxford University Paperback, pp. 38,
    47, 51, 80, 90-91, 94, 98-100, 104, 110, 112, 118, 119,
    134, 142, 166, 183.
        Emphasizes the influence of Synge's individual person-
    ality and the realistic or "strong" nature of his plays
    and poems. Includes several scattered comments on Synge's
    works.

126

1969

12   PITTOCK, MALCOLM.   "Riders to the Sea."   ES, 49, no. 5 (Octo-
      ber), 445-449.
          Maurya's vision is implausible: its effect depends upon
      the audience's assenting to the superstitions of the is-
      landers.

13   PRICE, A[LAN].   Riders to the Sea, The Playboy of the Western
      World (J. M. Synge).   Notes on English Literature.   Oxford:
      Blackwell, 87 pp.
          A basic introduction to the two plays, integrating back-
      ground material with literary analysis.   Contains several
      "Questions" about the works.   "It is movingly ironic that
      after praising Christy as a hero...she [Pegeen Mike] flatly
      rejects him when he actually is what she fancied him to
      be."

14   ROYAL IRISH ACADEMY DUBLIN, COMMITTEE FOR THE STUDY OF ANGLO-
      IRISH LANGUAGE AND LITERATURE.   Work in Progress: Handlist
      No. 1.   Dublin: Royal Irish Academy, 23 pp., passim.
          The first year of a publication which began in mimeo-
      graphed form and by 1974 had assumed a traditional format.
      Obvious disadvantage is that many of the works listed never
      did "progress."   But the assets far outweigh the debits in
      providing a detailed grouping of works in Anglo-Irish--
      including masters' theses.   Relies upon news sent in about
      ongoing projects, and, besides providing an excellent "at-
      mosphere" for Anglo-Irish studies, offers a meeting place
      for scholars with similar interests.   Information can be
      obtained by writing directly to the Committee for the Study
      of Anglo-Irish Language and Literature, Royal Irish Acad-
      emy, 19 Dawson Street, Dublin 2, Ireland.

15   SKELTON, ROBIN.   "J. M. Synge and The Shadow of the Glen."
      English, 18, no. 102 (Autumn), 91-97.
          Maintains that the play is a crucial transitional work,
      the first play which effectively dramatizes Synge's major
      themes, a highly original work, and a forerunner of black
      comedy.

16   _____, ed.   Riders to the Sea.   Dolmen Editions, 8.   London:
      Oxford University Press, 58 pp.
          Based upon the Houghton manuscript in Harvard Univer-
      sity.   Skelton's Introduction emphasizes the number sym-
      bolism in the play as well as commenting upon many other
      aspects of the work.   Abridged: 1970.1.

1969

17   SMITH, HARRY W. "Synge's Playboy and the Proximity of Vio-
     lence," QJS, 55, no. 4 (December), 381-387.
          Notes parallels between the peasants' thirst for vio-
     lence in The Playboy of the Western World and the violence
     of the 1960s: "The archetypal attitudes of Synge's mythi-
     cal villagers resemble our own."

18   SULLIVAN, MARY ROSE. "Synge, Sophocles, and the Un-making of
     Myth." MD, 12 (December), 242-253.
          A detailed examination of parallels between The Playboy
     of the Western World and Oedipus Rex centering upon the
     mythologizing and demythologizing of the protagonists,
     which demonstrates that "even in comedy he [Synge] was
     moving to the very borderline of tragedy."

19   SULTAN, STANLEY. "A Joycean Look at the Playboy of the West-
     ern World," in The Celtic Master: Contributions to the
     First James Joyce Symposium Held in Dublin, 1967. Edited
     by Maurice Harmon. Dublin: Dolmen, pp. 45-55.
          Points out Christocentric allusions in The Playboy of
     the Western World and sees as a cause of riots over the
     play "the hitherto neglected Anglo-Irish motif of the re-
     jected deliverer...," which it contains.

20   TINDALL, WILLIAM YORK. A Reader's Guide to Finnegans Wake.
     New York: Farrar, Straus and Giroux, pp. 108, 198, 251,
     298.
          Relates The Playboy of the Western World to the father-
     killing theme in the Wake.

21   UNTERECKER, JOHN. Voyager: A Life of Hart Crane. New York:
     Farrar, Straus and Giroux, p. 219.
          Crane writing in 1921 stated: "After one has read
     'Bartholomew Fair' it isn't so hard to see where Synge got
     his start--a start toward a husky folk-element in the
     drama."

22   WARNER, ALAN. "The Poet as Watcher." Threshold, 22 (Summer),
     64-70.
          Synge as a writer needed objectivity and artistic dis-
     tance and should not be criticized for his impersonality.

23   WATSON, GEORGE, ed. "Edmund John Millington Synge, 1871-
     1909," in The New Cambridge Bibliography of English Litera-
     ture. Vol. 3. 1800-1900. Cambridge, England: at the
     University Press, 1934-1938.
          Secondary bibliography runs through 1965. Also, gives
     primary data on Synge's works, plus notes on his letters

and diaries and collections of his writings. Cites five
bibliographies of criticism on Synge.

24   WEBSTER, MARGARET. The Same Only Different: Five Genera-
       tions of a Great Theatre Family. New York: Knopf, p. 237.
          Brief reference to The Playboy of the Western World as
       an example of "new theatre" that was "stirring" outside of
       London in 1907.

25   WHITAKER, THOMAS R., ed. The Playboy of the Western World:
       A Collection of Critical Essays. TCI. Englewood Cliffs,
       New Jersey: Prentice-Hall, 125 pp.
          Reprints 1911.80, 83; 1946.6; 1947.7; 1953.10; 1961.3,
       11; 1965.19. Abridges 1939.2; 1959.6; 1960.14; 1963.8;
       1967.6.

26   WHITING, FRANK M. An Introduction to the Theatre. Third
       edition. New York: Harper & Row, pp. 99-100, 124, 148.
          Synge's satire "is never cruel, nor is it a satire on
       the Irish alone."

27   WICKSTROM, GORDON MINTON. "The Deirdre Plays of AE, Yeats,
       and Synge: Patterns of Irish Exile." Dissertation Ab-
       stracts, 29 (May-June), 4027A.
          The three Deirdre plays demonstrate the "tensions that
       exist between Ireland and her children--tensions that
       drive many of them into exile from the homeland."

                           1970

1   CLARK, DAVID R., ed. John Millington Synge: Riders to the
       Sea. The Merrill Literary Casebook Series. Columbus,
       Ohio: Charles E. Merrill, 136 pp.
          Reprints 1947.2; 1955.2; 1964.18; 1969.10. Abridges
       1913.3; 1951.5; 1959.4; 1961.9; 1964.8; 1965.15; 1969.16.

2   DAVIE, DONALD. "The Young Yeats," in The Shaping of Modern
       Ireland. Edited by Conor Cruise O'Brien. New York:
       Barnes & Noble, pp. 140 151.
          About Christy Mahon in The Playboy of the Western
       World: "Is the figure that Synge created to be given the
       love and admiration that should be denied to the creations
       of Thomas Davis?" The reception given to the play "is
       not quite such a shameful blot on the 'scutcheon as people
       commonly believe."

1970

3   FLANNERY, JAMES W. <u>Miss Annie F. Horniman and the Abbey Thea-</u>
<u>tre</u>. The Irish Theatre Series 3. Dublin: Dolmen, pp. 7,
17, 19, 22, 24-28, 34.
    Records Miss Horniman's dislike of Synge and, in passing
references, documents Synge's involvement in the behind-
the-scenes activity of the Abbey.

4   FLOOD, JEANNE. "The Pre-Aran Writings of J. M. Synge."
<u>Éire</u>, 5, no. 3 (Autumn), 63-80.
    Examination of the "Autobiography," the "Vita Vecchia,"
and the "Étude Morbide" in the light of Synge's attempts
to reconcile the passionless objectivity of the artist with
his need to face the demands of physicality and sensuality:
"...Synge must allow his own creative imagination to con-
front the terrifying dynamism of the physical universe
within which man exists."

5   FRENCH, FRANCES-JANE. <u>The Abbey Theatre Series of Plays: A</u>
<u>Bibliography</u>. Dublin: Dolmen; Chester Springs, Pennsyl-
vania: Dufour Editions, pp. 13-15, 26-28.
    Deals with the original Abbey Theatre Series of fifteen
volumes and the later Abbey Theatre Series of nine unnum-
bered volumes in providing descriptive bibliographical
material for <u>The Well of the Saints</u> and <u>The Playboy of the</u>
<u>Western World</u>.

6   HOGAN, ROBERT, ed. <u>Towards a National Theatre: The Dramatic</u>
<u>Criticism of Frank J. Fay</u>. The Irish Theatre Series 1.
Dublin: Dolmen, pp. 9-10, 106.
    Calls Arthur Griffith "the brilliant editor of <u>The United</u>
<u>Irishman</u> and the formulator of the policy of Sinn Féin."
Cites Frank Fay as the probable author of the statement
that Synge and other Irish writers were led to "work at
writing plays" by the "formation of a company to act plays
by Irish authors...."

7   HOLLOWAY, JOSEPH. <u>Joseph Holloway's Irish Theatre</u>. Vol. 3.
<u>1938-1944</u>. Edited by Robert Hogan and Michael J. O'Neill.
Dixon, California: Proscenium Press, pp. 10, 11, 21, 59,
78, 87, 104.
    Records Richard Best's comments on Synge, among these
that Synge "got his dialect from Dr. Douglas Hyde's translation of <u>Love Songs of Connacht</u> and not from the Aran
people." Of the 1907 performances of <u>The Playboy of the</u>
<u>Western World</u>: "a slice of life drawn direct from nature."
<u>See</u> 1968.15; 1969.5.

8   McMAHON, SEÁN. "Clay and Worms." Éire, 5, no. 4 (Winter), 116-134.

Examines Synge's works in detail to refute the charge that Synge was "morbid."

9   MARCUS, PHILLIP L. Yeats and the Beginning of the Irish Renaissance. Ithaca and London: Cornell University Press, pp. 20, 33, 103, 121, 129, 205-207, 274-275, 280.

Several passing references to Synge define how the controversy over The Playboy of the Western World influenced Yeats's break with the "popular" audience.

10   MIKHAIL, EDWARD HALIM. "Sixty Years of Synge Criticism, 1907-1967: A Selective Bibliography." BB, 27, no. 1 (January-March), 11-13; 27, no. 2 (April-June), 53-56.

Lists books and articles about Synge and divides into the following seven parts: "Bibliographies," "General Studies," "Individual Plays," "Introductions to Editions," "Unpublished Material," "Recordings," and "Background to the Plays."

11   PYLE, HILARY. "J. M. Synge," in Jack B. Yeats: A Biography. London: Routledge & Kegan Paul, pp. 87-99.

Discusses Jack Yeats and Synge in the Congested Districts and several other aspects of their relationship. For example: "Yeats also advised Synge about the jockey costume for Christy Mahon in The Playboy...." In addition, relates an episode in which Synge told of the janitress of the Abbey Theatre calling Synge a "bloody old snot" for having written The Playboy of the Western World with the word "shift."

12   ROBSON, W. W. Modern English Literature. London and New York: Oxford University Press, pp. 54, 59, 107.

Brief comparisons of Synge with Büchner, D. H. Lawrence, and Powys.

13   SALMON, ERIC. "J. M. Synge's Playboy: A Necessary Reassessment." MD, 13, no. 2 (September), 111-128.

Examines in detail six major themes in the work that have been ignored or understated by previous critics and shows how they are embodied in Synge's language: "Only the cultivation of a sensitivity of the same order as that of the play itself can release the explosive and magnificent energies of the Playboy's comic vision and vitality."

1970

14   SMITH, ELTON EDWARD. <u>Louis MacNeice</u>. TEAS, No. 99. New York:
        Twayne, pp. 101, 103.
           Maintains that "It was only through friendship with John
        Millington Synge and a knowledge of his writing that Yeats
        came to appreciate the value of brute vitality...."

15   SULTAN, STANLEY, ed. "Introduction," "Textual Notes," "Glos-
        sary," in <u>J. M. Synge: The Playboy of the Western World</u>.
        Barre, Massachusetts: Imprint Society, pp. 9-42, 121-122,
        123-130, 131-132.
           Maintains: "<u>Playboy</u> seems to me to contain the finest
        dramatic speech of any play in English since the time of
        Shakespeare." Adds: "The present edition of <u>The Playboy
        of the Western World</u> is based on the text registered by the
        Lord Chamberlain's office on April 27, 1907, as that of the
        original production at the Abbey Theatre, which records the
        changes to the play made in production."

16   SWANDER, HOMER D. "Shields at the Abbey: A Friend of Cath-
        leen." <u>Éire</u>, 5, no. 2 (Summer), 25-41.
           Several references to Arthur Shields' playing of Christy
        Mahon, one of the "ten greatest stage performances of mod-
        ern times...."

17   WOLFE, THOMAS. <u>The Notebooks of Thomas Wolfe</u>. Vol. 1.
        Edited by Richard S. Kennedy and Paschal Reeves. Chapel
        Hill: University of North Carolina Press, pp. 13, 113,
        135, 308.
           Demonstrates Wolfe's continuing interest in Synge. An
        entry in Pocket Notebook 2 (October 1926 to September 1927)
        says of <u>The Playboy of the Western World</u>: "The best play
        for poetry...." And in 1928, under "Term Paper, <u>Drama</u>"
        appears this assignment: "Compare the use of suspense,
        irony, and fate in <u>Riders to the Sea</u> with the use of them
        in <u>The Agamemnon</u>...<u>Oedipus the King</u>...or <u>The Trojan
        Women</u>...."

1971

1   ANON. "The 'Ascendancy Writer.'" TLS, no. 2 (July), 749-750.
           Cites the distortions of Synge's life and writings by
        critics, especially those stemming from a view of him as
        an Ascendancy man who lived among the people. Like Chek-
        hov, Synge was more interested in his private vision than
        in naturalistic sketches of peasant life. Reviews several
        books on Synge.

2   BORD FAILTE (IRISH TOURIST BOARD). Ireland of the Welcomes:
     Special John Millington Synge Issue, 19, no. 6 (March-
     April), 35 pp.
        Besides extracts from Synge's works, many photographs,
     and essays on contemporary Inishmaan and Kerry, the issue
     contains articles by Ann Saddlemyer and Lanto Synge. See
     1971.40, 49.

3   CARMODY, TERENCE F. "A Centennial Note: J. M. Synge, 1871-
     1909." Independent Shavian, 9:42.
        Sketches Synge's study of language, trips to the Aran
     Islands, and effects of his early death.

4   CLURMAN, HAROLD. "Theatre." London The Nation (25 January),
     pp. 124-125, 212-214.
        Does not find it surprising that audiences hissed The
     Playboy of the Western World in 1907: "This comedy in
     prose which is sheer poetry is also the sternest realism.
     For an Irishman steeped in his country's myth, the play's
     veracity must prove searing."

5   CORNIER, SIDSEL. John Millington Synge et Arne Garborg.
     L'Homme et son milieu naturel: Agressivité, passivité et
     harmonie. Caen: University of Caen, 199 pp.
        An overview of both authors' lives and works discussing
     such topics as their language and the role of nature in
     their work. Both developed their themes in a "société
     primitive."

6   DEANE, SEAMUS. "Synge's Poetic Use of Language." Mosaic,
     5, no. 1, 27-37.
        Synge's drama "incarnates its meaning in its language,"
     and Deane points out the "various devices of composition"
     by which Synge carries out his purposes.

7   EVERSON, IDA G. "Lennox Robinson and Synge's Playboy (1911-
     1930): Two Decades of American Cultural Growth." NEQ, 44
     (March), 3-21.
        Outlines the gradual acceptance of The Playboy of the
     Western World in America through Robinson's efforts, cul-
     minating in the production of the play by the Amherst
     Masquers in May, 1930.

8   FARRIS, JON R. "The Nature of the Tragic Experience in
     Deirdre of the Sorrows." MD, 14, no. 2 (September), 243-
     251.
        Taking issue with previous critics, who never specific-
     ally defined "tragedy" in the play, Farris holds that the
     "tragic experience" in the work follows from the irony that

1971

> "...Deirdre has a most intense joy in life, and that joy in
> life is to be the very cause of her death...self-fulfill-
> ment is ultimately self-destruction."

9 FERRIS, WILLIAM R., JR. "Folklore and Folklife in the Works
   of John M. Synge." NYFQ, 27, no. 4 (December), 339-356.
        Although the very people for whom Synge revived Irish
   folklore rejected him, "One cannot imagine a more natural
   articulation of folklore in literature than the work of
   Synge."

10 FRENZ, HORST. Eugene O'Neill. Modern Literature Monographs.
    New York: Frederick Ungar, pp. 103-104.
         O'Neill's "farmers, seamen, bums, and prostitutes, like
    the Irish peasants in J. M. Synge, speak a language of
    poetic musicality, full of unexpected naive, oblique images,
    which often fail to crystallize."

11 GERSTENBERGER, DONNA. "Bonnie and Clyde and Christy Mahon:
    Playboys All." MD, 14, no. 2 (September), 227-231.
         Bonnie and Clyde and The Playboy of the Western World
    both center upon the unlikely folk hero who is exalted by
    rural groups: the dispossessed mid-American of the De-
    pression and the deprived people of western Ireland.
    Audiences find both works disturbing, however, because of
    the sudden commingling of comedy and brutality in the two:
    "the greatest shock of recognition for the audience comes
    precisely at the moment of realizing that we who have
    laughed are also guilty."

12 GILL, BRENDAN. "The Theatre: Growing Old." NY, 46 (16 Jan-
    uary), 75.
         Review of the production of The Playboy of the Western
    World at the Repertory Theatre of Lincoln Center. The work
    no longer has the stature it once had: psychoanalysis has
    made Christy's "murder" of his father much less shocking,
    and Synge's diction is contrived, "sedulously cultivated
    lyricism."

13 GREENE, DAVID H. "Books & the Arts: 'That Enquiring Man,
    John Synge.'" London The Nation (30 August), pp. 150-152,
    213-215.
         Looking back over the years, Greene maintains: "It is
    difficult to realize that John Millington Synge was once
    the enfant terrible of Irish letters, considered by many
    of his contemporaries a slanderer of Irish womanhood, a
    Parisian flâneur passing himself off as an interpreter of
    Irish life."

14 _____. "J. M. Synge: A Centenary Appraisal." Éire, 6, no. 4
(Winter), 71-86.
In a paper read at the Synge Centenary Conference in
Dublin, April 27 to May 1, 1971, Green states: Synge's
"influence encouraged Irish dramatists who followed him to
look closely at the realities of Irish life, urban as well
as rural, and to use the poetic resources of the language
to the full."

15 _____. "Synge in the West of Ireland." Mosaic, 5, no. 1,
1-8.
Synge went to the Aran Islands not to discover a language which he already knew, but to enjoy the solitude of
the place, whose topography interested him more than its
inhabitants: "Synge...had nothing to learn from the people [on Aran], any more than Gauguin had in Tahiti. Both
the painter and the writer had brought their European attitudes with them, and the plays which Synge brought out
of Aran are as European as the paintings which Gauguin sent
home from Tahiti."

16 HENN, T. R. "John Millington Synge: A Reconsideration."
Hermathena, 112 (Autumn), 5-21.
A broad view of Synge's plays; the riots over The Playboy of the Western World, which, Henn feels, hastened
Synge's death; Synge's language; and Synge's philosophical
and theological ambivalence: "Behind most of the plays
there is what I would call an epic perspective, hinted at
rather than stated at a number of levels.

17 HEWES, HENRY. "The Theatre: Singed Hero." SatR (23 January), pp. 54, 75-76.
Calls the Lincoln Center presentation of The Playboy
of the Western World "a condemnation of women's compulsion
to destroy the heroes they inspire their men to be."
Scores the "preposterous situation" of the plot.

18 JOCHUM, K. P. S. "Maud Gonne on Synge." Éire, 6, no. 4
(Winter), 65-70.
Includes an obscure assessment of The Playboy of the
Western World written by Maud Gonne, which appeared in
French in Les Entretiens Idéalistes in January 1914. Ms.
Gonne denounced The Playboy of the Western World and felt
that Synge's plays were inferior to Yeats's since Synge
never understood the Irish soul.

1971

19   KALEM, T. E. "The Theatre: Synge's Wake." Time, 97, no. 3
      (18 January), p. 37.
           Criticizes the inept acting at Manhattan's Lincoln Cen-
      ter Repertory Theater: "Lesser and somewhat fragile dramas
      [like The Playboy of the Western World] are bulldozed into
      poetic rubble."

20   KAUFFMAN, STANLEY. "Stanley Kauffman on Theatre: The Playboy
      of the Western World." The New Republic, 164, no. 5
      (30 January), 24, 35.
           Calls the Lincoln Repertory production of The Playboy of
      the Western World "mediocre": "the play lives in its
      words--its Irish words." If the play "no longer looms as
      a major or revolutionary work, it is still a vivid example
      of the ethnic mode that was one way of revolt against the
      commercial theater at the turn of the century." Synge's
      play deals with the "dominant theme of this century--the
      increase of consciousness and its burdens."

21   KENNY, VINCENT S. Paul Green. TUSAS, No. 186. New York:
      Twayne, p. 6.
           Notes a parallel between The Last of the Lowries and
      Riders to the Sea.

22   KILROY, JAMES. The 'Playboy' Riots. The Irish Theatre Series
      4. Dublin: Dolmen, 101 pp.
           Not only reprints important newspaper accounts of the
      Dublin riots over The Playboy of the Western World in 1907,
      but also provides an enlightened commentary on the articles.
      For example, in Kilroy's Conclusion, we find this note:
      "no one seemed to find it either surprising or even amusing
      that when the Abbey company, in 1968, had a special audi-
      ence with the Pope, they presented him with a rare edition,
      bound in white leather of that play which once caused riots:
      The Playboy of the Western World." Reprints 1907.2, 3, 9,
      11, 14, 16, 17-19, 21-23, 28, 29, 32, 34-38, 40.

23   KILROY, THOMAS. "Synge the Dramatist." Mosaic, 5, no. 1,
      9-16.
           Synge's plays, which champion the isolated individual
      in his struggle against the "respectable" establishment,
      are Modernist in nature. Synge was not so much shaped by
      the Irish Theatre, with its late Romanticism, as he was by
      his own instinct for the contemporary: "...Synge's work is
      informed by a radical, anarchic spirit quite unlike any-
      thing in Lady Gregory or Yeats..., whose only counterpart
      is to be found outside Ireland, in the main tradition of
      modern drama."

24   KRAUSE, DAVID. "Sean O'Casey and the Higher Nationalism:
     The Desecration of Ireland's Household Gods," in Theatre
     and Nationalism in Twentieth-Century Ireland. Edited by
     Robert O'Driscoll. Toronto and Buffalo: University of
     Toronto Press, pp. 21-39.
         About the place of the man of genius in society: "Synge
     had raised the whole issue with his very first play...."

25   KROLL, JACK. "Theater: The Old Glory." Newsweek, 77
     (18 January), 79.
         About the Lincoln Center presentation of The Playboy of
     the Western World, calls the work: "a brilliant comedy
     whose humor is present at every moment in every detail...."

26   LEVITT, PAUL M. "The Whole Analysis: Riders to the Sea,"
     in A Structural Approach to the Analysis of Drama. The
     Hague and Paris: Mouton, pp. 84-116.
         An extensive examination of such matters as scene di-
     visions and the purposeful use of stage properties to dem-
     onstrate how "The impression of an unbroken cycle of death
     inevitably working itself out is a direct result of the
     organization of the play."

27   LYDON, J. F. "John Millington Synge: The Man and His Back-
     ground." Mosaic, 5, no. 1, 17-25.
         Traces several influences that allowed Synge to break
     away from his urban, Protestant-Ascendancy background:
     his isolation, his interest in science and in music, his
     loss of faith, and his journeys abroad. Synge's picture
     of the Irish peasant is based upon reality: "Yeats...
     idealised the peasant, having little knowledge of him at
     first hand. Synge did not." Synge's perceptions stemmed
     from his physical closeness to the tramps and mountain men
     of Wicklow.

28   MacANNA, THOMAS. "Nationalism from the Abbey Stage," in
     Theatre and Nationalism in Twentieth-Century Ireland.
     Edited by Robert O'Driscoll. Toronto and Buffalo: Uni-
     versity of Toronto Press, pp. 66-88.
         Comments briefly on Synge's troubles with nationalists:
     "Synge had shown the beautiful Cathleen bereft of green
     cloak and golden crown...."

29   METWALLY, ABDALLA A. "Synge's When the Moon Has Set," in
     Studies in Modern Drama. Vol. 1. Beirut: Beirut Arab
     University, pp. 38-59.
         Argues that in spite of its rejection by Yeats and Lady
     Gregory, "this first play of his holds in embryo the main
     characteristics of his later dramas."

1971

30　MEYER, MICHAEL.　Ibsen: A Biography.　Garden City, New York:
　　　　Doubleday, pp. 58, 273, 656-657.
　　　　　　"Ibsen himself thought Peer Gynt too Norwegian ever to
　　　　be appreciated abroad, much as Synge felt about The Playboy
♦　　　of the Western World...." Says that the two plays have
　　　　much in common, e.g. "their ebullient rhythms and extrava-
　　　　gant imagery."

31　MIKHAIL, E. H.　"Two Aspects of Synge's Playboy."　CLQ, 9,
　　　　no. 6 (June), 322-330.
　　　　　　The two aspects are Synge's "Deliberate Workmanship" in
　　　　the play and the many parallels between the work and Peer
　　　　Gynt.　Both are "pre-eminently occupied with a quest in
　　　　search of Self...."

32　O'DOHERTY, BRIAN.　"Jack B. Yeats: Promise and Regret," in
　　　　Jack B. Yeats: A Centenary Gathering.　The Tower Series
　　　　of Anglo-Irish Studies 3.　Edited by Roger McHugh.　Dublin:
　　　　Dolmen, pp. 86-87.
　　　　　　Complains that "Synge's language has a built-in mirror--
　　　　it is constantly reflecting itself.　It is narcissus lan-
　　　　guage, always regarding its own quirkiness, and is thus
　　　　next door to condescension."

33　O'DRISCOLL, ROBERT, ed.　Theatre and Nationalism in Twentieth-
　　　　Century Ireland.　Toronto and Buffalo: University of
　　　　Toronto Press, pp. 21-39, 66-88, 89-101, 114-133.
　　　　　　See individual entries: 1971.24, 28, 34, 43.

34　_____.　"Two Lectures on the Irish Theatre by W. B. Yeats,"
　　　　in Theatre and Nationalism in Twentieth-Century Ireland.
　　　　Edited by Robert O'Driscoll.　Toronto and Buffalo: Uni-
　　　　versity of Toronto Press, pp. 89-101.
　　　　　　Records Synge once stating to Yeats: "Style is from
　　　　the shock of new material."

35　OLIVER, CAROL HOEG.　"The Art of J. M. Synge: A Develop-
　　　　mental Study."　DAI, 32A:979A.
　　　　　　Concerned more "with the process by which experience
　　　　becomes art than with documentation," this study traces
　　　　polarities throughout Synge's works.

36　ROBINSON, PAUL NEWMAN.　"Medieval Aspects in the Plays of
　　　　John M. Synge."　DAI, 32A:3327A.
　　　　　　Traces relationships of Synge's plays, "especially his
　　　　peasant drama, to themes and attitudes which prevailed in
　　　　Western culture during the Middle Ages." The Playboy of
　　　　the Western World, for example, involves "the theological

justification by medieval theologians who lessen the cul-
pability of sins of passion such as that committed by
Christy Mahon against his father."

37 ROLLINS, RONALD G. "Portraits of Four Irishmen as Artists:
Verisimilitude and Vision." IUR, 1, no. 2, 189-197.
Discusses Synge's use of revealing details in Riders to
the Sea. Also, his stay on the Aran Islands influenced
his view of life as "an attempt by man to find shelter and
sympathy in a lighthouse or cottage on an island that was
constantly being eroded...."

38 RUSSELL, BRENDA LEE. "The Influence of the Saga Tradition on
the Irish Drama: 1900-1920." DAI, 32 A:3328A-29A.
In Deirdre of the Sorrows "the lovers choose death
rather than living on to witness the slow decline of their
passion."

39 SADDLEMYER, ANN. "'Infinite Riches in a Little Room'--The
Manuscripts of John Millington Synge." Long Room [Trinity
College Dublin], 1, no. 3 (Spring), 23-31.
Capitalizing upon Synge's obsession with keeping records of his revisions, article describes the high points
of the Synge holdings at Trinity College, especially the
notebooks. Finds that most of the changes reveal Synge's
emphasis on language, not particularly on characterization. See also 1971.50.

40 _____. "John Millington Synge: Poet and Playwright of the
Western World." Ireland of the Welcomes: Special John
Millington Synge Issue, 19, no. 6 (March-April), 6-12.
Though basically a sketch of Synge's life and works,
the essay does include important photographs of Synge and
his activities. "Synge became a cornerstone in Yeats's
private mythology...."

41 _____, ed. Letters to Molly: John Millington Synge to Maire
O'Neill, 1906-1909. Cambridge: Belknap of Harvard University Press, 330 pp.
Containing approximately four hundred letters, this
volume is an essential source of biographical information
about Synge's last three years. As Ms. Saddlemyer states,
"Here for the first time we are privileged to observe the
whole man." The Introduction traces the role of the various women in Synge's life, cites the influence of Synge's
repressive family, provides detailed background on Molly's
own family, describes troubles in the Abbey acting set
caused by the Molly Allgood--Synge engagement, and fills

1971

in lacunae in Molly's life after Synge's death. Judging
from comments in his letters, Synge thought the debate over
The Playboy of the Western World a "mistake" and the opponents "low ruffians." He was so consumed with his passion
for Molly during the week of the rioting in 1907, however,
that his judgments about crowd reaction to The Playboy of
the Western World are few and perfunctory. See 1974.25.

42   ____, ed. Some Letters of John M. Synge to Lady Gregory and
W. B. Yeats. Selected by Ann Saddlemyer. Dublin: Cuala,
92 pp.
        "The fifty-six letters included in this selection trace
Synge's participation in...theatrical upheavals, from his
first visit to Coole in 1898 and the hesitant enquiries
about his own early submissions, to his final role as resi-
dent director and producer." Last letter is dated 3 January 1909; Synge died on 24 March of this year. An entry
from April, 1905 speaks with reservation of the Mayo people
and might foreshadow his treatment of them in The Playboy
of the Western World. Several entries describe Synge's
difficulties with Deirdre of the Sorrows. In general, this
brief collection contains some material important to an
understanding of Synge's work.

43   ____. "Stars of the Abbey's Ascendancy," in Theatre and
Nationalism in Twentieth-Century Ireland. Edited by Robert
O'Driscoll. Toronto and Buffalo: University of Toronto
Press, pp. 114-133.
        Sees in Christy's constant battles with his "Da" the
"unending struggles of the Irish dramatic movement...."

44   SKELTON, ROBIN. "Introduction" and "Notes on the Text," in
J. M. Synge: Some Sonnets from "Laura in Death" after the
Italian of Francesco Petrarch. Edited by Robin Skelton.
Dublin: Dolmen, pp. 7-23, 24.
        Traces personal influences, especially Synge's dealings
with women, on his translations of Petrarch. Cites the
"strength and delicacy" of Synge's renderings.

45   ____. J. M. Synge and His World. A Studio Book. New York:
Viking, 144 pp.
        Pictorial biography which offers over one hundred photo-
graphs of Synge, his family, his literary associates,
Irish actors, cities and towns where Synge spent his time,
political figures of the day, Synge artifacts (such as his
library cards--on one of which his middle name is mis-
spelled--and his typewriter), a few drafts of his works,
etc. Some of the more important pictures include the

following: an eviction scene, with a battering ram used
against a peasant's cottage; stark pictures of the Aran
Islands, including one of three islanders in a curragh and
another of an old woman sitting next to a cold hearth; a
cabin in Wicklow similar to the one used as the setting
for In the Shadow of the Glen; and several caricatures of
Synge and others around the time of the rioting over The
Playboy of the Western World. Includes a brief chronology
and bibliography, notes on the pictures, and an Index.

46   _____. The Writings of J. M. Synge. Indianapolis and New
      York: Bobbs-Merrill, 190 pp.
          Contains individual chapters on each of Synge's six
      plays, on the early work, on When the Moon Has Set, on The
      Aran Islands, on Synge's verse plays, on the essays, and
      on Synge's poetry. Skelton shows how Synge's early work,
      including When the Moon Has Set, contains all of his later,
      major themes; regards The Aran Islands as expressive of a
      value system found in the plays as well; argues that
      Riders to the Sea was written in part as an antidote to
      Yeats's romanticism and traces, extensively, mythic ele-
      ments in the play; explores In the Shadow of the Glen as
      a precursor to black comedy; views The Tinker's Wedding as
      expressive of the "movements of May" in conflict with the
      Establishment; defines the literary worth of Luasnad, Capa
      and Laine; argues that The Well of the Saints "expresses
      more distinctly than any other of Synge's plays his belief
      in individualism, his distrust of conventional idealism...";
      maintains that Synge, in his essays, believed that Ireland
      could gain universal truth by studying its impoverished
      peasants; examines the use of Christocentric elements in
      The Playboy of the Western World and points out the influ-
      ence of Don Quixote on the work; delineates speech patterns
      in Deirdre of the Sorrows and shows why the play fails
      dramatically, contrasting it with Yeats's Deirdre; and de-
      fines the nature of Synge's persona in his poems while
      tracing elements of his poetry in Yeats's writing. Skelton
      feels that "while J. M. Synge was indeed passionately con-
      cerned with what was essentially Irish, and emotionally
      involved in working for the cultural renaissance of his
      country, his work is, in any serious sense of the word,
      international, for he tackled fundamental crises of the
      human spirit...."

47   STENERSON, DOUGLAS C. H. L. Mencken: Iconoclast from Balti-
      more. Chicago and London: University of Chicago Press,
      pp. 139, 143.

1971

> Points out that Mencken "reserved his greatest enthusi-
> asm for Ibsen, Hauptmann, Sudermann, Wedekind, Andreyev,
> and Synge."

48   STEPHENS, LILO. "Introduction," in J. M. Synge: My Wallet
of Photographs. Arranged and introduced by Lilo Stephens.
Dublin: Dolmen, pp. vii-xvi.
Provides brief notes on the fifty-three pictures in the
collection.

49   SYNGE, LANTO. "'Uncle John.'" Ireland of the Welcomes:
Special John Millington Synge Issue, 19, no. 6 (March-
April), pp. 13-15.
Comments favorably on Synge's religious nature and his
musical abilities. Also, Synge "mixed well and was wel-
comed in any house he visited."

50   TRINITY COLLEGE, DUBLIN. The Synge Manuscripts in the Library
of Trinity College Dublin. Dublin: Dolmen and Trinity
College Library, 56 pp.
Trinity College houses the largest collection of Synge's
worksheets for the plays, letters, other manuscripts,
diaries, etc., and this description is indispensable for
the serious student of Synge. Divides into "Manuscripts
and Typescripts," "Notebooks," "Diaries," and "Correspondence." Contains a short but informative chronology and an
introduction (written by Nicholas Grene) which has an interesting note on the dating of the items. See also:
1971.39.

51   WARNER, ALAN. "Astringent Joy: The Sanity of Synge."
WascanaR, 6:5-13.
Opposes the view that Synge is pessimistic by contrast-
ing Beckett's All That Fall with The Playboy of the Western
World.

52   WILLIAMS, J. E. CAERWYN. "Introduction," in Literature in
Celtic Countries. Edited by J. E. Caerwyn Williams.
Taliesin Congress Lectures. Cardiff: University of
Wales Press, pp. 5-19.
"Synge is remarkable in that he made the attempt to
express the life not of his English-speaking but of his
Irish-speaking compatriots." Finds an analogy in Goethe
for Synge's stress on folk materials.

1972

1 ALEXANDER, JEAN. "Synge's Play of Choice: The Shadow of the Glen," in A Centenary Tribute...Sunshine and the Moon's Delight. Edited by S. B. Bushrui. Foreword by A. Norman Jeffares. New York: Barnes and Noble, pp. 21-31.
Traces the "transformation" of the characters through a reconciliation with Eros and the force of nature: "the play is basically concerned with the acceptance of risk for the sake of vital existence."

2 BERROW, HILARY. "Eight Nights in the Abbey," in J. M. Synge: Centenary Papers 1971. Edited by Maurice Harmon. Preface by Roger McHugh. Dublin: Dolmen, pp. 75-87.
Synthesizes several accounts of the disturbances over The Playboy of the Western World in 1907.

3 BIGLEY, BRUCE MICHAEL. "Perspectivism in Ibsen, Synge, and Hofmannsthal: An Essay in the History of Modern Drama." DAI, 33A:2361A.
Discusses The Playboy of the Western World and Deirdre of the Sorrows in relation to the "shift in mode that occurred in the drama in the decades surrounding 1900...."

4 BLISS, ALAN J. "The Language of Synge," in J. M. Synge: Centenary Papers 1971. Edited by Maurice Harmon. Preface by Roger McHugh. Dublin: Dolmen, pp. 35-62.
Answers the various allegations raised against Synge's use of dialect and maintains: "Synge, like many other writers before him and after him, was creating a special language to suit his special artistic purpose...."

5 _____. "A Synge Glossary," in A Centenary Tribute...Sunshine and The Moon's Delight. Edited by S. B. Bushrui. Foreword by A. Norman Jeffares. New York: Barnes and Noble, pp. 297-316.
"The purpose of this Glossary is to record all the non-Standard words and phrases and all the non-Standard meanings used by J. M. Synge in his Poems and Plays...." Bliss fills in lacunae, corrects previous errors--including an erroneous gloss of a term by Synge himself--and classifies the non-Standard words and usages into seven categories. The 282 head-words in the Glossary are arranged alphabetically; each entry cites the possible derivation of the word and its location in Synge's work.

6 BOGARD, TRAVIS. Contour in Time: The Plays of Eugene O'Neill. New York: Oxford University Press, pp. 119, 234, 419.

1972

Interesting note on the delayed production of The Playboy of the Western World in November, 1911. Also, compares
the language in O'Neill's Hughie to that of Synge's Aran
Islands peasants.

7   BROWN, MALCOLM. The Politics of Irish Literature: From
     Thomas Davis to W. B. Yeats. Seattle: University of
     Washington Press, pp. 11-12, 14, 16, 295, 317, 350, 359,
     365, 383, 389.
          Places The Playboy of the Western World in a cluster of
     five "poetical disputes," and Christy Mahon among the "mad
     peasants" of the early years of the Revival. Speaks of the
     "fresh individuality" of Synge's "Aranman." Finds an his-
     torical allegory of Ireland's rising up in In the Shadow
     of the Glen. And sees in Synge the "profane joy" of
     Stephen Dedalus in A Portrait of the Artist as a Young Man.

8   BUSHRUI, S. B., ed. A Centenary Tribute to John Millington
     Synge, 1871-1909: Sunshine and The Moon's Delight. Fore-
     word by A. Norman Jeffares. New York: Barnes & Noble,
     356 pp.
          Besides the Jeffares Foreword and a "Centennial Poem"
     by Marcus Smith, consists of twenty-two essays on Synge
     and "A Synge Glossary" by Alan Bliss (1972.5). The twenty-
     one page "Select Bibliography" lists standard critical
     books and articles and includes several entries in foreign
     languages. Bushrui's own essay, "Synge and Yeats," shows
     how Synge "entered Yeats's imaginative consciousness and
     became an integral part of it...." See individual entries:
     1972.1, 5, 10, 11, 13, 23, 24, 27, 28, 32, 37, 41, 42, 44,
     46, 47, 50, 53, 59, 64, 67, 69, 72, 76.

9   CASEY, DANIEL J. "An Aran Requiem: Setting in Riders to the
     Sea." AntigR, 9 (Spring), 89-100.
          Discusses elements in the play which make it much more
     than a factual or realistic study of life and death on the
     Aran Islands.

10   CLARK, DAVID R. "Synge's 'Perpetual Last Day': Remarks on
     Riders to the Sea," in A Centenary Tribute...Sunshine and
     The Moon's Delight. Edited by S. B. Bushrui. Foreword by
     A. Norman Jeffares. New York: Barnes & Noble, pp. 41-51.
          Brief discussion of imagery from the Book of Revelation
     in Riders to the Sea, then an examination of critical opin-
     ion which maintains that the play is not classically trag-
     ic but too pathetic. Clark argues that the work does
     indeed have "the tragic rhythm."

11 COXHEAD, ELIZABETH. "Synge and Lady Gregory," in <u>A Centenary</u>
    <u>Tribute...Sunshine and The Moon's Delight</u>. Edited by S. B
    Bushrui. Foreword by A. Norman Jeffares. New York:
    Barnes and Noble, pp. 153-158.
        Lady Gregory must not be regarded as a mere copy of
    Synge but rather as his complement: a playwright in her
    own worthy manner. In fact, the degree of collaboration
    among Irish Renaissance dramatists has been greatly exag-
    gerated. Lady Gregory defended <u>The Playboy of the Western</u>
    <u>World</u> to the height of her abilities even though she dis-
    liked the work: "She was a Victorian, and of her time;
    Synge was an Edwardian, and ahead of his. Christy, the
    Playboy, looks forward to the beatniks and hippies of
    today."

12 DEANE, SEAMUS. "Synge's Poetic Use of Language," in <u>J. M.</u>
    <u>Synge: Centenary Papers 1971</u>. Edited by Maurice Harmon.
    Preface by Roger McHugh. Dublin: Dolmen, pp. 127-144.
        Traces "verbal oppositions" in Synge's work, e.g. those
    in <u>The Well of the Saints</u> "transformed" a "metaphor of de-
    cay" into an "assertion of vitality."

13 DUNCAN, DOUGLAS. "Synge and Jonson (with a parenthesis on
    Ronsard)," in <u>A Centenary Tribute...Sunshine and the Moon's</u>
    <u>Delight</u>. Edited by S. B. Bushrui. Foreword by A. Norman
    Jeffares. New York: Barnes and Noble, pp. 205-218.
        Explores several similarities between Jonson and Synge,
    especially their use of peasant dialect for poetic and
    dramatic purposes. Jonson, however, stressed characteri-
    zation and evolved a distinct idiom for each personage,
    while the language of Synge's peasants is homogeneous. An
    extended comparison between <u>The Tinker's Wedding</u> and <u>Bar-</u>
    <u>tholomew Fair</u> reveals their affinities and differences,
    e.g. "The chief spokesman for the instinctual life is in
    both cases a hard-drinking, pipe-smoking, old woman...."
    The digression concerning Ronsard is meant to show how
    Synge consciously used the poetry of a predecessor, even
    though he did impose upon Ronsard's descriptions of nature
    and the countryside his own artistic and philosophical
    strictures.

14 DURBACH, ERROL. "Synge's Tragic Vision of the Old Mother and
    the Sea." MD, 14, no. 4 (February), 363-372.
        Although Maurya embodies the archetypal figure of the
    <u>Pietà</u>, she is not merely pathetic, but truly tragic. And
    the tragic theme of <u>Riders to the Sea</u> is manifested
    through ironically opposing symbols, with Maurya seen in

1972

part as the sea, which is both the provider and the taker
of life. "The entire play moves...towards a synthetic
vision of existence in which images of life and death in-
termingle in a series of diverse variations." Some of the
antinomial symbols include the spinning wheel, the white
boards, the nets, and the bread.

15 FACKLER, HERBERT VERN. "The Deirdre Legend in Anglo-Irish
Literature, 1834-1937." DAI, 33A (September-October),
1166A.
    Shows how Synge's play is "perhaps the most effective
dramatic treatment" of the Deirdre legend.

16 FLOOD, JEANNE A. "Thematic Variation in Synge's Early Peasant Plays." Éire, 7, no. 3 (Autumn), 72-81.
    Examines several parallels among three plays begun in
1902: Riders to the Sea, In the Shadow of the Glen, and
The Tinker's Wedding. For example, in the first and third
a mother officiates at a major event in a son's life, and
in all three plays there is a contrast between life in
a shelter and life in external nature. In the Shadow of
the Glen partially reconciles the sexual polarities in
the plays between the male figures and the lethal feminine
types.

17 GASKELL, RONALD. "Synge: Riders to the Sea," in Drama and
Reality: The European Theatre since Ibsen. London:
Routledge & Kegan Paul, pp. 99-105.
    Riders to the Sea demonstrates Synge's stress on the
physical, the passionate; yet it rises to a higher, almost
religious plane at its conclusion.

18 GREENE, DAVID H. "J. M. Synge--A Centenary Appraisal," in
J. M. Synge: Centenary Papers 1971. Edited by Maurice
Harmon. Preface by Roger McHugh. Dublin: Dolmen,
pp. 180-196.
    An extensive examination of Synge's prose to shed light
on his enigmatic personality.

19 _____. "Yeats's Prose Style: Some Observations," in Modern
Irish Literature: Essays in Honor of William York Tindall.
Edited by Raymond J. Porter and James D. Brophy. The Library of Irish Studies, No. 1. Iona College Press,
pp. 301-314.
    Mentions Yeats's misunderstanding of the true virtues
of Synge's prose style.

20   HARMON, MAURICE, ed. J. M. Synge: Centenary Papers 1971.
     Foreword by Maurice Harmon. Preface by Roger McHugh.
     Dublin: Dolmen, 215 pp.
        Inspired by the Synge Centenary Commemoration in Dublin
     from April 27 to May 1, 1971, this volume consists of ele-
     ven essays on Synge. See individual entries: 1972.2, 4,
     12, 18, 22, 26, 31, 54, 55, 65, 70.

21   HART, WILLIAM. "Synge's Ideas on Life and Art: Design and
     Theory in The Playboy of the Western World." Yeats Stud-
     ies, 2:35-51.
        Maintains that the "formal design of the Playboy de-
     rives ultimately from a general philosophy of life and art
     which shaped Synge's theory of poetry and drama."

22   HENN, T. R. "The Prose of John Millington Synge," in J. M.
     Synge: Centenary Papers 1971. Edited by Maurice Harmon.
     Preface by Roger McHugh. Dublin: Dolmen, pp. 108-126.
        Shows how Synge's prose style accords with the type of
     subject which moves him, whether it be Synge's description
     of nature or his frequent morbidity.

23   _____. "Riders to the Sea: A Note," in A Centenary Tribute...
     Sunshine and The Moon's Delight. Edited by S. B. Bushrui.
     Foreword by A. Norman Jeffares. New York: Barnes and
     Noble, pp. 33-39.
        Discusses "background" aspects of the Aran Islands,
     Synge's possible use of Biblical imagery, the symbolic
     importance of the physical objects in the cottage, and then
     asks the question: "[W]hy did her [Maurya's] blessing for
     Bartley stick...in her throat.... Is Michael the beloved
     son....?"

24   HOGAN, ROBERT. "The Influence of Synge in Modern Irish
     Drama," in A Centenary Tribute...Sunshine and The Moon's
     Delight. Edited by S. B. Bushrui. Foreword by A. Norman
     Jeffares. New York: Barnes and Noble, pp. 231-244.
        Criticizes the bland treatment of Synge's plays in re-
     cent years and argues for a fidelity in the production of
     his works which "throws into bold relief the sensuality
     of the plays and their grotesquerie." Traces the influen-
     ces of Synge--admittedly tenuous--upon George Fitzmaurice,
     Bryan MacMahon, Michael J. Molloy, and (in his first three
     plays) John B. Keane. Today, "perhaps it does not matter
     if Synge's manner be lost.... It is only the richness and
     joy that matter, and in those qualities Synge has given
     his real legacy to the men who came after."

1972

25   HULL, KEITH N. "Nature's Storms and Stormy Natures in Synge's
      <u>Aran Islands</u>." <u>Éire</u>, 7, no. 3 (Autumn), 63-71.
           Synge's Aran Islanders are far from simplistic. His
      book reveals their mystical relationship with nature, which
      is often characterized by their fear of its hostility;
      their stress on passion; the complexity of their attempts
      to counter their fate; and their sometime cruelty, which
      arises when the unity between them and nature is temporar-
      ily abrogated.

26   HUNT, HUGH. "Synge and the Actor--A Consideration of Style,"
      in <u>J. M. Synge: Centenary Papers 1971</u>. Edited by Maurice
      Harmon. Preface by Roger McHugh. Dublin: Dolmen,
      pp. 63-74.
           Discusses such issues as the initial difficulty of the
      Irish Players in speaking Synge's lines and the "violence"
      of the speech.

27   JEFFARES, A. NORMAN. "Foreword," in <u>A Centenary Tribute...</u>
      <u>Sunshine and The Moon's Delight</u>. Edited by S. B. Bushrui.
      New York: Barnes and Noble, pp. 9-15.
           Discusses the complexities of Synge's family life, es-
      pecially those surrounding his mother.

28   KAIN, RICHARD M. "The <u>Playboy</u> Riots," in <u>A Centenary Trib-</u>
      <u>ute...Sunshine and The Moon's Delight</u>. Edited by S. B.
      Bushrui. Foreword by Norman A. Jeffares. New York:
      Barnes and Noble, pp. 173-188.
           Summarizes views (both favorable and unfavorable) of
      <u>The Playboy of the Western World</u> following its presenta-
      tion at the Abbey Theatre by examining the chief newspapers
      and periodicals of the time: "the...reviews and notes are
      taken from a scrap-book of clippings, original ownership
      unknown, now in the author's [Kain's] possession." The
      clippings deal with the calling in of the police to insure
      a hearing for <u>The Playboy of the Western World</u>, William
      Boyle's withdrawing of his plays from the Abbey, the sur-
      prisingly large number of defenses of Synge's play and
      other events.

29   KEE, ROBERT. <u>The Green Flag: The Turbulent History of the</u>
      <u>Irish National Movement</u>. New York: Delacorte Press,
      p. 452.
           Describes Griffith as often grim, and, citing as an
      example his opposition to <u>In the Shadow of the Glen</u> and
      <u>The Playboy of the Western World</u>, says, "it is difficult
      to resist the impression...that he was sometimes narrow-
      minded and lacking in humour and that his one great

characteristic was his relentless doggedness." In his
quarrel with Synge and Yeats "he emerges poorly as a puri-
tanical critic...."

30 KELLOGG, CHARLES ALFRED. "Ambiguity of Tone in the Plays of
    J. M. Synge." DAI, 33A:2380A.
        Traces Synge's ambiguous judgmental tone to show the re-
    lationship between the structure of his works and his lit-
    erary theory.

31 KILROY, THOMAS. "Synge and Modernism," in J. M. Synge: Cen-
    tenary Papers 1971. Edited by Maurice Harmon. Preface by
    Roger McHugh. Dublin: Dolmen, pp. 167-179.
        Argues that Synge "cannot be simply accommodated within
    the early Abbey Theatre Movement and left there"; nor can
    he be placed without some squeezing into "the wider tradi-
    tion of modern European drama."

32 KLEINSTÜCK, JOHANNES. "Synge in Germany," in A Centenary
    Tribute...Sunshine and The Moon's Delight. Edited by S. B.
    Bushrui. Foreword by A. Norman Jeffares. New York:
    Barnes and Noble, pp. 271-277.
        Even though The Well of the Saints was produced in Ber-
    lin as early as 1906, as part of a reaction against Natu-
    ralism, Synge's works are not well known in Germany today.
    Difficulties reside in the inability of the Germans to
    translate Synge's idiom and the Socialists' use of Synge's
    works as anti-fascist propaganda, e.g. as in Brecht's Die
    Gewehre, which distorts Synge's Riders to the Sea. The
    East Berlin translation of The Playboy of the Western
    World, for instance, emphasizes Christy as killer and in-
    terprets Pegeen's closing words to mean that the last mur-
    derer in the West is now gone and that an era of peace
    will come about.

33 KOPPER, EDWARD A., JR. "Lady Gregory and Finnegans Wake."
    WN, NS 9, no. 6 (December), 103-107.
        Lists several references to The Playboy of the Western
    World, to Riders to the Sea, and to the Fay Brothers in
    Finnegans Wake. Maintains that the famous Letter of the
    Wake is, on one level, "a missive sent to Yeats from Lady
    Gregory as she escorted the Irish players through America
    during the Playboy riots in the season of 1911-12."

34 KRAUSE, DAVID. "The Barbarous Sympathies of Antic Irish
    Comedy." MHRev, 22 (April), 99-117.
        Knowing intuitively what Freud defined explicitly, the
    skeptical Synge was "attracted to precisely those wild

1972

pagan customs which he had been conditioned by his religion
to fear." Discusses the Satanic and profane joy in Synge's
plays. Christy Mahon and his "comically barbaric va-
grants...pursue their liberating sins with unrepentent high
spirit and low comic rebellion."

35 LAURENCE, DAN H., ed. <u>Bernard Shaw: Collected Letters, 1898-
1910</u>. New York: Dodd, Mead, pp. 453, 714, 861.
Includes a pejorative comment on the acting of <u>The Playboy of the Western World</u> at the Great Queen Street Theatre
on June 10, 1907.

36 LEBLANC, GÉRARD. "Ironic Reversal as Theme and Technique in
Synge's Shorter Comedies," in <u>Aspects of the Irish Theatre</u>.
Cahiers Irlandais 1. Edited by Patrick Rafroidi, Raymonde
Popot, and William Parker. Paris: University of Lille,
pp. 51-63.
Examines such elements as antithesis and "antinomic
worlds" in <u>In the Shadow of the Glen</u> and <u>The Tinker's
Wedding</u>, "whose concentration and single-mindedness make
even clearer the interplay of dramatic gestures, attitudes
and speech which is the core of the pattern of reversal."
Although Synge begins a "new kind of drama," his work
"simply moves on and stops, leaving all ambiguities and
tensions unresolved."

37 _____. "Synge in France," in <u>A Centenary Tribute...Sunshine
and The Moon's Delight</u>. Edited by S. B. Bushrui. Foreword by A. Norman Jeffares. New York: Barnes and Noble,
pp. 265-270.
The influence of Synge in France has been slight, with
only <u>Deirdre of the Sorrows</u> and <u>The Playboy of the Western
World</u> arousing any significant attention. French produc-
ers of the former capture mainly the dreaminess and mist
which they think Ireland consists of, and they often turn
characters in the latter into buffoons or dull rustics.
All translations of Synge are out of print in France.

38 LERNER, LAURENCE. "Homage to Synge." <u>Encounter</u>, 38, no. 1
(January), 62-67.
Reviews several books on Synge. "And in these days,
when we are told on all sides that true art is revolutionary...it should give us pause to remember that the
police were called to the Abbey Theatre to give a great
dramatist a hearing against the yells of popular frenzy."

39 McHUGH, ROGER. "Theatre: The Synge Centenary." Art in Amer-
ca, 60 (March-April), 90-93.
    Has several photos of the centenary celebration produc-
    tions of Synge's work at the Abbey Theatre, including one
    of The Tinker's Wedding.

40 McMAHON, SEÁN. "The Road to Glenmalure." Éire, 7, no. 1
(Spring), 142-151.
    By using such source material as Irish topography and
    Synge's prose writings, McMahon traces the "path along
    which Synge journeyed to reach the cottage of Dan and Nora
    Burke...."

41 MALEH, GHASSAN. "Synge in the Arab World," in A Centenary
Tribute...Sunshine and The Moon's Delight. Edited by S. B.
Bushrui. Foreword by A. Norman Jeffares. New York:
Barnes and Noble, pp. 245-252.
    Arab translators of Synge's plays see an affinity be-
    tween the Aran World and Ireland during its Renaissance:
    engagement in a "struggle for freedom, unity and national
    identity." Synge's language, however, has often been mis-
    construed. One Arab translator, for example, uses the
    title "The Spoilt Youth of the West" for his version of
    The Playboy of the Western World.

42 MARTIN, AUGUSTINE. "Christy Mahon and the Apotheosis of Lone-
liness," in A Centenary Tribute...Sunshine and The Moon's
Delight. Edited by S. B. Bushrui Foreword by A. Norman
Jeffares. New York: Barnes and Noble, pp. 61-73.
    Christy's leaving Mayo and Pegeen at the end of The
    Playboy of the Western World represents a victory of the
    Dionysiac view of life over the Apollonian, his "escape to
    freedom between the Scylla and Charybdis of loneliness on
    the one hand and domination on the other." Martin defines
    three groups of characters in the play by the Apollonian
    vs. Dionysiac polarities. Christy's departure with his
    father, for example, embodies his rejection of the "pseudo-
    Dionysian Michael James."

43 MEDINE, PATRICIA DAVIS. "The Art of John Millington Synge."
DAI, 32A (May-June), 6937A.
    Analyzes the techniques used by Synge to render the
    "'mysterious external world' in an intensely personal ex-
    pression...."

1972

44   MERCIER, VIVIAN. "The Tinker's Wedding," in A Centenary Trib-
      ute...Sunshine and The Moon's Delight. Edited by S. B.
      Bushrui. Foreword by A. Norman Jeffares. New York:
      Barnes and Noble, pp. 75-89.
          The play is marred by the tinkers' violent treatment of
      the priest--who is basically sympathetic, though not overly
      intelligent--and the audience, contrary to Synge's inten-
      tion, is forced to regard him as a martyr and to lose sym-
      pathy with the tinkers. Essay also discusses prelapsarian
      symbolism in The Tinker's Wedding and in The Well of the
      Saints and the distance between Dublin audiences and the
      rural fictional characters of Synge's plays.

45   MIKHAIL, E. H. A Bibliography of Modern Irish Drama, 1899-
      1970. Foreword by William A. Armstrong. Seattle: Uni-
      versity of Washington Press, 62 pp., passim.
          Lists books, periodicals, etc. which treat Irish writers
      generally. Though few entries refer to Synge by name, he
      is of course considered in many of the entries. Listing is
      alphabetical, according to the critics' names.

46   MOORE, JOHN REES. "Synge's Deirdre and the Sorrows of Mortal-
      ity," in A Centenary Tribute...Sunshine and The Moon's
      Delight. Edited by S. B. Bushrui. Foreword by A. Norman
      Jeffares. New York: Barnes and Noble, pp. 91-105.
          The heroine's "passionate conviction that something
      within her is not dust" causes her to vibrate "in tragic
      tension."

47   MUNROE, JOHN. "J. M. Synge and the Drama of the Late Nine-
      teenth Century," in A Centenary Tribute...Sunshine and The
      Moon's Delight. Edited by S. B. Bushrui. Foreword by A.
      Norman Jeffares. New York: Barnes and Noble, pp. 219-230.
          In their "simplicity," necessitated by the physical re-
      strictions of the Irish Theatre itself, and in their
      stress upon the inner person, Synge's plays differ from
      the elaborate productions of the late nineteenth century
      English theater. Synge offers an alternative to the arti-
      ficiality of nineteenth century "closet" drama and the
      reductionism of Naturalism.

48   NASH, VINCENT. "The Well of the Saints: Language in a Land-
      scape." LWU, 5:267-276.
          Argues that the meaning of the play is much more com-
      plex than the simple opposition of helpful illusion to un-
      pleasant reality.

1972

49   O'BRIEN, CONOR CRUISE. States of Ireland. New York: Random
      House, Pantheon Books, pp. 52, 71-74.
          Includes a lengthy comment on six groups of people in
      The Playboy of the Western World, considered alphabetic-
      cally.

50   O'DRISCOLL, ROBERT. "Yeats's Conception of Synge," in A Cen-
      tenary Tribute...Sunshine and The Moon's Delight. Edited
      by S. B. Bushrui. Foreword by A. Norman Jeffares. New
      York: Barnes and Noble, pp. 159-171.
          Synge inspired Yeats by his ability to reconcile the
      spiritual and the physical worlds, and the "tragic ecstasy
      that Yeats saw in Synge's life and work is closely linked
      in Yeats's mind with his concept of the mask...." Yeats
      felt that Synge's high passions found an objective cor-
      relative in the externals of the Aran Islands. Synge be-
      came for Yeats a symbol of the self-sufficient artist, "an
      apocalyptic agent...a perfect symbolist, an artist who used
      the external world to express subjective moods."

51   OREL, HAROLD. "Synge's Concept of the Tramp." Éire, 7, no. 2
      (Summer), 55-61.
          Relates Synge and his characters to the vagrants of the
      Victorian Age, i.e. to Arnold's scholar-gypsy.

52   ORR, ROBERT H. "The Surprise Ending: One Aspect of J. M.
      Synge's Dramatic Technique." ELT, 15:105-115.
          Maintains that the surprise endings in Synge's plays
      are artistically justified and come from the confrontation
      between the "affirming temperament" and the "restrictive...
      one."

53   OSHIMA, SHOTARO. "Synge in Japan," in A Centenary Tribute...
      Sunshine and The Moon's Delight. Edited by S. B. Bushrui.
      Foreword by A. Norman Jeffares. New York: Barnes and
      Noble, pp. 253-263.
          Cites translations of Synge's works in Japanese and ac-
      counts for the popularity of each. For example, The Play-
      boy of the Western World "moves us in Japan through its
      vigorous and effective atmosphere."

54   ÓSÚILLEABHÁIN, SEÁN. "Synge's Use of Irish Folklore," in
      J. M. Synge: Centenary Papers 1971. Edited by Maurice
      Harmon. Preface by Roger McHugh. Dublin: Dolmen,
      pp. 18-34.
          Discusses specific elements of Irish folklore in Synge's
      work such as Heroic Tale-Types and Motifs and concludes,

1972

"Synge has emerged as a reliable collector of traditional
lore in the course of his visits to parts of Wicklow,
Kerry, Galway, and Mayo."

55 Ó TUAMA, SEÁN. "Synge and the Idea of a National Literature,"
in J. M. Synge: Centenary Papers 1971. Edited by Maurice
Harmon. Preface by Roger McHugh. Dublin: Dolmen,
pp. 1-17.
    Discusses elements of true Irish life that Synge has
incorporated into his plays, e.g. the fatalism of Maurya,
and finds "highly successful" Synge's "attempt to recreate
West of Ireland life...." Maintains that "Synge is possi-
bly the only major writer of the Anglo-Irish nation to have
achieved satisfactory identification with the historic
Irish ethos."

56 PALMER, D. J. "Drama," in The Twentieth-Century Mind: History, Ideas, and Literature in Britain. Edited by C. B.
Cox and A. E. Dyson. Vol. 1: 1900-1918. London and New
York: Oxford University Press, pp. 447-474.
    Synge is the "one dramatist of European stature produced
by the Irish theatre," and even he wrote only "one undoubted masterpiece [The Playboy of the Western World]."

57 POLLARD, M., comp. "International Association for the Study
of Anglo-Irish Literature: Bibliography Bulletin." IUR,
2, no. 1, 79-110.
    The first publication of a project begun in 1970.
Listings are for the most part under individual authors,
though publication does contain much "general" information.
For example, under the heading "Ireland 1970," we find
"Irish Bibliographical Aids." Articles on Synge appear in
Arabic, Gaelic, and Japanese. As M. Pollard, Chairman of
the IASAIL subcommittee, states, "It is the aim of this
subcommittee to produce an annual bibliography listing
every publication concerned with Anglo-Irish literature
which has appeared during the previous year." Pollard admits stressing more arcane criticism in this, the first
issue, but hopes in the future to include more English and
American sources of criticism. At the time of this writing, this indispensable research tool had appeared three
times.

58 PORTER, RAYMOND J. "Language and Literature in Revival Ireland: The Views of P. H. Pearse," in Modern Irish Literature: Essays in Honor of William York Tindall. Edited by
Raymond J. Porter and James D. Brophy. The Library of
Irish Studies, No. 1. New York: Iona College Press,
pp. 195-214.

1972

Discusses Pearse's attitude towards The Playboy of the Western World. Though more enlightened than most of his contemporaries, Pearse attacked the work on a moral basis and spoke of Synge as possessing "a sort of Evil Spirit..." which was "called into existence" by the Irish dramatic movement. See 1973.13.

59   PRICE, ALAN. "A Survey of Recent Work on J. M. Synge," in A Centenary Tribute...Sunshine and The Moon's Delight. Edited by S. B. Bushrui. Foreword by A. Norman Jeffares. New York: Barnes and Noble, pp. 279-296.
An analysis of full length books on Synge and collections of his works, and a survey of such critical issues as Synge's use of myth, his place in playwriting tradition, and his relationship with other writers. Price laments that Ireland itself has produced so few critical appraisals of Synge and that assessments of Synge's works tend to be scattered.

60   RAJAN, BALACHANDRA. "Yeats, Synge, and the Tragic Understanding." Yeats Studies, 2:66-79.
Summarizes the use of the Deirdre legend by AE, Lady Gregory, Yeats, and Synge and goes on to maintain that Synge's "effort is to state within the particularities of human joy and loss what are for him the cadences of being."

61   REID, ALEC. "Comedy in Synge and Beckett." Yeats Studies, 2:80-90.
Points out several external similarities between the two and maintains that in both Synge and Beckett "the double vision of the comic writer goes hand in hand with the tragic poet's demand for our emotional involvement."

62   REYNOLDS, LORNA. "The Rhythms of Synge's Dramatic Prose." Yeats Studies, 2:52-65.
A detailed scansion of Synge's language patterns in relation to the Elizabethans and to the Authorized Version of the Bible.

63   ROY, EMIL. "J. M. Synge," in British Drama Since Shaw. Carbondale and Edwardsville: Southern Illinois University Press; London and Amsterdam: Feffer & Simons, pp. 54-67.
Approaches Synge's works psychoanalytically, pointing out, for example, the "culinary metaphors" in Synge's Prefaces. Cites the renunciation of "heterosexual love for homoerotic competition" by Synge's "more vigorous males." Sees in the "alcoholic fantasies" of Synge's weaker male characters a parallel with life in the womb.

1972

And discusses the complexity of characterization in The
Playboy of the Western World and in Deirdre of the Sorrows.

64 SADDLEMYER, ANN. "Art, Nature, and 'The Prepared Personality':
    A Reading of The Aran Islands and Related Writings," in A
    Centenary Tribute...Sunshine and The Moon's Delight.
    Edited by S. B. Bushrui. Foreword by A. Norman Jeffares.
    New York: Barnes and Noble, pp. 107-120.
       Details the "systematic arrangement" of Synge's prose.
    Synge was influenced "by the aesthetic doctrines of...
    great nineteenth century synthesizers...." His final
    theories, however, were formed of his own blending of
    life's contrasting elements.

65 _____. "Deirdre of the Sorrows: Literature First...Drama
    Afterwards," in J. M. Synge: Centenary Papers 1971.
    Edited by Maurice Harmon. Preface by Roger McHugh. Dub-
    lin: Dolmen, pp. 88-105.
       Sketches the background of Deirdre of the Sorrows in
    Synge's last days and traces the theme of time's passing
    in the play. The work is "a twilight play, beginning in
    the darkness of storm clouds and ending in the stillness
    of death."

66 _____. "Synge and Some Companions, with a Note Concerning a
    Walk Through Connemara with Jack Yeats." Yeats Studies,
    2:18-34.
       Details the development of the Synge myth then goes on
    to point out affinities between Synge and Jack Yeats, e.g.
    their love of western Ireland.

67 SIDNELL, M. J. "The Well of the Saints and the Light of This
    World," in A Centenary Tribute...Sunshine and The Moon's
    Delight. Edited by S. B. Bushrui. Foreword by A. Norman
    Jeffares. New York: Barnes and Noble, pp. 53-59.
       Defines the complexity of the blindness motif in the
    play, finding analogues in Tiresias, Oedipus, and Glouces-
    ter.

68 SKELTON, ROBIN. J. M. Synge. The Irish Writers Series.
    Lewisburg, Pennsylvania: Bucknell University Press, 89 pp.
       General view of Synge's works which discusses such is-
    sues as his rejection by women--seen in his early work;
    Synge's theme of Irish "cultural confusion," in all the
    plays; his view of the vagrant, expressed especially in
    In the Shadow of the Glen; the "rebellious mother" motif,
    seen most clearly in Sarah Casey; and Christocentric sym-
    bolism and Synge's visit to the Congested Districts as

1972

background materials for <u>Riders to the Sea</u>. About Synge's verse: "Synge's own personal experience was as much central to his mature plays as it was to his earliest works, and it was at the very heart of all his poetry." And of Synge's contemporary significance: "The tinkers of Synge's plays are...dropouts."

69 SMITH, MARCUS. "Centennial Poem," in <u>A Centenary Tribute...</u> <u>Sunshine and The Moon's Delight</u>. Edited by S. B. Bushrui. Foreword by A. Norman Jeffares. New York: Barnes and Noble, p. 19.
Sees Synge as an enduring presence.

70 STALLWORTHY, JON. "The Poetry of Synge and Yeats," in <u>J. M.</u> <u>Synge: Centenary Papers 1971</u>. Edited by Maurice Harmon. Preface by Roger McHugh. Dublin: Dolmen, pp. 145-166.
Sketches the background of Synge's poems from their beginnings. About the influence of Synge on Yeats: "When Synge the poet showed Yeats the way forward into his later style, he was but redirecting him along a road he had already taken under guidance from Synge the playwright."

71 STARKIE, WALTER. "Memories of John Synge and Jack Yeats." <u>Yeats Studies</u>, 2:91-99.
These memories of a "declining septuagenarian" portray Synge as a "lonely man" and as a "man of mystery" who provided Starkie with the "most exciting experience" of his youth, the 1907 production of <u>The Playboy of the Western</u> <u>World</u>. Reprints with slight revision 1963.10. Reprinted: 1977.7.

72 SYNGE, LANTO M. "The Autobiography of J. M. Synge," in <u>A</u> <u>Centenary Tribute...Sunshine and The Moon's Delight</u>. Edited by S. B. Bushrui. Foreword by A. Norman Jeffares. New York: Barnes and Noble, pp. 121-140.
Examines Synge's views of nature, religion, and music to show that the <u>Autobiography</u> "is among his most interesting works."

73 TÁKACS, DALMA SAROLTA. "J. M. Synge as a Dramatist." DAI, 32A (May-June), 6457A.
Synge's interest in his plays is not in ideas but in human beings; his stress on characterization makes his works universal.

74 TANIGUCHI, JIRO. "Critical Analysis of Dialogue in Synge's Plays" and "Explanatory Notes," in <u>A Grammatical Analysis</u> <u>of Artistic Representation of Irish English, with a Brief</u>

1972

Discussion of Sounds and Spelling. Revised and enlarged
edition. Tokyo: Shinozaki Shorin, pp. 286-309, 310-377.
    Provides a detailed scansion of Synge's plays plus
charts detailing such matters as "Types of Feet" and "Total
of Feet Syllable." References to Synge are scattered
throughout the book.

75 TRACY, ROBERT. "Ireland: The Patriot Game," in The Cry of
    Home: Cultural Nationalism and the Modern Writer. Edited
    by H. Ernest Lewald. Knoxville: University of Tennessee
    Press, pp. 39-57.
        Compares Brendan Behan's sympathy for the criminal to
    the Aran Islanders' compassion for the hunted man, as re-
    told by Synge's accounts of his visits there.

76 WARNER, FRANCIS. "A Note on the Poems of J. M. Synge," in A
    Centenary Tribute...Sunshine and The Moon's Delight.
    Edited by S. B. Bushrui. Foreword by A. Norman Jeffares.
    New York: Barnes and Noble, pp. 141-152.
        Discounts the importance of Synge's poems while comment-
    ing on their simplicity of diction and their theme of the
    contrast between love and death.

77 WHITAKER, THOMAS R. "Notes on Playing the Player." CentR,
    16, no. 1, 1-23.
        Comments on audience-player interaction in The Playboy
    of the Western World.

                              1973

1 ECKLEY, GRACE. "Truth at the Bottom of a Well: Synge's The
    Well of the Saints." MD, 16, no. 2 (September), 193-198.
        The play expresses the dual truth that self-realization
    is more important than physical appearance and that a short
    life lived intensely surpasses a long and weary existence.
    "To parallel Martin's self-assertion in Lucifer-like re-
    bellion, Mary Doul establishes her own kingdom of the
    mind...." "...Synge combines in this one play the symbols
    of holy water on the eyes and reflective water in a pool
    to develop his preference for confronting one's fate in
    one's own fashion and in a short, full life...."

2 FERRAR, HAROLD. Denis Johnston's Irish Theatre. The Irish
    Theatre Series 5. Dublin: Dolmen, pp. 7, 8, 17, 21, 131.
        Denis Johnston "has superbly heeded Synge's famous plea:
    'On the stage one must have reality, and one must have
    joy.'"

3   FOSTER, LESLIE D. "Heroic Strivings in <u>The Playboy of the</u>
     <u>Western World</u>." <u>Éire</u>, 8, no. 1 (Spring), 85-94.
          Although Christy is definitely not a Christ figure, he
     is in many respects an epic or national hero, whether
     ironic or not; and Synge lends the play epic stature in
     part by his emphasis on geographic directions--north,
     south, east, and west.

4   GARDNER, PHILIP. <u>Norman Nicholson</u>. TEAS, No. 153. New York:
     Twayne, pp. 113, 121.
          Notes the importance of Nicholson's admiration for
     Synge's "dramatic language."

5   KENT, CONSTANCE KEMLER. "Stasis and Silence: A Study of
     Certain Symbolist Tendencies in the Modern Theatre." DAI,
     34A (December), 3404A-405A.
          Examines Synge's use of symbolism to augment his belief
     that drama must be both "poetic" and "true."

6   LARKIN, PHILIP, comp. "J. M. Synge: 1871-1909," in <u>The Ox-</u>
     <u>ford Book of Twentieth-Century English Verse</u>. London:
     Oxford University Press, Clarendon Press, p. 106.
          Includes "A Question" and "Winter: With Little Money
     in a Great City."

7   LAUTERBACH, EDWARD S. and W. EUGENE DAVIS. "John Millington
     Synge," in <u>The Transitional Age: British Literature,</u>
     <u>1880-1920</u>. Troy, New York: Whitston Publishing Company,
     p. 285.
          Lists fifteen critical works on Synge and gives a brief
     summary of his importance, with the somewhat safe state-
     ment that his plays "now are ranked among the finest of
     the first decade of the Abbey Theatre...."

8   LEECH, CLIFFORD. "John Synge and the Drama of His Time."
     MD, 16, nos. 3 and 4 (December), 223-237.
          Comments on the relationship between the dialogue of
     Synge's plays and the Anglo-Irish language of the time.
     Emphasizes the "harshness" of Synge's works by discussing
     links between the plays and points out analogues between
     Synge and dramatists outside Ireland and Britain. "Synge
     is...our only twentieth-century playwright in the English
     language who has given us, with high authority, the accent
     of country life."

1973

9   MICHIE, DONALD M. "Synge and His Critics." MD, 15, no. 4
     (March), 427-431.
         Examines chronologically stages of critical opinion con-
     cerning Synge's worth: the early years, when Synge was
     attacked by the Nationalists, overly praised by Yeats, and
     treated as an established writer in Europe; the reaction
     against the adulation of Synge in the twenties; the bal-
     anced view of Synge in the thirties and the forties; and
     the present interest in Synge, which is due to the revived
     interest in Yeats's plays: "Scholars' present assessment
     of Synge is that he is one of the best dramatists that
     Ireland has produced, but that he must necessarily be clas-
     sified as a minor playwright...."

10   MORRIS, ALTON C., BIRON WALKER, and PHILIP BRADSHAW, eds.
     "John Millington Synge, The Playboy of the Western World,"
     in Imaginative Literature: Fiction, Drama, Poetry. Second
     edition. Chicago, San Francisco, Atlanta: Harcourt,
     Brace, and Jovanovich, pp. 220-221.
         Points out that : "In a reader survey reported in the
     London Observer in 1966, The Playboy of the Western World
     was included as one of the twenty plays written since 1900
     in which the main trends of the theater in this century
     could be most clearly discerned."

11   MURPHY, SHEILA ANN. "A Political History of the Abbey Thea-
     tre." Literature and Ideology, 16:53-60.
         Passing reference to Annie Horniman's intention to build
     the Abbey Theatre around Yeats--not Synge.

12   O'CASEY, EILEEN. Sean. Edited with an Introduction by J. C.
     Trewin. London: Pan Books, pp. xvi, 31-32, 258.
         In her single days, Mrs. O'Casey acted as a keener in
     Riders to the Sea. O'Casey himself called the play, to
     quote his wife: "a lovely melody of pain...."

13   PORTER, RAYMOND J. P. H. Pearse. TEAS, No. 154. New York:
     Twayne, pp. 54-56.
         Repeats Pearse's lengthy comment about The Playboy of
     the Western World. See 1972.58.

14   REYNOLDS, LORNA. "Collective Intellect: Yeats, Synge and
     Nietzsche." E&S, 26:83-98.
         Yeats saw Synge as the ideal artist in Nietzsche's con-
     ception of life as drama.

1973

15 RODGERS, W. R., ed. "J. M. Synge," in <u>Irish Literary Por-</u>
<u>traits</u>. Introduction by Conor Cruise O'Brien. New York:
Taplinger, pp. 94-115.
First broadcast in 1952, the article contains some im-
portant biographical details provided by Synge's nephew,
Edward Stephens, by Oliver Gogarty, by the publisher George
Roberts, and by others. Roberts discusses how his printer
begged him to omit the word "bloody" from the edition of
<u>The Playboy of the Western World</u>. Roberts also adds
some important data about the physical danger to Synge of
his being in the theater during the riots over this play.
Reprinted: 1977.7.

16 SKELTON, ROBIN. "J. M. Synge." EDH, 37:95-107.
Synge's works reflect his personal life, his own rebellion against middle class values.

17 WARNER, ALAN. <u>Clay is the Word: Patrick Kavanagh, 1904-1967</u>.
Dublin: Dolmen, pp. 28, 30, 81, 82, 101, 117.
Cites Kavanagh's attacks on Synge, which led him to
speak of the "atrocious formula" of Synge's dialogue and
to see Synge as motivated by hate. To Kavanagh: "One
phrase of Joyce is worth all Synge as far as giving us the
cadence of Irish speech...."

18 WEBSTER, BRENDA S. <u>Yeats: A Psychoanalytic Study</u>. Stanford,
California: Stanford University Press, pp. 125-126, 156,
212, 219-220.
"It was the 'energy and abundance' he [Yeats] saw in
Synge that provided Yeats with a balance to sterility in
both literature and politics." And: "Yeats transformed
his sense of loss and pain at Synge's approaching death
into a concern that Synge might not be able to finish his
last play."

19 WINTERS, YVOR. <u>Yvor Winters: Uncollected Essays and Reviews</u>.
Edited and introduced by Francis Murphy. Chicago: The
Swallow Press, pp. 147-148, 259-260.
In 1929, Winters described <u>In the Shadow of the Glen</u> and
<u>Deirdre of the Sorrows</u> in terms of a shifting of "moods"
typical of an Elizabethan Age work. These realignments
occur within and among groups of characters. For example,
in the opening of <u>In the Shadow of the Glen</u> Nora and Michael are pitted against Dan and the Tramp, a pattern
which changes by the end of the play. In 1933, Winters
wrote: "Synge is largely disappointing, however...like
most prose-poets and some other poets, he dilutes his perception with a vast excess of mannerism...."

1973

20 WINZELER, CHARLOTTE M. "The 1910 'Ghost Edition' of Synge's
    Plays." Library, 28, no. 2 (June), 158-159.
       By examining the holdings at Lilly Library, provides
    evidence that there never was a 1910 single-volume edition
    of Synge's plays.

1974

1   BLOTNER, JOSEPH. Faulkner: A Biography. Vol. 1. New York:
    Random House, pp. 208, 331-332; Vol. 2, pp. 1003, 2087.
       Faulkner could quote Synge from memory and argued that
    his strength came in part from his depiction of a definite
    "locality." Faulkner compared The Emperor Jones to The
    Playboy of the Western World. Included among the books
    that Faulkner bought for the winter of 1938 were Synge's
    complete works.

2   DITSKY, JOHN M. "All Irish Here: The 'Irishman' in Modern
    Drama." DR, 54, no. 1 (Spring), 94-102.
       In The Playboy of the Western World "the figure of the
    coming rebellion against a conformist tradition is the
    displaced Irish Everyman, Christy Mahon, Christian Man...."

3   EDWARDS, BERNARD LAURIE. "The Vision of J. M. Synge: A Study
    of The Playboy of the Western World." ELT, 17, no. 1, 8-
    18.
       Discusses the various implications of Christy's search
    for self in the play.

4   FARRIS, JON ROGERS. "The Hard Birth of The Playboy of the
    Western World." DAI, 35A:3735A.
       Limns the process of composition of the work by analyz-
    ing the over one thousand pages which constitute Synge's
    thirteen typescript drafts of the play.

5   FAULK, C. S. "John Millington Synge and the Rebirth of Com-
    edy." SHR, 8, no. 4 (Fall), 431-448.
       Places Synge's works in many cultural traditions, with
    analogues ranging from Oedipus to Wagner: "The success of
    Synge's comedy is in its exorcism of pity."

6   GOLDRING, MAURICE. "Le Mythe d'une civilisation rurale dans
    la Renaissance littéraire irlandaise." Pensée, 177:117-
    126.
       Mentions that Synge feared the industrialization of the
    Aran Islands: "il était conscient du conflict entre sécu-
    rité matérielle et richesse d'imagination...."

7   GRENE, NICHOLAS. "Synge's Creative Development in The Aran
Islands." Long Room [Trinity College Dublin], pp. 30-36.
      An "examination of the note-book and manuscript drafts
of The Aran Islands in the Trinity College Dublin collection" undertaken in an attempt "to show something of
Synge's creative development in the period of the Aran
visits, 1898-1902." Synge's revisions demonstrate how he
made his book more immediate, and Grene traces "this tran-
sition from a reported to a dramatic form of presentation."
Synge's dialect is a blend of Aran Islanders' expression
and his own, individualized unique vision.

8   _____. "Synge's The Shadow of the Glen: Repetition and Al-
lusion." MD, 17, no. 1 (March), 19-25.
      Several patterns of repetition reinforce Synge's theme
of desolation, decay, and aging: Dan's repetition of
overheard conversation, the anti-pastoral sheep motif, the
symbolism of the "shadow" in the glen, and references to
three off-stage characters: Mary Brien, Peggy Cavanagh,
and--most importantly--Patch Darcy.

9   GUTIERREZ, DONALD. "Coming of Age in Mayo: Synge's The
Playboy of the Western World as a Rite of Passage." HSL,
6, no. 2, 159-166.
      Discusses the work as a "puberty rite of passage," in
which Christy passes from "boyhood to manhood."

10   HOGAN, ROBERT. "John Synge and Jack Yeats," JML, 3, no. 4
(April), 1031-1038.
      Comments on ten recent books on the two and adds, "It
might well be time for a critical moratorium on Synge."

11   HUNT, HUGH. The Theatre and Nationalism in Ireland. The
Professor W. D. Thomas Memorial Lecture. Swansea: Uni-
versity College of Swansea, 21 pp., passim.
      Many comments on the reception of The Playboy of the
Western World, including a comparison with Osborne's Look
Back in Anger (1956).

12   HUNTER, JEAN COMISKEY. "The Primitive Vision of John Millington Synge." DAI, 35A (August), 1047A-48A.
      Discusses folkloric, savage, and primitive elements in
Synge's plays by bringing together "evidence from psychology, anthropology, religion, and comparative literature...."

1974

13 INNES, CATHERINE LYNETTE. "Through the Looking Glass: Achebe, Synge and Cultural Nationalism." DAI, 34A (May-June), 7234A.
    Examines the language and the father/son theme in The Playboy of the Western World in relation to the Irish struggle for cultural independence.

14 JEFFARES, A. NORMAN. "Ireland," in Literatures of the World in English. Edited by Bruce King. London and Boston: Routledge & Kegan Paul, pp. 98-115.
    Brief references to Synge, whose "delight" in the Irish peasant's "wildness was given head in The Playboy of the Western World...."

15 KENNY, HERBERT A. Literary Dublin: A History. New York: Taplinger; Dublin: Gill and Macmillan, pp. 132, 181, 189-190, 191-196, 276-277, 323.
    Passing references to the controversy surrounding Synge and his scholarly rebirth in 1971.

16 LEBLANC, GÉRARD. "J. M. Synge in Paris." CahiersI, 2-3: 191-213.
    Part of an ongoing effort to define the nature of both the French influences on Synge and his "contacts" with Paris.

17 LEVITT, PAUL M. J. M. Synge: A Bibliography of Published Criticism. New York: Barnes & Noble, a Division of Harper & Row, 224 pp.
    Following an eight-page Introduction that sketches the issues that Synge critics have addressed, the volume is divided into two main sections. Part 1, "Books and Periodicals," contains (eliding some subdivisions) a bibliography of Synge criticism; Synge biography; general dramatic criticism and general literary criticism; criticism of each of Synge's plays; Synge's non-dramatic prose works and his poetry and translations; passing references to Synge; introductions to editions of Synge's works, and recordings, letters and poems about Synge. Part 2, "Newspapers," cites entries ranging from The Aberdeen Free Press to The Washington Times. The newspapers are arranged by city in order to facilitate use of microfilm. The index to the book covers thirteen pages. Work is complete through 1969, though some items are added after that time. Book is indispensable to a thorough study of Synge. See 1974.31.

1974

18 MEIR, COLIN. The Ballads and Songs of W. B. Yeats: The Anglo-
    Irish Heritage in Subject and Style. New York: Barnes &
    Noble, a Division of Harper & Row, pp. 68, 76, 78, 90, 110,
    113.
        Several passing references to the bases of Synge's syn-
    tax and to his demand for "vital verse."

19 MURPHY, BRENDA. "Stoicism, Asceticism, and Ecstasy: Synge's
    Deirdre of the Sorrows." MD, 17, no. 2 (June), 155-163.
        Takes issue with two critical commonplaces about the
    work: that the Deirdre of the original legend was rarefied
    and delicate and that the play reflects virtually undis-
    tilled autobiography. Goes on to demonstrate that the "in-
    terplay of the three motifs of stoicism, asceticism, and
    ecstasy to convey the major theme of death as the transcend-
    ence of time and decay, and the corresponding minor theme
    of the sorrow of giving up the beauty of nature and love,
    produces at the same time a beautiful work of art and a
    moving dramatic experience."

20 NOLTE, WILLIAM H. H. L. Mencken Literary Critic. Middletown,
    Connecticut: Wesleyan University Press, pp. 9, 12, 27, 39,
    58, 153.
        Mencken thought The Playboy of the Western World "the
    greatest modern comedy...."

21 O'CASEY, SEAN. The Sting and the Twinkle: Conversations with
    Sean O'Casey. Edited by E. H. Mikhail and John O'Riordan.
    London: Macmillan; New York: Barnes & Noble, a Division
    of Harper & Row, pp. 31, 33, 130.
        Contains a few passing comments on Synge.

22 Ó hAodha, Micheál. "Synge and the Abbey Play" and "Synge's
    Successors," in Theatre in Ireland. Totowa, New Jersey:
    Rowman and Littlefield, pp. 40-59, 60-76.
        Traces the actualities of Synge's work against the back-
    ground of distortion concerning the plays, both early and
    recent. For example, "behind the Iron Curtain, Christy
    Mahon has been frequently portrayed as a Marxist revolu-
    tionary who has raised a loy...against petit-bourgeois
    capitalism." Second article states: "...Synge's unique
    mastery of peasant idiom created a situation in which more
    than half the strength of what was and still is largely
    accepted as an Abbey play resided in its dialogue."

23 POWER, ARTHUR. Conversations with James Joyce. Edited by
    Clive Hart. New York: Barnes & Noble, a Division of
    Harper & Row, pp. 33-36.

1974

> Joyce found the dialogue of Synge's peasants to be
> artificial. Abridged: 1977.7.

24 ROBINSON, PAUL N. "The Peasant Play as Allegory: J. M.
Synge's The Shadow of the Glen." CEA, 36, no. 4 (May),
36-38.
Traces elements of the medieval Everyman in the play.
For example, Nora is Everyman and her husband, time.

25 SADDLEMYER, ANN. "On Editing Synge's Letters." TN, 28,
no. 2, 58-59.
Concentrates on problems encountered while editing Letters to Molly (1971.41). Relates that Synge was interested
far more in the actors' performances that in the audiences'
reaction.

26 SKENE, REG. The Cuchulain Plays of W. B. Yeats: A Study.
New York: Columbia University Press, pp. 77-81, 148.
Traces the influences of the riots over The Playboy of
the Western World on Yeats's The Green Helmet.

27 SOLOMON, ALBERT J. "The Bird Girls of Ireland." CLQ, 10,
no. 5 (March), 269-274.
Examines the "wading-girl" image in George Moore, Joyce,
and Synge.

28 SPONBERG, ARVID FREDERIC. "J. M. Synge: Man of the Theatre."
DAI, 35A:477A-78A.
Maintains that the physical, "external requirements" of
stage and audience affected Synge in some ways but did not
influence the vision of life that he presented.

29 STEPHENS, EDWARD. My Uncle John: Edward Stephens's Life of
J. M. Synge: Edited by Andrew Carpenter. London: Oxford
University Press, 237 pp.
This book, taken from the mammoth typescripts concerning
Synge written by his nephew, is an indispensable source of
information about the playwright's personal life. Though
it does not add much to our knowledge of Synge's public
affairs and though it seems to be written as much against
the repressive influences of Synge's mother and her Establishment friends and relatives as it is for Synge's memory,
it does fill in many gaps left in the Greene-Stephens biography. Carpenter's Introduction is useful in providing
background material on the Stephens typescript; and, at
several points, Carpenter summarizes long and tedious epi-
sodes in Stephens's narrative. Carpenter divides Synge's
life into three parts: 1871-1892, 1893-1900, and 1901-
1909.

30 SULLIVAN, JAMES T. "A Gay Goodnight: A Study of Irish Trag-
    edy." DAI, 35A (December), 3773A.
        Emphasizes the gaiety in Riders to the Sea. Maurya
    "transcend[s] her situation with a gay attitude."

31 THORNTON, WELDON. "Review: Paul Levitt, J. M. Synge: A
    Bibliography of Published Criticism." JIL, 3, no. 2, 51-
    55.
        Deals mainly with the organizational problems in
    Levitt's book, while noting its completeness and reliabil-
    ity. See: 1974.17.

                            1975

1   ALLEN, MICHAEL. "Provincialism and Recent Irish Poetry: The
    Importance of Patrick Kavanagh," in Two Decades of Irish
    Writing. Edited by Douglas Dunn. Chester Springs, Penn-
    sylvania: Dufour, pp. 23-36.
        Synge is yoked with Lady Gregory and Yeats as one who,
    in the young Kavanagh's eyes, had turned Dublin into a
    "literary metropolis."

2   ATLAS, JAMES. "The Prose of Samuel Beckett: Notes from the
    Terminal Ward," in Two Decades of Irish Writing. Edited
    by Douglas Dunn. Chester Springs, Pennsylvania: Dufour,
    pp. 186-196.
        Mentions that Beckett has "acknowledged the influence
    of Synge"; he has drawn, especially, from "the sprawl and
    wit" of Synge's speech.

3   DAVIE, DONALD. "Austin Clarke and Padraic Fallon," in Two
    Decades of Irish Writing. Edited by Douglas Dunn. Chester
    Springs, Pennsylvania: Dufour, pp. 37-58.
        Brief mention of the fact that Synge's poems are often
    "furnished with...cottage properties...."

4   DEANE, SEAMUS. "Irish Poetry and Irish Nationalism," in Two
    Decades of Irish Writing. Edited by Douglas Dunn. Chester
    Springs, Pennsylvania: Dufour, pp. 4-22.
        Riots over The Playboy of the Western World came from a
    "noisy collision" between "literary men of genius and...
    propagandists...."

5   DUNN, DOUGLAS, ed. Two Decades of Irish Writing: A Critical
    Survey. Chester Springs, Pennsylvania: Dufour, pp. 4, 5,
    26, 54, 114, 154, 188, 190, 192, 231.
        Contains several brief references to Synge. See individ-
    ual entries: 1975.1, 2, 3, 4, 9, 12.

1975

6   FLANNERY, JAMES W.   "W. B. Yeats and the Abbey Theatre Com-
    pany." ETJ, 27:179-96.
        Details Synge's opposition to Yeats's proposal to take
    "continental municipal theatres as a model" and to use
    English actors at the Abbey.

7   FREE, WILLIAM J.   "Structural Dynamics in Riders to the Sea."
    CLQ, 11, no. 3 (September), 162-168.
        Sees the play as not simply an elegy but as a work sus-
    tained by dramatic conflict within the family. Develops
    the crucial role of Cailteen [sic].

8   FRENCH, WARREN. John Steinbeck. TUSAS, No. 2.   Second edi-
    tion. Boston: Twayne, a Division of G. K. Hall, p. 36.
        At the funeral service for John Steinbeck after his
    death in December, 1968, Henry Fonda, "who had played Tom
    Joad in the film version of The Grapes of Wrath, read Ten-
    nyson's poem 'Ulysses' and selections from J. M. Synge and
    Robert Louis Stevenson...."

9   GARFITT, ROGER. "Constants in Contemporary Irish Fiction,"
    in Two Decades of Irish Writing. Edited by Douglas Dunn.
    Chester Springs, Pennsylvania: Dufour, pp. 207-241.
        Synge and O'Casey capitalized on the "instinctive drama-
    tic sense" of the Irish community.

10 GRENE, NICHOLAS. Synge: A Critical Study of the Plays.
    Totowa, New Jersey: Rowman and Littlefield, 206 pp.
        Believing that Synge has now reached the point of criti-
    cal eminence at which he can be called by his surname alone,
    Grene writes the "first full study to concentrate exclu-
    sively on the plays." He eschews full discussion of the
    prose and the poetry, feeling that this material is impor-
    tant mainly as a basis of understanding the plays. Besides
    detailed evaluations of the individual plays, Grene's book
    contains such chapters as "The Landscape of Ireland,"
    "Synge's Aran," and "The Development of Dialect." Cites
    many parallels and contrasts between and with Synge and
    European dramatists.

11 HABICHT, WERNER. "John Millington Synge," in Englische Dicht-
    er Moderne: Ihr Leben und Werk. Edited by Rudolf Sühnel
    and Dieter Riesner. Berlin: Erich Schmidt, pp. 180-192.
        Sketch of Synge's work, which divides into five sections;
    the third (3 pp.) discusses The Aran Islands. Part 4 in-
    cludes an interesting comparison with Lady Gregory's plays.

12 HEANEY, SEAMUS. "The Poetry of Patrick Kavanagh: From Mona-
    ghan to the Grand Canal," in <u>Two Decades of Irish Writing</u>.
    Edited by Douglas Dunn. Chester Springs, Pennsylvania:
    Dufour, pp. 105-117.
        Kavanagh looked upon the "romantic nationalist revival
    of Synge and Yeats as 'a thoroughgoing English-bred lie....'"

13 KELSALL, MALCOLM. "Introduction" and "Appendix," in <u>The Play-</u>
    <u>boy of the Western World</u>. The New Mermaids. London:
    Ernest Benn, pp. ix-xxxiii, 86-87.
        Analyzes the play against the background of Irish Ren-
    aissance politics. Includes a comparison between Lady
    Gregory and Synge. Appendix reprints "John McGoldrick and
    the Quaker's Daughter."

14 _____. "The <u>Playboy</u> before the Riots." ThR, 1 (October),
    29-37.
        A detailed analysis of how the actors in the play con-
    tributed to the disturbances: "What must be faced, how-
    ever, is the gloom of William Fay's vision of Synge as the
    first of modern Irish realists, and a writer of satires,
    and that Synge went along with this view in production."
    Given the intractability of playwright and actors, "the
    riots were natural, even, dare one suggest, healthy."

15 KORNELIUS, JOACHIM. "Authorspecific and Groupspecific Vari-
    ation of Style-Markers in 'Irish Renaissance' Drama." FJS,
    8:33-46.
        Includes <u>When the Moon Has Set</u> with the six major plays
    in discussing such matters as "The Frequency Distribution
    of Lengths of Sentences," "The Measurement of Complexity of
    Sentence Structure," and "The Frequency Distribution of
    Lengths of Dialogues."

16 LEAMON, WARREN. "Yeats, Synge, Realism, and 'The Tragic Thea-
    tre.'" SoR, 11 (January), 129-138.
        Explains why Yeats praised so lavishly the language of
    Synge's characters and underestimated their complexity.

17 LEVITT, PAUL M. "The Two Act Structure of <u>The Playboy of the</u>
    <u>Western World</u>." CLQ, 11, no. 4 (December), 230-234.
        Synge was forced by theatre conventions to design the
    work in three acts: the play should be in two acts, with
    the first entrance of Old Mahon as the dividing point.

18 MIKHAIL, E. H. <u>J. M. Synge: A Bibliography of Criticism</u>.
    Foreword by Robin Skelton. Totowa, New Jersey: Rowman &
    Littlefield, 227 pp.

1975

This work is comprehensive and scholarly and is an indispensable source for criticism on Synge. The list of
"some 2500 items" divides into the following categories:
"Bibliographies," "Books by J. M. Synge and Their Reviews,"
and "Criticism on J. M. Synge." The third category is
further divided into "Books," "Periodicals," "Reviews of
Play Productions," "Unpublished Material," "Recordings,"
and "Background." The first of two indexes lists references to works by Synge; the second, names of critics arranged alphabetically. See 1976.28.

19 NONOYAMA, MINAKO. "La función de los símbolos en Pelléas et
Mélisande de Maeterlinck, Bodas de sangre de Lorca y Riders
to the Sea de Synge." REH, 9, no. 1, 81-98.
Sees the central theme in all three works as man's con-
frontation with the inevitability of his death.

20 O'CASEY, SEAN. The Letters of Sean O'Casey, 1910-1941.
Vol. 1. Edited by David Krause. New York: Macmillan,
pp. 89, 120, 128, 148, 153, 166, 167, 200, 297, 379, 419,
421, 577, 683, 904.
Letters evidence O'Casey's admiration for Synge and his
identification with him on the problem of censorship.
They also present a few interesting facts about Synge's
writing. For example, a letter dated October 4, 1930 from
Lady Gregory mentions: "Prague played one of Synges [sic]
plays long ago--and the then Director of the theatre...
spent some days getting 'local color'...."

21 O'HANLON, THOMAS J. The Irish: Sinners, Saints...and Other
Proud Natives of the Fabled Isle. New York and London:
Harper & Row, pp. 47, 58, 129, 282.
Contrasts Synge's peasant with that of Patrick Kavanagh
in his novel Tarry Flynn.

22 PURDY, ANDREW JAMES. "Mannerism in the Plays of J. M. Synge."
DAI, 35A:5422A.
Accounts for the unique strength of Synge's writings by
seeing them as early twentieth century examples of "manner-
ist art."

23 ROSENBLATT, ROGER. "The Back of the Book: J. M. Synge."
The New Republic. Part 1, 173 (4 October), 30-32; Part 2,
173 (11 October), 31-33.
Sketches the troubled reception of The Playboy of the
Western World in preparation for the December 11 public
broadcast of the work.

24   SADDLEMYER, ANN. "The Irish School: John Millington Synge (1871-1909)," in English Drama (Excluding Shakespeare): Select Bibliographical Guides. Edited by Stanley Wells. London: Oxford University Press, pp. 261-262.
     Contains seven entries under "Text" and twenty-two under "Critical Studies and Commentary."

25   _____. "John Millington Synge in Europe." EI, 4:27-30.
     Lists twenty entries under "Synge's European Calendar" and then provides brief descriptions of thirteen "European Correspondents and Acquaintances." Calls for help from people knowing something of Synge's European residence—for a planned definitive edition of the letters.

26   TOWNLEY, ROD. The Early Poetry of William Carlos Williams. Ithaca and New York: Cornell University Press, pp. 33, 46.
     Cites the possible influence of Synge on Williams' 1909 one-act play "A September Afternoon."

1976

1   BENSTOCK, BERNARD. Paycocks and Others: Sean O'Casey's World. Dublin: Gill and Macmillan; New York: Barnes & Noble, a Division of Harper and Row, pp. 180, 201, 254, 256, 292, 302.
     O'Casey saw in Synge's characters, "'the call of a brave heart for the fullness of life.'" Comments on O'Casey's opinion of The Playboy of the Western World.

2   CARPENTER, ANDREW. "Two Passages from Synge's Notebooks." Hermathena, 120 (Summer), 35-38.
     Traces Synge's mysticism and his view of women in parts of the manuscript collection of Trinity College which went into "On a Train to Paris."

3   DANIELS, WILLIAM L. "AE and Synge in the Congested Districts." Éire, 2, no. 4 (Winter), 14-26.
     Follows Synge and George Russell to "the south coast of Galway and the Belmullet area of Mayo in order to watch them stirring the same pot." Synge's view of the peasant of the Congested Districts tended to be "pessimistic."

4   DONOGHUE, DENIS. "Being Irish Together." SR, 84, no. 1 (January-March), 129-133.
     "Synge and the minor writers of the Irish literary revival were not strong enough to counter Yeats's incantatory rhetoric...."

1976

5   FLANNERY, JAMES W. "Yeats and the Abbey Theatre Company," in
    W. B. Yeats and the Idea of a Theatre: The Early Abbey
    Theatre in Theory and Practice. New Haven and London:
    Yale University Press, pp. 212-238.
        Discusses such behind-the-scene matters as Synge's op-
    position to bringing Continental plays to the Abbey, his
    disagreement with Yeats over the Fay Brothers, and the
    trouble caused in the company by Synge's engagement to
    Molly Allgood. Book prints for the first time some impor-
    tant manuscript materials.

6   FLOOD, JEANNE. "Synge's Ecstatic Dance and the Myth of the
    Undying Father." AI, 33, no. 2 (Summer), 174-196.
        An important study which uses the tools of psychoanaly-
    sis and Synge's own working materials to account for the
    change in Synge's artistic development after his trips to
    the Aran Islands.

7   GIELGUD, JOHN. Early Stages. New York: Taplinger, p. 46.
        Under "1922-23" describes a setting for Deirdre of the
    Sorrows "consisting almost entirely of a few light tree-
    trunks cut in three ply...."

8   GLANDON, VIRGINIA E. "Index of Irish Newspapers, 1900-1922."
    Part 1. Eire, 2, no. 4 (Winter), 84-121.
        Valuable in assessing the impact of newspaper comments,
    both hostile and sympathetic, about Synge's writings--be-
    cause it describes, besides publication dates, such matters
    as places where circulated and editorial policy. About
    The United Irishman, for example: "Irish-Ireland[,] Sinn
    Féin"; and "Among nationalists throughout Ireland and
    abroad."

9   JEFFARES, A. NORMAN. "Coughing in Ink." SR, 84, no. 1 (Jan-
    uary-March), 157-167.
        Comments on Synge's friendship with Yeats.

10 KAIN, RICHARD M. "General Works," in Anglo-Irish Literature:
    A Review of Research. Edited by Richard J. Finneran.
    New York: The Modern Language Association of America,
    pp. 1-23.
        A description of important sources of information about
    Anglo-Irish literature. Any serious student of this field
    must read Kain's analysis. Included in the chapter, for
    example, is a comment on Richard J. Hayes's monumental
    Manuscript Sources for the History of Irish Civilization
    (1965). Some of the sources cited by Kain are listed in

this Synge bibliography; but, since none of the works deal
solely with Synge, there has been no attempt made to in-
corporate them all.

11 _____. "The Image of Synge: New Light and Deeper Shadows."
SR, 84, no. 1 (January-March), 174-185.
   Surveys recent criticism on Synge after stating: "The
Yeats image of Synge became the definitive interpretation,
with the result that criticism remained static for fifty
years after his death...."

12 _____ and JAMES H. O'BRIEN. George Russell (A.E.). The Irish
Writers Series. London: Associated University Presses;
Lewisburg, Pennyslvania: Bucknell University Press, p. 32.
   Mentions that the public attacks on Synge led to the
resignations of Maud Gonne, Douglas Hyde, and Russell, all
vice-presidents, from the Irish National Theatre Society.

13 KNOWLSON, JAMES. "Beckett et John Millington Synge." Gambit,
7, no. 28, 65-81.
   Notes Beckett's admiration for Synge and cites several
parallels between them, e.g. their awareness of death, the
similar "comédie noire" elements in their work, their use
of Christocentric and color symbolism, and the difficulty
of placing their plays in an established genre. Beckett
differs from Synge, however, in the vastness of his (Beckett's) scope.

14 KOPPER, EDWARD A., JR. Lady Isabella Persse Gregory. TEAS,
No. 194. Boston: Twayne, a Division of G. K. Hall,
pp. 55-59.
   Over twenty references to Synge throughout the volume
emphasize Lady Gregory's defense and encouragement of him
in spite of her dislike of The Playboy of the Western World.

15 KORNELIUS, JOACHIM. "Hinweise zur Aussprache irischer Namen
im Dramen-Werk J. M. Synges." NM, 77:638-647.
   Lists proper names found in Synge's plays with a guide
to pronunciation, an indication of where each appears in
the plays, and a brief description of each entry.

16 LUCAS, F. L. "John Millington Synge," in The Drama of Chek-
hov, Synge, Yeats, and Pirandello. New York: Phaeton
Press, pp. 147-237.
   After a lengthy examination of Synge's Irish antecedents
and of his plays, Lucas concludes: "Synge may be...minor.
But there are certain minor writers--such as Sappho, or
Beddoes--who remain, none the less, unique." Dismisses

1976

> The Tinker's Wedding as inferior, synthesizes a good deal
> of background material on The Playboy of the Western World,
> and calls Deirdre of the Sorrows "a play with first-rate
> passages rather than a first-rate play."

17 McMAHON, SEÁN. "'Leave Troubling the Lord God': A Note on
     Synge and Religion." Éire, 11, no. 1 (Spring), 132-141.
          Synge was interested in preserving artistic freedom, not
     primarily in denouncing religion, though he had little time
     for the Irish clergy.

18 O'BRIEN, EDNA. "Mother Ireland." SR, 84, no. 1 (January-
     March), 34-36.
          "Ireland for me is moments of its history...a few people
     who embody its strange quality,...a line from a Synge
     play...."

19 O'DONNELL, BEATRICE. "Synge and O'Casey Women: A Study in
     Strong Mindedness." DAI, 37A (August), 699A-700A.
          Examines the reasons that Synge and O'Casey portrayed
     strong-minded women in their works.

20 OREL, HAROLD. "A Drama for the Nation," in Irish History and
     Culture: Aspects of a People's Heritage. Edited by Har-
     old Orel. Lawrence, Manhattan, Wichita: University Press
     of Kansas, pp. 251-269.
          Contains an overview of the problems caused in Dublin
     by Synge's controversial plays: "...Synge's candor...
     added insult to the injury of a theater without sixpenny
     seats for the 'common people' of Ireland...."

21 PERKINS, DAVID. A History of Modern Poetry: From the 1890s
     to the High Modernist Mode. Cambridge, Massachusetts and
     London: The Belknap Press of Harvard University, pp. 79,
     81, 209, 213-214, 226, 232, 253, 255, 259, 260-261, 265,
     267, 275, 281, 300, 341, 361, 456, 579-580.
          Stresses Synge's opposition to "traditional" poetry.
     Synge's own power is seen in "Danny."

22 PIERCE, JAMES CLAITIVE. "Romantic Quest Out of the Natural
     World: A Study of the Plays of John Millington Synge."
     DAI, 36A (January), 4478A-79A.
          Examines Synge's six published plays to show that
     Synge, "morbidly obsessed with the oppressive finality of
     the natural world, was driven in a passionate quest of
     aesthetically transcending the absolute boundaries of that
     world...."

1976

23   PLUNKETT, JAMES. "A Great Occasion." SR, 84, no. 1 (January-
     March), 1-33.
          In this short story, Plunkett writes that Synge's "prose
     was beyond praise, though his plays were in questionable
     taste."

24   ROSENBLATT, ROGER. "The Journal of Stephen MacKenna." SR,
     84, no. 1 (January-March), 133-142.
          Comments on MacKenna's appreciation of The Well of the
     Saints and The Playboy of the Western World.

25   SHIVERS, ALFRED S. Maxwell Anderson. TUSAS, No. 279. Bos-
     ton: Twayne, a Division of G. K. Hall, pp. 22, 32, 37.
          Cites Synge as one of Anderson's continuing favorite
     authors.

26   TAYLOR, RICHARD. The Drama of W. B. Yeats: Irish Myth and
     the Japanese Nō. New Haven and London: Yale University
     Press, pp. 8,15.
          Brief comment on the "cadenced prose" of Synge.

27   THORNTON, WELDON. "J. M. Synge," in Anglo-Irish Literature:
     A Review of Research. Edited by Richard J. Finneran.
     New York: The Modern Language Association of America,
     pp. 315-365.
          This indispensable chapter provides not only a presenta-
     tion of a good deal of important criticism on Synge but
     also a judicious commentary on the material. Its nine sec-
     tions are devoted to such topics as "Correspondence,"
     "Bibliography," and "Poetry." Section 6, "Studies of the
     Drama," starts with criticism of In the Shadow of the Glen
     and ends with Deirdre of the Sorrows. Focus is on major
     writings about Synge.

28   _____. "Reviews: E. H. Mikhail, J. M. Synge: A Bibliography
     of Criticism." JIL, 5, no. 2 (May), pp. 131-135.
          Finds that Mikhail's book (1975.18) is "in the main
     complete and reliable...." Adds ten items.

29   TUOHY, FRANK. Yeats. New York: Macmillan, pp. 9, 14, 103,
     121-124, 137, 140-141, 148, 175, 190, 192, 216-217.
          Comments on the Synge-Yeats relationship, including the
     differences between Yeats and Russell over The Playboy of
     the Western World. An 1895 portrait of Synge appears on
     page 121.

30   YEATS, W. B. Uncollected Prose of W. B. Yeats. Vol. 2. Re-
     views, Articles and Other Miscellaneous Prose, 1897-1939.
     Edited by John P. Frayne and Colton Johnson. New York:
     Columbia University Press, 543 pp. passim.

1976

Contains close to one hundred (indexed) references to
Synge. Reprints many previously uncollected materials
dealing with Yeats and Synge, many of them from newspapers
now difficult to come by. Reprints: 1900.1; 1903.12;
1907.41; 1910.6; 1911.84; 1912.38; 1913.19; 1924.10;
1926.3; 1933.3.

1977

1 ALCORN, JOHN. The Nature Novel from Hardy to Lawrence. New
   York: Columbia University Press, p. 62.
      Refers to the "spirit of place" in Riders to the Sea,
   which "provides an eloquent testimony" to the "search for
   roots in the soil...."

2 BIGLEY, BRUCE M. "The Playboy of the Western World as Antidrama." MD, 20, no. 2 (June), 157-167.
      Seeing the work as a "Bildungsdrama" allows the reader
   to understand Synge's attitude towards Christy and his
   imaginative use of realistic data. Also, the play is
   "truly antidrama, a form which undercuts its own conven-
   tions and refuses to resolve the problems it raises."

3 DAVIS, ROBERT BERNARD. George William Russell ("AE"). TEAS,
   No. 208. Boston: Twayne, a Division of G. K. Hall, p. 133.
      "AE preferred Stephens to Synge and O'Casey because
   Stephens writes of the heroic past while the other two de-
   scribe the purely human condition of Ireland's present."

4 FALLIS, RICHARD. The Irish Renaissance. Syracuse: Syracuse
   University Press, pp. 4, 32-33, 96, 102-108, 110-111, 114-
   115, 122-123, 127, 129, 132, 140, 171, 179-180, 185, 187,
   199, 208, 241.
      Focuses on the Irishness of Synge's work. Includes a
   summary of various interpretations of The Playboy of
   the Western World. Comments on Synge's influence on Yeats's
   poetry.

5 HARMON, MAURICE. Select Bibliography for the Study of Anglo-
   Irish Literature and Its Background: An Irish Studies
   Handbook. Port Credit, Ontario: P. D. Meany, pp. 82, 84,
   108, 110, 131, 138, 143.
      A briefly annotated listing of source materials for
   Irish studies, including sections on Bibliographies of
   Bibliographies, Irish and Anglo-Irish Language, and biblio-
   graphies for individual writers. Contains a forty page
   chronology.

6   LAGO, MARY. "Irish Poetic Drama in St. Louis." TCL, 23,
      no. 2 (May), 180-194.
         Briefly mentions actors' resignations over In the
      Shadow of the Glen.

7   MIKHAIL, E. H., ed. J. M. Synge: Interviews and Recollec-
      tions. Foreword by Robin Skelton. New York: Barnes &
      Noble, a Division of Harper & Row; London: Macmillan,
      152 pp.
         Reprints 1907.21; 1911.60, 80, 83; 1921.3; 1924.3, 4,
      10; 1926.1; 1949.5; 1964.17; 1972.71; 1973.15. Abridges
      1911.79; 1921.8; 1935.6; 1937.3; 1955.7; 1963.10; 1967.10;
      1974.23.

8   _____. Lady Gregory: Interviews and Recollections. London:
      Macmillan, pp. 33-40, 41, 42-45, 52-56, 57, 59, 70-73, 81,
      83, 85, 107.
         Includes several passing references to Synge.

9   MIKHAIL, E. H. "Synge, John Millington (1871-1909)," in
      English Drama, 1900-1950: A Guide to Information Sources.
      Vol. 2 in the American Literature, English Literature, and
      World Literatures in English Information Guide Series.
      Detroit: Gale, pp. 277-279.
         Includes (throughout the volume) over fifty references
      to works dealing with Synge. The Synge Section itself lists
      fifteen sources of bibliographical information about Synge.

10   MIKHAIL, E. H., ed. W. B. Yeats: Interviews and Recollec-
      tions. Vol. 1. Foreword by A. Norman Jeffares. London:
      Macmillan; New York: Barnes & Noble, a Division of Harper
      & Row, 54, 77-78, 82-84, 85-86, 173.
         Contains copious notes after each reprinted selection.
      Reprints 1907.40; 1911.82; 1912.37, 38; 1964.4.

11   SADDLEMYER, ANN. "Synge and the Doors of Perception," in
      Place, Personality and the Irish Writer. Edited by Andrew
      Carpenter. Irish Literary Studies, 1. New York: Barnes
      & Noble, a Division of Harper & Row, pp. 97-120.
         Traces Synge's desire for "heightened consciousness" in
      his writings, both prose and poetry. Synge was not morbid
      but, from the beginning, sought freedom and a higher world
      of perception.

12   SEYMOUR-SMITH, MARTIN. "Synge, John Millington (1871-1909)"
      in Who's Who in Twentieth Century Literature. New York:
      McGraw-Hill, pp. 357-358.

1977

"With Pirandello...Brecht..., and O'Neill...[Synge]
forms the great quadrumvirate of twentieth-century dramatists."

13   SKELTON, ROBIN. "The Politics of J. M. Synge." MR, 18,
no. 1 (Spring), 7-22.
Synge was not "unfitted to think a political thought";
rather, "he was not a 'party man.'" Traces affinities with
William Morris and discusses such matters as Synge's detes-
tation of capitalism. Also, the Saint in The Well of the
Saints has much in common with the "political reformer."

14   STERNLICHT, SANFORD. John Masefield. TEAS, No. 209. Boston:
Twayne, a Division of G. K. Hall, pp. 27-28, 88, 90, 92,
104-105, 123.
Describes Masefield's friendship with Synge from their
first meeting in January, 1903 until their last in 1907.
Masefield admired the "tragic Irish spirit" captured in
The Playboy of the Western World. Points out Synge's influence in Masefield's The Tragedy of Nan, "a three-act,
prose folk tragedy in the style of Synge...."

Index

179

Fechter, Paul, 1957.7
Ferrar, Harold, 1973.2
Ferris, William R., Jr., 1971.9
Figgis, Darrell, 1911.42;
    1912.16-17
Finneran, Richard J., 1976.10
Firkins, O. W., 1920.2-3
"The First Lady of Ireland,"
    1912.29
Fisher, John, 1960.3
Flannery, James W., 1970.3;
    1975.6; 1976.5
Fletcher, John Gould, 1937.2
Flood, Jeanne Agnes, 1968.11-12;
    1970.4; 1972.16; 1976.6
"Flowers and Timber: A Note on
    Synge's Poems," 1957.2
"Folklore and Folklife in the
    Works of John M. Synge,"
    1971.9
Forces in Modern British Litera-
    ture, 1947.12
Ford, Boris, 1964.5
Ford, Ford Madox, 1911.43
"Form as Agent in Synge's Riders
    to the Sea," 1964.18
Foster, Leslie D., 1973.3
Fox, R. M., 1955.4
Frankenberg, Lloyd, 1964.17
Fraser, G. S., 1965.9
Fraser, Russell A., 1960.4
Frayne, John P., 1976.30
Frechet, René, 1968.13
Free, William J., 1975.7
Freedley, George, 1947.1
French, Frances-Jane, 1970.5
"French Influences on Synge,"
    1968.18
French, Warren, 1975.8
Frenz, Horst, 1971.10
Frenzel, Herbert, 1932.5
Freyer, Grattan, 1948.2; 1964.5
Fricker, Robert, 1964.6
The Frontiers of Drama, 1964.3
Frye, Northrop, 1957.8
Fuller, Eunice, 1911.44

G

Galsworthy, John, 1912.18-19;
    1913.8
Ganz, Arthur, 1967.8
Garab, Arra, 1965.10

Gardner, Philip, 1973.4
Garfitt, Roger, 1975.9
Gascoigne, Bamber, 1966.8
Gaskell, Robert, 1964.7
Gaskell, Ronald, 1963.6; 1972.17
Gassner, John, 1954.1-2
The Genius of the Gael: A Study
    in Celtic Psychology and Its
    Manifestations, 1913.6
The Genius of the Irish Theater,
    1960.2
"George Moore on the Irish Thea-
    tre," 1911.64
Gerstenberger, Donna, 1963.7;
    1964.8; 1965.11; 1971.11
Gibbon, Monk, 1937.1
Gibbs, Wolcott, 1946.3
Gielgud, John, 1976.7
Gilbert, Stuart, 1966.12
Gilder, Rosamond, 1947.6
Gill, Brendan, 1971.12
Glandon, Virginia E., 1976.8
Gogarty, Oliver St. J., 1937.3;
    1973.15
The Golden Labyrinth: A Study of
    British Drama, 1962.8
Goldring, Maurice, 1974.6
Goodwin, K. L., 1966.9
Gordon, Jan B., 1969.4
Gorki, Maxim, 1924.2
"The Gospel According to Synge,"
    1968.30
A Grammatical Analysis of Artis-
    tic Representation of Irish
    English, with a Brief Discus-
    sion of Sounds and Spelling,
    1972.74
Grebanier, Bernard D. N., 1949.1
Greene, David H., 1946.4; 1947.7-
    9; 1948.3; 1957.9; 1959.5;
    1961.4; 1971.13-15; 1972.18-
    19
Greene, Graham, 1935.7
Gregory, Lady, 1911.45-46;
    1912.20; 1913.9-10; 1947.10
Grene, Nicholas, 1971.50; 1974.7-
    8; 1975.10
Griffith, Arthur, 1903.4-7;
    1904.4; 1905.3-6; 1907.22, 39
    See also Shanganagh
Grigson, Geoffrey, 1962.6
Gunnell, Doris, 1912.21